PRAISE FOR BOB HARDCASTLE AND *MONEY MINUTES*

"Bob Hardcastle is passionate about the work he does — advising individuals on how to manage their financial affairs and achieve their financial goals. His gift is his ability to translate his 40 years of experience into common sense advice that all can understand."
— **Chuck Kadlec, Managing Director and Chief Investment Strategist for J & W Seligman**

"Bob Hardcastle is Mr. Money in St Louis. His Money Talks show is the most famous, long established financial radio show in the city and he has guided his clients wonderfully through up and down markets for decades. His latest book, drawn from years of his experience with clients, offers invaluable advice that will make everyone a far better investor!"
— **Jordan E. Goodman, America's Money Answers Man and author of *Everyone's Money Book***

"Bob Hardcastle explains in third grade, seventh month terminology all aspects of saving, investing and gifting. Bob is truly a friend of the investor, making his suggestions easy to understand and easily adaptable. Go buy this book — you will regret it if you don't!"
— **Dr. J.T. "Dock" Houk (CEO, National Heritage Foundation)**

"When's the last time you read a financial advice book that quotes Emily Bronte', Scarlett O'Hara and the Beatles? Half the battle in getting your financial house in order is finding an adviser who speaks a language you can actually understand. Bob Hardcastle is that adviser."
— **Mike Jensen, former Chief Financial Correspondent of NBC News**

"I've known Bob Hardcastle since his first day in the business 43 years ago. Throughout all these years his primary goal has been gaining knowledge so that he can in turn pass it on to his clients. His latest book takes sophisticated information and applies a common sense approach, which further illustrates his philosophy, "people don't care about how much you know until they know you care."
aDale Young, Distribution Vice President, Columbus Life Insurance Company

D1372580

"In this technological era of information bombardment, Bob Hardcastle's latest book provides simple steps on charting a proven course for financial survival and health. Like a good cup of coffee with a trusted friend, Bob shares his experience and insight in an easily understood, relaxed manner. Why not spend a couple of hours with Bob. You'll enjoy his company and benefit from his wisdom."
— **Ed Buerger, Executive Director,**
Southern Illinois University Alumni Association

"He's done it again! Bob has underscored the need for the investor to be able to articulate their personal and family goals, seek and evaluate input from professionals, and be patiently disciplined while creating their desired financial future. This is a must read for the serious investor."
— **Dr. Walter V. Wendler, Former Chancellor,**
Southern Illinois University Carbondale

"I've known Bob Hardcastle since our days just out of college and have followed his career with great interest and admiration. Few are as qualified to write about the subject of money management as Bob. This book is a must read for financial planners and investors alike!"
— **Don Urban, Co-founder and former President, LifeUSA Insurance Co.**
(now Allianz Life of North America)

"Bob calls all the right signals clearly. It is then up to the reader to follow through with the right play and score a successful financial goal."
— **Joe Gibbs, Head Coach of the Washington Redskins**

"We're extremely proud to have Bob as a member of our Leadership council. His no-nonsense approach to making financial planning easy to understand is something that not only helps consumers nationwide, but he's also helping shape the whole financial planning industry by setting standards which all advisors can hope to obtain."
— **Jim Brown, CPA, Founder of American Financial Marketing, Inc.**

"Bob Hardcastle is like a trusted friend you can turn to for great financial advice. He takes time to help you understand the mechanics of investing for your future. With Bob you won't feel as though you are being scolded for not having properly done your financial planning. Bob's insight and guidance will put you in the driver's seat when it comes to your personal financial picture."
— **Susan Wilson Solovic, CEO, SBTV.com (Small Business Television)**

ABOUT THE AUTHOR

Named to America's Top 100 Investment Advisors List by *Registered Representative* magazine in August of 2007, Bob Hardcastle, a registered investment advisor, has been helping investors and businesses quickly and simply solve their money concerns for over 40 years. Thousands of investors, businesses and clients have benefited from his timely and his easy-to-understand explanations of complex investment and wealth-building techniques in individual consultations, as well as through his weekly syndicated radio programs, his TV segments and his books. Bob's other books include *Bob Hardcastle's Money Talk* **(AMACOM Books)**, *Wealth Enhancement* **(The Institute),** and *21st Century Wealth* **(Quantum Press)**. He also writes weekly investment columns for St. Louis newspapers.

Anthony Vlamis (intellagent@att.net) is a writer, author and former Wall Streeter with over 30 years in business and professional publishing. He's the author/co-author of a number of business books, including *Business The Yahoo Way* **(Capstone Publishing),** *Smart Leadership* **(AMACOM Books)** and *Investing With Options*.

David Caldwell

Money Minutes

8/9/11

How to Grow and Manage Your Money
One Easy Idea at a Time

Best Wishes

Bob Neubert

Money Minutes.
How to Grow and Manage Your Money One Easy Idea at a Time.

Copyright © 2008 by Robert Hardcastle with Anthony Vlamis.

All rights reserved.

Printed in the United States of America.

No part of this book may be used or reproduced in any manner whatsoever without written permission, except in the case of brief quotations embodied in critical articles or reviews. For information, contact York House Press, Ltd., 70 West Red Oak Lane, White Plains, N.Y. 10604.

www.yorkhousepress.com

For more information, please contact York House Press.

Phone: 914.764.0800
Fax: 914.764.5159
E-mail: info@yorkhousepress.com

Book design by Concise Marketing & Communications
www.beconcise.com Cover image, Dreamstime.

Library of Congress Control Number: 2007943757
ISBN-13: 978-0-971956-2-4
ISBN-I0: 0-9791956-2-4

This book is available at a special discount when ordered in bulk quantities.
For information, contact York House Press.

Money Minutes

How to Grow and Manage Your Money
One Easy Idea at a Time

• • • • • • • • •

Robert Hardcastle
with
Anthony Vlamis

Acknowledgements

There are so many people to thank when looking back over a 40-year investment career. However, in the more immediate timeframe, there are some very special people to whom I would like to pay tribute.

First, I'd like to thank Jan, my wife of 43 years and friend of 53 years. Thank you because I Love You!

Then there are our children, Jody and Scott, who are both in the investment field. It thrills dad to know, in some respect, you are following in my footsteps.

To our grandchildren, Rachel, Ashley, Jordan, David and Ally, what more do grandparents need than to be with their grandkids.

My Delta Force team has been phenomenal in all they have done to help me succeed throughout the years. I want to pay special thanks to Chris and Jay, who have been by my side for over 20 years. Also, a very special thank-you goes to Barb, who consistently takes my dictation and makes it flow.

I also want to express a very special thanks to Tony Vlamis, who worked with me on my first book, **Bob Hardcastle's Money Talk** and has taken a great interest in rewriting, researching, adding original material, Web, and Internet material to this book.

I want to thank Jordan Goodman, who is known throughout the world as a real investment guru. I greatly appreciate him contributing the Foreword of this book.

And, I thank you for reading my book. I hope as you read through these **Money Minutes** you will get some encouraging ideas on how you can feel more comfortable with your money and succeed financially in life.

Best wishes.

Bob Hardcastle

How thankful I am in so many ways and to so many people: In work, to be writing and working for such a first-class man as Bob Hardcastle; in life to be blessed with a really golden family—a "really smart" loving wife and "partner", Connie, who is also the love of my life; a growing family of grandkids—Philip, Marley, Maura, and Eve—following on the heels of our sons, Mark and Paul and daughters-in-law, Natalie and Paige, and; to Steven "Alexander", our youngest son who is making his own tracks in the financial world and life, and yet to experience all the joys of family extension and connection that are to come to him. And finally, to my sister, Suzanne. She has been a life-long supporter and business partner. I envy no one as having more prospects and riches.

Energy and Light...

Anthony Vlamis

Table of Contents

SECTOR INVESTING

SOCIAL SECURITY

TAXES

THEFT

Why The Money Minutes Guide Will
Improve Your Personal Finance Know How

There was a time when a fool and his money were soon parted,
but now it happens to everybody.

— Adlai Stevenson

Put a few hundred people in a room and probably 80% of them can tell you what the most popular TV shows are. But ask how much they are saving for retirement what their social security benefits will be or how much of their current income is needed to retire on without changing their current lifestyle and you won't see many hands raised. That's because we don't give enough thought to our saving, spending and retirement options. No surprise there. It's all getting too complicated. So many people just throw up their hands and figure like literature's famous procrastinator Scarlet O'Hara from Gone With The Wind, "I'll worry about it tomorrow."

Yet various surveys have shown that money, and more often debt, is the greatest source of worry for most of us. So who needs a survey to tell us what we already know.

It starts so innocently. You pick up a credit card here, a credit card there, buy a few needed things and pay off a good part of the balance but leave some owing until next month. A few years in and you have steady credit balances that may go up or down but rarely get paid off anymore. You tell yourself it's manageable and everybody has a little debt.

Then you get married and start thinking about a home. Before you know it you have saved enough for a down payment on a comfortable but modest residence complete with a 30 year mortgage and a sizable chunk of debt. But hey, you are a homeowner, like the majority of us; right?

Next your union is blessed with a few kids. Before you know it the years fly by, the kids are getting ready for college and you realize with the steadily increasing cost of higher education you haven't saved nearly enough to get them all the way through. So you take out a few education loans. A few thousand here and a few thousand there and pretty soon, as Everett McKinley Dirksen used to way, it adds up to real money.

After decades of borrowing money you never seem to have enough of just to take care of life's necessities, you find yourself in middle age or closing in on retirement. Only now you have a debt nightmare on your hands. It's really more like a day-mare because money woes don't just wake you up at night. They crowd your thoughts all day long.

Finally, you get close enough to retirement to think you are home free, but when you put the pencil to paper you realize that getting out of the rat race at 65 to troll the beaches of warmer climes, cast to a cruising bonefish, or just plain laying on the warm sun drenched sands at the beach may not be in the cards. Especially if you are one of the lucky people who have longevity in your family plus good health, no serious chronic diseases to deal with, and you live a healthy lifestyle. Part blessing, part curse some would say.

Sound familiar? It may because this is the case with a great many working families.

And so many of the clients I have advised over the past four decades.

So where does that leave you?

Peter Drucker, the godfather of management technology, put it this way: *"You can either take action or you can hang back and hope for a miracle."*

Scarlett O'Hara would have loved the hanging back and hoping for a miracle part. However, if you have read this far, you probably aren't the Scarlett O'Hara type. You are the type who takes action. If only you knew where to start. That's a good thing. At least you are self-aware and recognize the kind of problems you could have if you don't rein in certain behaviors or change direction.

Life throws us a lot of curves from the financial mound and if you don't make some preparation or plan in advance for things like education, savings, investment, retirement and eldercare, you are pretty much destined to be swinging wildly at what gets thrown at you and getting nowhere in later years.

Sure I know friends and associates who are working well into their 70s and beyond. But they are the lucky ones. They are healthy, working at a job they really like a lot or engaged in an activity they are passionate about. But if you look around at many of the elders who are working in the places you shop, behind the mask of cordiality is a person feeling trapped, with no choice but to keep on working. Let's face it; that's a depressing place to be in your golden years.

And that is a major part of why I wrote this book: To get main street regular readers to stop and think about the personal financial matters they have to deal with in a simple straightforward fashion and see that they can take action and start a new plan that will make life easier down the road.

Given the busy lives and lifestyles most of us lead, a book that boils down a few hundred or so of the most important money and personal finance issues into simple words and facts with some simple actionable ideas and plans might make our financial lives simpler. Down the line, it can help us get a feeling of control over money issues shaping a certain sense of self that is inwardly reassuring. That feeling can be directed outwardly and affect family and friends in a positive way, too. And who knows, you may just sleep better at night.

I talk a lot about debt in the book. Why debt? Because debt is a lot like Emily Bronte's Mrs. Rochester. She's locked up in the attic and plumb crazy. But nobody wants to talk about her much less confront her. It's just too painful and scary. Debt is truly an albatross around the necks of many people. It will literally make you sick. I have seen this in my own experience so many times, with people from all walks of financial life. Fixing debt problems can truly change your life. Financial health is wealth and wealth brings financial well being that spills over into other areas of your life.

In this book you'll find some practical and not so painful ways to confront debt and make it go away eventually. All it takes is a plan and the persistence to deal with it on a systematic basis. It doesn't matter whether you have a little debt or a pile of credit cards; there are concrete ways inside to remedy the situation.

Retirement is another event we are all looking forward to. However, no matter how good our intentions may be the majority of us come up short on the funds and planning side. That makes our stretch lap a wild and anxious ride. To ease that stretch run takes some basic knowledge about what your savings and planning options are. Nothing too complicated mind you, but if you will take just a few of the really simple steps described in the one page nuggets that follow, you'll end up well ahead of most friends and colleagues in the retirement derby.

You've heard by now that most people die without a will. I'm not so sure how true this is anymore. If you don't have a will, it could make your whole probate and estate process more complicated instead of easier. Of course, you won't have the problem then but your family will.

The Beatles Paul McCartney—that's Sir Paul to you Anglophiles—wrote a number called "Silly Love Song," The song goes on about whether the world really needs another love song. And then, of course, launches off into Paul's "'nother" love song. Some of you might be thinking the same about personal finance; with good reason.

There are many many books on personal finance. A lot of them were written by financial reporters. They are a lot like the TV weather reporters. Certainly they are good platform people. They reach out to a lot of folks with information, but they are not meteorologists. They report on what their advisory services feed them. Interpretation is not usually a part of their portfolio.

Many others who have written books are TV celebrities and they bring a lot of awareness to the personal finance arena. That's good for the general public. However, the media stars don't have clients. And that is a key difference between my writing and most of the rest of the books out there. For 40 years I have been in—blessed you might say—the day-to-day business of talking to, reviewing and advising and providing professional financial advice to clients who pay for my services or listen to me on radio—some even see me on TV—and who have problems to solve. I doubt I'd still be in this business if my advice wasn't sound—or at the very least did no harm.

More important, the advantage of having and advising clients and being in the trenches with them every day is that I know from experience the narrow ten per cent of finance and money matters that really concern people. I know from repeated requests over the past 40 years what they want and need to know to manage their finances better.

Foreword

by Jordan E. Goodman, personal finance expert, America's Money Answers Man at **www.moneyanswers.com**

I have known Bob Hardcastle for well over 20 years and respect him as one of the most balanced and insightful financial advisors and broadcasters in the country. He is the host of one of the longest running financial radio shows in American history. No matter whether the economy, stock and bond markets are booming or crashing, Bob always has a keen sense of perspective that his clients and listeners respect. Bob has worked with many of his clients for decades and they keep coming back for more advice because he so often gets it right. When the stock market is soaring, he usually is the voice of caution that prevents his clients from pouring their money in at the top. When the markets are tanking, Bob soothes his clients' jangled nerves and keeps them from panicking and selling out at the bottom.

This is the kind of advice that Bob Hardcastle offers to you, the reader of Money Minutes, in this book. Bob has heard every possible question that could have been asked about personal finance in his many years on radio and TV in the St. Louis market. This book is a compilation of the very best questions and the very best answers on every topic that the average American wonders about. Bob speaks to you like he is in your kitchen talking to you over your morning coffee. No jargon, no long lectures, just the facts that you need to make smart financial decisions.

Just a few of the topic areas that Bob covers in this book are: getting out of debt, financing college, getting the best mortgage, making the best real estate moves, minimizing taxes legally, funding IRAs and other retirement accounts, completing wills and other estate plans and even planning for your funeral.

Because the information is provided in bite-sized nuggets, you can get exactly what you need quickly on any topic of personal finance. Use Money Minutes and thrive!

Jordan Goodman,
America's Money Answers Man
www.moneyanswers.com

Money Minutes

ANNUITIES—THE GOOD, THE BAD, AND THE UGLY

Few topics in financial advisory circles stir up as much mud in the water as annuities.

First, there are many different types of annuities. An annuity is a contract backed by an insurance company that in return for a lump sum deposit a liquidation of a sum of money from a person's savings or a series of periodic contributions will guarantee a series of payments for a specified period of time. The guarantees are only as strong as the issuing insurance company.

Who Should Consider Annuities?

The simple direct answer is: People who want a guaranteed stream of income for a certain number of years or for life, no matter how long they live.

Are They Good Investments?

For the right investor with specific investment goals, annuities can be a great investment. However, it is easy to make mistakes when selecting an annuity, so it can't be done lightly. Some investors fail to do the proper research Knowing the different types of annuities, taking proper advantage of the tax consequences and benefits, and being fully aware of the holding periods are just a few things you need to do to make an annuity fit your investment or retirement program. As a guaranteed piece of the income stream during retirement, an annuity makes good sense for many people.

Many times I get asked about excess charges or surrender fees with annuities, and they can be real problems. So always know the details before you buy.

Money Sense: Questions you have to ask yourself

Here's the three-part question on annuities I use to help investors

1

decide whether or not an annuity is right for them:

- Do you have to have a guaranteed amount of money coming in for a specific period of time?
- Would you like the freedom to make money if your investment goes up and not lose money if your investment goes down?
- Would you be willing to pay extra for that kind of protection?

If the investor's answer is yes to at least two out of those three questions, then investing in an annuity is right for at least a portion of their retirement income.

FIXED ANNUITY SMARTS

A lot of investors need a portion of their money in guaranteed investments. Why? It's simple. Fixed annuities usually pay a higher guaranteed rate than other types of guaranteed investments like bonds, CDs, money market accounts or Treasuries (Treasury notes, bills, or bonds). However, the guarantees are only as strong as the issuing insurance company.

No Loss of Principal—Guaranteed

A fixed annuity guarantees owners they will not lose any of their principal if they maintain—meaning do not sell—the contract for a specific period of time called the penalty period. A fixed annuity also guarantees that the insurance company (issuer) will pay a certain minimum rate of interest and that there will be guaranteed dollar amount deposited in your account. Further, these payments will be guaranteed for a certain number of years, or even for the life of the annuitant (policy owner). The investment is 100% guaranteed. It's a contract between you and the issuing insurance company.

Guaranteed Rates May Not Be Guaranteed Forever

Of course there is usually a look back at the guaranteed rate after a period of time. After all, a company cannot guarantee to pay the owner a rate of, say, 7% per year if the company is earning only 5% on the money invested with it.

The Single Most Important Factor
in Considering Fixed Annuity Contracts

No, it's not the rate of interest paid each year. Nor is it the length of time the rate is guaranteed. First and foremost are the financial strength and reputation of the company behind the contract. It doesn't matter how much the guaranteed rate is if the company isn't rock solid financially. So don't be fooled by higher rates from a second-tier insurer.

Can Any Money Be Withdrawn without Penalties?

Usually an investor can withdraw 10% per year out of an annuity without a penalty. If the investor withdraws more than that, there is a penalty on all additional funds above 10%. It is important to check out what the penalty period is. It might decrease over time. For example there may be a penalty period of 5 years or 10 years or longer but the penalty may be sliding from say 5% down to 1% and then 0% after the five-year period.

What about Hidden Charges?

So long as the investor stays through the penalty period there are no front-end charges although most contracts have internal fees and charges much like mutual funds have expense and management fees. However, fixed annuities will pay a specific rate of return over the life of the investment without any internal charges except the penalty for getting out early or withdrawing more than allowed each year. Always know the details before you buy.

SO WHEN ARE ANNUITIES RIGHT FOR YOU?

Good question. Our friends at Fidelity have a neat little 60-second Q & A page that will take you through the initial process of discovering whether an annuity is a good investment vehicle for at least part of your retirement assets.

You'll find the quick test at: *http://personal.fidelity.com/products/annuities/intro.shtml.cvsr?banner=%epid!&psite=overture&crtype=search&kw=annuity* .

Or simply go to *www.fidelity.com* and click through on the annuity information pages.

Among the Things You Need to Consider

Evaluating whether annuities are right for your situation or just "bunk" is simple. Ask yourself the following:

- How long you think you will live, taking into consideration the ages of your elder relatives and close family?
- How healthy you have been, how soon and for how long you will need a guaranteed income?
- How long a period is your money locked up or penalized upon withdrawal?

Once you have that figured out you can use the quick test above to affirm whether or not annuities make good sense. Just because there are horror stories out there, and some unscrupulous salespeople, or under-informed investors, don't ignore the annuity as one more financial vehicle in the arsenal of investments that may be suited to your purpose.

Also see *www.AARP.org* for general retirement and annuity contract information.

Money Minutes

PORTFOLIO MANAGEMENT 101 – ASSET ALLOCATION

Asset allocation is just another term for having a portfolio that's balanced in broad categories like stocks, bonds, annuities, fixed investments, real estate, insurance and so forth. There is a further breakdown into money you save outside your company benefit program (401K or 403B) and your traditional IRA or ROTH IRA program. The total of the assets in both these portfolios should be diversified to mange risk and buffer performance.

What's asset allocation based on?

As the jumping off point for financial portfolio management, asset allocation is the result of a process where the investor and the investment advisor work together to choose:

- The type of risk that's acceptable
- The amount of growth desired
- The timeframe for total return on the portfolio.

Even with an advisor in the picture, the investor has the final say. The advisor's job is to help establish the asset mix, pointing out what works best in the investor's scheme of things and also what kind of fine-tuning will work at different times to keep the portfolio in balance.

Opportunities to participate in various employee benefit programs will vary greatly if you work for a large company with many choices or are self-employed or work for a smaller company with fewer benefits.

Money Sense:
Age and family status have a good bit to do in coming up with an appropriate master strategy. So too are years till retirement. The retired person has pretty much got all the money they are ever going to have. There's little or no new money coming into the picture. The investor still working is going to add new money to the picture each year and the longer they have until retirement the more variable (with more inherent risk) investments are included.

Money Minutes

WHEN TO CONSIDER CHANGES IN ASSET ALLOCATION

What Triggers Changes in Asset Allocation?

Changes in future goals.

Life changing events are often a good reason to schedule a financial check-up to see if any fine-tuning should be done to enhance or modify portfolio performance. Events like the birth of a new child or grandchild, change of job accompanied by a large increase or decrease in salary, or a major health or financial emergency.

A change in your time horizon.

You are 52 yrs of age and you have decided that you won't work until you are 65 or the age at which you can collect full Social Security Benefits and officially retire from the workforce. Let's say you have decided to take retirement benefits at age 62. That means you'll need to change your portfolio, in particular asset allocation in the portfolio to deliver the target funds sooner. Originally you had in mind to work until age 65 and therefore portfolio performance had to meet a certain criteria to get you there.

Retirement.

Once you decide to retire, even if you have a balanced portfolio, it's time to reassess. If you haven't worked with an advisor before to establish general needs and a good asset mix to get what you need, then this is a key place and time to seek professional advice. Generally a person in retirement will have fewer variable investments and more guaranteed and fixed investments in their portfolio mix.

Is Asset Allocation The Same Thing As Diversification?

The easiest way to distinguish the two is this: Asset allocation is the business of dividing up your portfolio into a number of asset classes—stocks, bonds, real estate income properties, even cash in order to achieve a certain return and a certain value in the portfolio at a certain time with consideration for your risk tolerance. Diversification is how much money you put in each class to get you to the desired return by taking on the appropriate or least amount of risk to achieve the desired returns. However, neither asset allocation nor diversification can assure a profit nor protect against loss.

Money Sense:

Wondering if all retirees have the same asset allocation? No, not at all. Those with the biggest concerns are the ones having almost all their money in fixed or guaranteed investments. Back in the 80s when interest rates were high fixed income was returning double digit annual gains. Now many of these instruments have returned to the norm and are yielding under 6%. Retirees who are used to variable investment returns and understand or are willing and able to bear a little more volatility usually have the greatest returns and can continue to live the way they used to while in full retirement.

ASSET CLASS INVESTING

The key to good investing is having some balance in your portfolio. Asset class investing helps you do this. Each grouping of investments within a specific asset class share a similar risk and return profile.

Four major asset classes are:

Cash and cash equivalents; Fixed Income Investments; equity investments; and, tangibles.

Cash and cash equivalents.

These are cash or highly liquid investments that can be turned into cash immediately. Savings accounts, certificates of deposit, short-term Treasury bills, short-term bonds and money market accounts.

Fixed Income Investments.

These debt instruments have a fixed payment schedule. They are loans or debt such as government bonds, municipal bonds, corporate bonds, high-yield bonds and foreign bonds.

Equity investments.

Here you have ownership interest in an asset like a company. You are a part owner via the shares you hold. There are many categories of equity investments including U.S. Large Capitalization stocks (One Billion of more in sales), U.S. Medium Capitalization stocks (500Million to 1 Billion in Sales) and Small Cap stocks (under 500 Million in sales). There are also micro caps with various definitions but generally between 50 and 200 or 300 Million in sales.

Tangibles

Tangibles include real estate, precious metals and other commodities and collectibles—coins, stamps, antiques, decoys, to name a few.

Money Sense:

Here's a quick and easy asset class investment lesson: Balance is the key. Combine different asset classes within the same investment portfolio. Although it can't assure a profit, you can reduce the overall risk and price volatility of the portfolio. It is smoothed out within the portfolio. If you are entirely invested in one asset class and it goes up, great! However, when it goes down—and sure enough every asset class will go through a down period (except for cash)—you could lose a lot.

DEBT AND EXPENSES

Few things get good people in trouble more often in life than excess spending and too much consumer debt. So we are going to hammer on some vital points in this area. It is easy to take a ride on debt road. Credit card benders make offers almost daily especially when lending rates are low. When rates are low debt payments start out small and maybe you get the instant gratification of enjoying more life now than you really can afford. It feels pretty good—for a little while. However, the debt road often takes an ugly turn into a "tunnel" with many twists and turns leading you into deeper and darker territory and sometimes taking you to a dead end with no way out but last resort options like bankruptcy. That's no get out of jail free card either with the new laws passed in 2007.

There Are Some Big and Little Things
You Can Do To Avoid the Debt Trap

Guidelines for Avoiding Big Debt Traps

1. Say "no" to credit card promo offers. The "come-on" rates are low but the winner in the end is usually the lender. Two reasons for this: 1) unless you are highly disciplined and always pay your bills on time, the default rate imposed for late or missed payments will "bite" you hard. And that penalty rate may be applied to your remaining loan balance permanently. In the end your promotional rate of 1.9% or less could end up becoming nearly 30% if you are even 1 day late on a payment. So think twice here.

2. Never take out an I/O—interest only— mortgage loan. Perhaps the most tempting of all jumbo creative lending devices adapted form the commercial lending arena is the interest only loan. The reason it is so compelling is that you can afford a much bigger mortgage. Here's an example: A $200,000 mortgage with a 5.5% interest rate will only cost you $916.67 per month. A conventional mortgage at the same interest rate will cost you $1135.58 per month. That's a difference of $218.91 per month.

13

At 7% an I/O will cost you 1166.67 per month versus $1330.60 per month for a conventional loan. A monthly difference of $263.93. Quite a difference. Some I/O mortgages even have artificially low "teaser rates" up front. When the teaser term is over; your mortgage principal actually goes up. That's called negative amortization!

Money Sense:

With an I/O loan you are paying interest only. The full amount you borrowed—the principal of the loan—is still owed at the end of the loan term which can be up to 30 years or whenever the loan is paid off. With a conventional loan each month a certain portion of your payment goes toward paying back some of the money you borrowed from the bank and it reduces the amount you have to pay back to the lender when you terminate the mortgage in a sale. At the end of the mortgage term if you were to continue to make the payments until the end of the term you would have completely paid back the money you originally borrowed. That's equity buildup.

3. Don't consolidate consumer credit card debt into a home equity loan just to get the tax deduction on the interest. This is a subtle minefield that can really sink you permanently. It seems logical. You have credit card debt on which you are paying as much as 20% or more in interest per year. None of the interest is deductible. But if you own your own home you can just consolidate your credit card debt and pay it off with a loan against the equity or excess value over the loan amount that has built up in your home over the years just by writing a check. It automatically converts to a loan at a much lower rate of interest, perhaps prime rate—the lowest rate of interest that banks extend to their best customers—plus a little surcharge of ¼ or ½ percent. So the interest rate may be cut in half or more and you also get to deduct the interest on your home equity loan.

Sounds like Christmas in July; Not Really. The momentary holiday cheer will be short lived if you return to your same old credit card habits and charge up what you can't afford. Unchecked spending will just lead you to having a new pile of credit card debt plus the old debt now secured by a lien against your home.

4. Don't finance your vacations with credit card debt. Oh sure, you've worked hard all year and you deserve a break. If you want a break and can break your piggy bank, then take that vacation of your dreams and enjoy every minute of it. But if you have to put it all on plastic then the hole you dig will give you more worry than joy. And all I can say—and I can say it knowingly— is that being out of debt will give you more piece of mind than a 1 week vacation ever could.

5. Prepare for the seasonal debt traps. Added expenses for vacations, camp, pool and swim club memberships, summer school, even clothing needs can just wreck a family budget. The regular monthly expenses we are pretty used to but when there is a seasonal change and new things come along many families just get caught up in all the spending. They spend now and when the bills come due realize they don't have enough to cover the tab. That's the summer debt trap. The National Foundation for Consumer Credit says its offices see an increase in activity during the fall months as bills from summer purchases start to mount. Of course this should cause the family to prepare to cut back on the holiday purchases in December, but in many cases, the reality is they won't cut back and their finances start going downhill taking the family deeper and deeper into debt and a large January hangover.

Money Sense:

Is there a way around this? Yes. Start putting money away in advance. A little at a time on a regular basis will help keep a lid on things. Also consider some money saving ideas like driving instead of flying, packing a lunch in the cooler for the road, eating at family restaurants instead of the hotels, camping instead of hotels, purchasing air and travel tickets well in advance rather than paying full price at the last minute, staying over and traveling on the weekdays when hotel rates are lower or taking advantage of Saturday night stay-overs, if using the airlines to get a price break. It takes a little research. One really patient friend took a voluntary flight bump for his family of four in return for a $400 credit.

Money Minutes

SHREWD SIMPLE TIPS FOR SAVING MONEY AND GETTING A LEG UP ON DEBT

1. Go Cash and Carry.

Avoid installment or credit card debt or pay you tomorrow situations whenever you can possibly do so. Pay for what you have cash for and think twice about anything that you can't afford to pay for right now. Obviously things like cars or houses or home improvements you won't have the cash for but for regular monthly expenses, think cash and go. In short, don't take on any more credit card debt

2. Don't have a savings account and carry credit card balances at the same time.

Seems obvious but so many people have a savings fund earning interest at passbook rates of a few per cent per month and they also carry credit card balances with interest rates as high as 20%. 2 per cent earned on savings. 20 per cent cost on debt. What's the trouble with that equation? Use your savings money earning only 2 per cent to pay off your installment debt costing 20 per cent.

3. Make more than the minimum monthly payments.

Make more than the minimum monthly payments on current consumer debt or you'll just drive yourself deeper into the debt tunnel. The only way out is to backtrack to zero debt or as close to it as you can get.

4. Brown bag it and save a bundle.

Ponder this. A person who eats lunch out five days a week, at a typical cost of $5 per lunch—and you can't do that every place in the country any more—could save a lot of money. Over a 25 year period and just brown bagging it 2 days per week, you'd save $520 per year. At an 8% annual return compounded weekly, you could amass a total of $42,519 just by bringing your lunch

17

two times a week. Why even a banker would notice that kind of money.

5. **Begin a regular savings plan as soon as you have zero debt.**

Even a simple to set up monthly savings bond program will help you start accumulating a nest egg for the future. But there is no time to tinker with your future financial health. Start changing ways today.

DEBT COUNSELING:
THE CURE FOR A DEBT HABIT YOU JUST CAN'T SHAKE

Consumers are Tapped Out

Some would say that consumers have done more than their fair share propping up the economy these past 10 years. For just the second time since the Great Depression Americans have spent every penny they made. The savings rate recently was zero per cent. So long as the economy hums along, no problem. But if the economy slows it could be trouble.

How much debt should you have?

It depends. The consensus of experts says about 10% of your take home pay not including your mortgage. But if you are consistently spending more than you take in and your debt payments keep mounting above the 10% guideline, you are headed for a lot of debt that can take years and years to pay off.

Overspending just isn't an isolated trouble spot. But if you are overspending and then a legitimate emergency arises, like major car repairs, a medical problem , or just a wedding, graduation, birthday, wedding or anniversary, then you are off the deep end.

Chronic Overspending Can be a Behavioral Problem

Overspending is often a behavioral problem that's been almost compulsive for years and the individual is in such deep debt they have no idea how to get back on their feet

Money Sense:

If you see yourself in the mirror here then admit it and seek out competent help. It's no shame. There are professional organizations such as the Consolidated Credit Counseling Service, *www.consolidatedcredit. org* a non profit organization that can help a person in debt find ways to resolve their problem, change their spending habits, and get out of the debt tunnel back into the light.

Money Minutes

IS THERE A WAY OUT WHEN YOU HAVE
TOO MANY CREDIT CARDS WITH HIGH BALANCES?

Here are some suggestions:

1. First, admit you have a debt problem. And resolve that you are going to re cover from it. Take a serious and disciplined approach toward cleaning up your situation. Otherwise some of the suggestions we make could just backfire and get you into such a world of trouble you'll be loading up the double-barrel and trying to find where I live.

2. If you are in a position to get a new low interest credit card with a promotional fee that allows you to transfer the balances from higher interest bearing credit cards, go for it and make the transfers. Some cards even offer interest free promotional rates for balance transfers. If you can get a piece of that you are off to a really good start in the quest to get liquid again.

3. Pay the minimum on the low interest rate card and pay as much as you can on the highest rate cards first. For instance, Card A low or no interest promo. Card B 12.95% interest. Card C 15%. Card D 19.99%. Pay the minimum on Card A and then pay as much you can on the balances on B, C and D. If you have a substantial balance and too many cards as above, pay the minimums on A, B and C and pay as much as you can on D to get it completely paid off first. Then start doing the same thing with B and C until C is eliminated. Then work on B. Once that's gone, start paying off your debt on A.

Money Sense:

Aside from what has been suggested above watch out for predatory lending offers. Before you know it you'll have several or more new credit cards with balances transferred to lower teaser interest rates while not closing down the original accounts you paid off in the first place. One slip or missed payment due date on the new cards and you may end up with a jacked-up interest rate from that date forward plus the late charge fee, even if you make monthly payments much higher than the minimums. And if you don't close out the zeroes out account, guess what, chances are you'll end up using it again, sooner or later.

MONEY MISERY

There's an old saw that goes like this:

The best way to help poor people is to not be one of them.

Granted, this sounds like tough love, but there is a lot of wisdom behind it. It's a little like the emergency message you get on the airplane. If an emergency situation develops and the oxygen masks drop down, before putting a mask on your child or aged or inform co-passenger, make sure you (the older, active and healthiest one,) put your mask on first, and then position the mask on those you are caring for. If you are too weak to help, all may suffer or perish needlessly.

20% Of Americans Have Money Issues...

If you think that only poor people have money problems, you'd be wrong. Statistics show 20% of Americans as a nation had trouble meeting basic needs at least once during the year. And slightly over 8 Million were families with incomes over $45,000 per year.

Where Do People Get Financial Help When Needed?

Three of four surveyed people said they'd get help from family or friends. But the Census Bureau reports only 17% actually got help that way or from the government. The reality is your family and friends may not be able to be there for you most of the time.

What's the solution?

Save, save, save.

And save even more if you can. Why? When any type of crisis hits you'll have something to fall back on. Paul Orfalea, who sold his mega successful copy company, Kinko's, to FedEx said in his book *Copy This*, there are only a few rules for business success: Save money, surround yourself with competent people; then get out of their way. Asked if he ever had any failures he said sure but I never had any debt. He financed his business schemes with savings. If they worked, great. If not he packed it in, saved up some more money, and started up again with the next venture.

Seek debt counseling.

The resources here are so numerous and there are many services that aren't there to serve your best interest. If you have used a financial adviser in the past, seek them out and explain your situation. They will probably have several recommendations. If not there consult at websites that have broad recognition and a very public platform, such as *The Motley Fool* — *www.fool.com* — or Microsoft's MSN Money at *http://moneycentral. msn.com/home.asp.* Here as with your own personal financial adviser, you'll get unbiased advice that could literally save your financial boat from getting swamped.

Money Sense:

If you want to avoid money misery, and I know I have said it before, save, save, save. You'll be so glad you did. And finally, don't wait and don't procrastinate over the problems. You need to get over the embarrassment of the situation and get help early. If your home mortgage is involved, talk to the lender, sooner rather than later. They actually have programs for remediation.

CREDIT OR DREAD-IT CARDS:
SURVIVAL FOR COLLEGE STUDENTS ON PLASTIC

Induction into the hall of debt starts early ...

- 83% of undergraduate students have at least one credit card
- The average college student carries credit card debt with an average balance of just over $3,000.
- 10% of students have balances exceeding $7,000

In many cases we are talking teenagers preoccupied with classes, living in a dorm or cramped off campus apartments, with no steady income, and little understanding of or formal budgeting skills. Can credit cards be good for them?

Credit cards can be useful. They are a convenient way to pay for school supplies, books and emergencies or to establish some kind of credit history that comes in handy later on. What's been a problem is the persistent on campus marketing of credit cards. So much so that some schools have banned it. Others are offering credit card debt seminars as part of orientation.

Money Sense: Real Simple Suggestions for Students Using Credit Cards:

- Learn the credit card basics like grace periods, late payment penalties, finance charges and minimum payments.

- Shop around for the best card rates. And avoid teaser or come-on rates. A list of student credit cards is available at www. cardtrak.com.

- Maintain only one credit card and keep the balance low.

- Pay off the balance each month or at least pay off more than the minimum to avoid running up excessive interest charges.

- Create a budget for the school year to better understand how credit cards can be used in the spending plan.

• Avoid late payments like the plague. Mail your payment at least 5 days before the due date. Late charges are high and reported to credit reporting companies. They also alert other creditors that you are falling behind on payments.

• Get the excellent free booklet "Budgeting 101: Your Money Guide for Getting Through School" from Consolidated Credit Counseling Services at **1-800-320-9929** or *http://www. consolidatedcredit.org/* .

WAYS TO PAY OFF TOO MUCH DEBT

Lowering and Eliminating Debt

Lowering and finally eliminating debt should be the first step in a household budget program. But anyone who has more than one credit card and is thinking of lowering their debt needs a plan. There are options.

Option 1. Find the lowest interest rate card possible, consolidate debt and then pay it off. Sounds good but before you go for it get a calculator and see what the cost saving is.

Money Sense Alert:

Be certain you are not a late payer or your teaser rate could disappear and you may be hit with a steep late payment fee as well. Remember, too that teaser rates only apply for a fixed period of time and then they revert to a higher rate. Miss one payment and you could end up paying as much as 18% or 21% or more on the remaining balance plus the late charge which very likely will cost you more than the interest rate you are currently paying over the long term.

Few people actually do switch cards and take advantage of the consolidating balances and saving features.

If you don't get the balance paid off and the teaser rate expires? You could end up with an even higher rate than you are currently paying. You could call the issuer and try negotiating a lower rate of interest or if you have sizable debt on more than one card and you don't feel comfortable getting the whole thing under control, try a credit counseling service or talk to your professional adviser about the best approach to paying down your debts.

Option 2. Seek professional help. Counseling services are available locally—check your Yellow Pages—and over the Internet. Smart Money has a credit card interest calculator on its site. www.

smartmoney.com. to help with the necessary calculations. But be sure the counseling service you choose isn't just a "front" for a loan operation and inquire about fees for services provided. On the plus side there are services that may be able to negotiate a lower interest rate on credit card balances as well as stretched out payments without penalty fees, and in there somewhere is a shot at getting out of the hole.

Option 3. Cut expenses first and divert the saved money to debt payment. Ask yourself every time you reach into your pocket, say for that flat screen TV on sale or the gourmet coffee or eating lunch out, "Do I need this?" Diverting expense money into debt reduction could cut hundreds or even thousands off your debt each year. And the sigh of relief you'll breathe is the sigh of financial freedom. Cost: Momentary deprivation. Value: Priceless.

WATCH YOUR CREDIT SCORE
AND KNOW WHAT AFFECTS IT

Switching to a New Credit Card with a new company could cost you in the ratings.

First you have a shorter history, less than one year, when you apply for a new card. That has a negative effect on your score. Second let's say you have $5,000 of debt outstanding on a card with a $6,000 limit. That's 83% of your credit limit. You are almost maxed out or limited out on the card. The effect on your FICO score is negative.

Keep balances below 50% of your total credit limit.

Over 50 % damages your score the most.

Avoid Late payments.

So often I hear people say, I have the money in my checking account but I just didn't get around to paying the bill on time. This costs you two ways. First many companies charge late fees and can legally collect them. Second it can be reported to the credit tracking companies and end up in your record as a penalty to your credit score. Should you have a good reason for missing a payment, some emergency or other legitimate excuse, do contact the companies you are late with and offer an explanation. That will often control any permanent damage that could result to your rating.

Keep old cards active even if you have paid off the balances.

If you have a card with a good and long history but no open balances, charge something on it at least every quarter or three months. Keep it small and then pay it off. The card will remain active and your score is affected positively because in the aggregate you show a higher credit balance and overall lower percentage of credit available usage. Also the credit card software algorithms score you higher for a card in good standing that has been open for a longer period of time. But they have to be considered active for it to count. So keep old cards alive with periodic small purchases for the positive shot they give your rating.

29

Keep cards in good standing open.

If you close a card you could hurt your score by lowering your overall debt to credit ratio. Your credit available is reduced and your remaining balances now represent a higher percentage of available credit. Seems foolish but that's the way it works. If you have 3 cards with $15,000 in available credit—$5,000 each—and close one with $5,000 and your total debt is say $5,500, now your available credit is $10,000 with $5,500 in outstanding debt. Your debt ratio went from 37% to 55%. Result: Lower credit score even though your intentions were good.

Pay off purchases each month.

If you find a credit card that won't charge interest if you pay off current month purchases, use that card and make sure you pay off the purchases completely each month. You'll have the use of their money interest free and a terrific payment history as well.

Money Sense:

If you have open balances on say 5 cards, spread your payments out over all the cards but weigh more heavily toward the ones with the highest balances and the highest interest rates. If you can't pay off all balances each month, the best of all worlds, make sure you don't have a very high balance on just one card, even if your payments are on time and the interest rate is the lowest because it will keep your FICA score lower than if you had all balances below 50%. If one card gets too high take advantage of the teaser low interest balance transfer offers. Just make sure you keep making payments on time otherwise it could cost you in the long run.

CUTTING THE FAT OUT OF YOUR EXPENSES

"Houston, we have a problem"...

Most of us know how to make money; but hanging on to it is something else. How to cut down on those monthly expenses we keep running on automatic is tougher than chewing on an overcooked piece of rump roast. Maybe this is one too many clichés but I wanted to challenge myself with a simple but shrewd thought on expense cutting.

If there was one antidote to uncontrollable spending habits, what would it be? After a minute or so of brain twisting I remembered an old 60s expression: Question Authority. And then the bulb went off. It's really simple. Start by:

Questioning Before You Spend ....

Spending is so habitual it is almost unconscious for many of us. Heading to the restaurant three times a week because it is easy, trading in the car for a new one when the payments are up, refinancing to pull more equity out of the house to buy a boat, or simply being self-indulgent. Expense control starts with a little self awareness or attention to what we are doing.

Just ask, "Do I really need this?" Buying only what we need will help us spend less and save more. If you need it, not just want it, buy it in the most economical way. If not, don't buy. Just try it and see. Take a few small examples:

> **Entertainment:** Rent a movie and watch it at home. You'll save the cost of going to the theatre not to mention the cost of the soda, popcorn and candy (way less than half price at home) which usually adds up to more than the price of the movie ticket.

> **Food:** Lunch. Bag it a few times a week and put the money in a jar. A store bought sandwich is around $7 in major cities and a home made one is perhaps $3. Big difference. Dinner. Instead of going to restaurants four times a month, make it two or three. Pocket the difference and you've paid a phone bill. Cut back the

31

second round of drinks when out and again, meaningful money is saved.

Home: Refinance your mortgage at lower interest. Put the saved interest in savings or better yet, pay down the rest of your debt with it. Wins both ways.

Gas: Always pay for gas with cash. Putting gasoline on a credit card will add potentially hundreds of dollars of interest payments to your cost unless you pay credit card expenses off in full every month.

RUB OUT MONEY WORRIES

As singer songwriter Jimmy Buffett croons "we are the people our parents warned us about". Money woes and the constant worrying about money will lead to emotional and physical problems.

But there are some good alternatives to being constantly preoccupied about money. Put all three of them into play and it will set you free.

Turn your home into a wellness center. Now what I mean by that is around 68% of families own their homes and those homes are also the source of their biggest headaches. The cure for home worry syndrome is to pay off your mortgage, as quickly as possible. If you pay an extra $50 a month on a $200,000, 7%, fixed rate 30 year loan you can knock $36,000 off your interest payments. And that could get rid of a lot of your money worries.

Thinking further into the future, your future that is, open a ROTH IRA. Today! With the traditional IRA you put pre tax money in but you take out taxable money in the future. With the ROTH you put in after tax money now and take out nothing but tax free money later. If you start early the taxes you pay now will likely be a lot less than the taxes you'd pay down the line on a traditional IRA at a time when you'd rather have no tax worries. Take care of your retirement years now and you'll have many worry free retirement years later.

Slash debt to the bone. Use any and all means possible to end this malignant anxiety. Speak to your banker about mortgage possibilities. Perhaps you can lower your mortgage rate. Consolidate credit card debt into one lower rate card. Rededicate yourself to spending on needed items only and paying off new purchases before the interest rate clock starts ticking.

Go long term on your investments and add to them as often as possible.

Money Sense:

A lot of money worries are psychological and may be caused by bad habits and unconscious behavior—usually spendthrift behavior that goes against our emotional and psychological grain. Getting to a place where you are comfortable, knowing what that comfort level is, and staying in that zone will go a long way toward easing money worries.

33

Money Minutes

BUYING WITHOUT MONEY

Each year about 8 Billion dollars of trade transactions occur without the exchange of money. That's called "bartering"

Depending on your age you might be saying, "What's barter, Bob?" In the old days if you had chickens and I had a cow, I could exchange some fresh milk for some of your eggs. With the growth of the Internet, bartering has mushroomed into more than a one to one business and now barter is being done on a worldwide scale.

A few ways to barter are:

1. My eggs for your milk or cheese. We decide what's a fair trade.

2. Your legal services for my bookkeeping and accounting. Figure hourly rates for these and a fair trade ratio, 1.5 to 1 or so if there is a great disparity in the standard rates for such services.

3. Mothers swapping no longer needed but serviceable items like cars seats, strollers or cribs for booster chairs or toddler beds.

4. A beautician may trade hairstyling with a computer literate client in return for computer troubleshooting and repair—or computer lessons.

5. Swapping goods and services for "trade dollars" instead of real money. The seller sets a price on their goods or services that is comparable with the actual fair market price of the merchandise or service. The buyer then offers services or goods they feel are comparable.

6. Barter clubs. Here members join with the express purpose of trading goods and services with other like minded people.

Goods and services traded or swapped via barter are considered the same as a cash transaction by the IRS and any "trade dollars" earned should be reported to the IRS. If you barter through a club the IRS is tracking those exchanges and the clubs have to issue 1099s. If you traded private math tutoring for a tune up on your car, no problem; however, be careful

35

about making it a business without reporting to the tax authorities.

Money Sense:

There are many bartering sites on the Web like *http://www.tradeaway. com* and books you can find on Amazon, such as Let's Trade: A Book About Bartering, from Money Matters, by Nancy Loewen and Brian Jensen. Today the expression one individual's junk is another's treasure has never been so true. Look at the number of transactions on e-Bay, referred to by some as the world's largest garage sale.

HOLIDAY PREPARATION—
EIGHT WAYS TO SAVE ON HOLIDAY SPENDING

1. Keep track of your spending. It can help you understand where you are financially with your expenditures. It can also keep you from spending money that you don't have.

2. Before buying a present for someone ask yourself "Am I buying this because it is a need or just to give as a present? Preplanning here can save you big.

3. Make a list with five columns. Person, gift budget, gift idea, how you'll pay for the gift, and the pay off plan. Could be mom, $100, clothes, credit card, 90 days. Or Jose, $25, tie, cash, paid on purchase. Making a list in August will help you plan your holiday expenditures better. With a list you can also take advantages of early bird sales, going out of business and end of season as well as pre season sales.

4. Avoid getting caught up in a seasonal shopping frenzy. Don't buy without thinking. Scale down your list. Make fruit or other gift baskets instead. Or buy gift certificates—saving time and money on unwanted gifts as well as gasoline.

5. Donate a stock that is up sharply for the year. You save by not paying short or long term capital gains and the recipient gets something of real value that you paid less for.

6. Donate money to charity with a credit card. If you do it at the end of the year, you get to take the deduction in the current year although you won't end up paying for it until next year.

7. Have an in house New Year's Eve Party instead of going out to overpriced galas. You can even have everyone pitch in and bring something.

8. Ship gifts early so you'll avoid the rush and the pressure to ship 2

day or overnight or express to make sure it arrives on time.

9. Think about craft or hand made kind of gifts you can make that are relatively inexpensive to create and whose perceived value will be far beyond your cost to create.

10. Shop online for "clearance" items. The Internet stores have become like department stores and they have clearance items on sale most times. Examples are Eddie Bauer, LL Bean, Macys, and Wal-Mart to name just a very few. In addition, at places like e-Bay you may find name brand year round clothing at clearance and below clearance prices. It's more like wholesale online buying.

SHOPPING SMART FOR TRAVEL BARGAINS

Travel Myths versus Realities

Myth 1:
Wait until the last minute and you'll get the best airfares, best room rates and best car rental rates.

Reality:
This may be a procrastinator's dream come true but the best way to save money traveling is by booking early. Recently a friend was on a business trip to Orlando—really!—flying out of LaGuardia Airport in New York. He used one of the cheap ticket services over the Internet and books 3 days prior to leaving. Cost: $399 for coach. On board he got chatting with his two seat mates. The woman next to him paid $329 and she booked a week earlier than he did. But the woman on the aisle paid just $150. She booked 3 months earlier through her travel agent.

Myth 2:
Shop on your own and you'll find the best bargains.
Every one loves a bargain and you'll come across some really great sounding deals if you spend enough time and research to look for them.

Reality:
Time has value, too. And if your time is precious or scarce, I really recommend your travel agent as a shortcut to money saving deals. They are professionals and they know about all sorts of deals. What's more, if you have no idea what you might want to do but you know for sure you really need a vacation, your travel agent can be a real storehouse of ideas. Just tell them how much you want to spend, a time frame for your vacation, they will ask you a few important questions and usually come up with a handful of ideas. And remember, they consult with you for free.

Myth 3:
Pick where and when you want to vacation and then shop to get the best value.

Reality:

If you can stay a little flexible on dates, day and even time of arrival and departure you can potentially save a significant amount of money on arrangements. Here again, a travel agent can be of tremendous help because they know where the opportunities are.

If you want to shop on line just for airline tickets—on which a travel agent makes very little booking— and you have computer access you can check the airlines directly or *www.cheaptickets.com, www.orbitz.com, www.travelocity.com* or *www.hotwire.com.* You can also check hotel room rates at some of the previous links or at *www.hotel.com.*

Money Sense:

No matter how much you need a vacation, and no matter how much you think you can make in monthly payments to pay for it later, don't take a vacation if you have to charge the whole thing. Long after the happy memories are gone those credit card payments will sting you every month. And a new link you'll want to check out is *www.kayak. com.* Kayak is a travel search engine that crawls other websites for the best deals available including all the airlines, hotels and so forth. Kayak doesn't book anything. When you find what you're looking for you go direct to the source and book there.

BANKRUPTCIES

Bankruptcies have been steadily increasing in the first part of this decade, both in the housing arena where foreclosures have increased and among individuals.

A new Bankruptcy Law passed in 2005, said to "toughen" the laws and requirements for those taking advantage of personal bankruptcy in order to get rid of personal and credit card debt. In a nutshell it means that lawyers will have more paperwork to do to for their clients and also have to provide more verification of their clients' finances. The result is there will be more lawyer time involved and more cost to file the application.

Under the new law people with above average incomes as determined by a "means test" will not be able to file under Chapter 7, allowing their debt to be completely wiped out. They'll have to file under Chapter 13 and submit to a 5 year repayment plan. In the State of New Jersey , for example, those with incomes above the state's median income—$87,412—who can pay at least $6000 over 5 years or $100 a month, would be required to file under Chapter 13.

Bottom Line: For most people, personal bankruptcy will still be possible, but the cost of filing under Chapter 7 will increase, and lawyers will want their money up front.

While no one is completely immune from having financial setbacks happen, it's a good idea to have a plan in place that will help you through financial adversity. A few good rules to follow that will keep you from the wolves are:

Money Sense:

- Have a financial cushion to tide you through the rough waters – losing a job, a major medical expense, disability or other hardship. Most of us haven't got more than 60 days of expenses covered with savings. Try to get it to at least 3 months or more. You won't regret it.

- A little tougher but still smart planning is never buy cars, computers or furniture or vacations on credit. Credit is a bad thing to use on a wasting asset that declines in value from the moment you own it.

- Placing vacations on credit is just bad money management. Vacations have no intrinsic value; just pure instant gratification.

CUT YOUR GASOLINE EXPENSES EVEN IF YOU CAN'T STOP DRIVING OR CAN'T BUY A HYBRID

Fools and Still Be Fooled—But Not For Much Longer

We had an oil embargo thirty some years ago with real gasoline and oil shortages, hours of standing in lines at gas pumps only to see the red flag go up and tempers flare up too, before we got to fill up. It lasted a few months and then all was back to normal. Cars slowly returned to high horsepower, more weight, and we super-sized our vehicles just like McDonald's fries. As the saying goes, fool me once, shame on you. Fool me twice, shame on me.

Finally it seems there are some signs that a change is in the wind with consumers, at the grassroots level, where it counts. Let's face it; ain't nobody but "us" can make us smarter fuel consumers.

The obvious best way to get a leg up on saving fuel is if you are about to trade in a vehicle.

Money Sense:

Go smaller to get more fuel efficient. Don't just buy looks. Check the published city and highway mileage ratings and check consumer magazines for the real mileage numbers from the road.

Hybrid is a good choice getting better, but not just yet. The front end –premium pricing—and back end—replacement battery—costs are too high to make it pay for itself.

Money Sense:

Beware buying any used hybrids from the early years. Battery replacement could run you well over $1,000 or more. For now the best alternative engine platform is diesel. Gas mileage is better. Plus there are fewer parts to service or replace.

Big ways to save fuel and money:

1. Car pool to work or the train station. If you see the same

people each morning on the train like so many of us do, think about asking if they'd want to share a ride to the train sometime. And if you drive to work try advertising in the local paper for someone to car pool with to the same destination. Around 90% of people drive one to a car. It's getting too expensive.

2. Contact human resources at work and ask to set up a bulletin board with postings for people who want rides, need rides or want to car pool. Every single bit counts.

3. Check for park and ride lots in your community. You could cut your driving by 80%, hop a bus or pick up passengers to jump into HOV (high occupancy vehicle) lanes that get you to work even faster—and cheaper.

4. Think diesel if you are in the market for a new car. The new platforms burn much cleaner, smell a lot better, and emit less unburned hydrocarbons into the air.

According to *www.erideshare.com* the average 40 mile a day commute costs $2600 per year or more now. Splitting the cost with just one other person in a car pool, you'd save $1300 or over $100 per month. Even if gas prices don't hurt that much, it's still smart to go thrifty on gasoline consumption. Our planet as well as our kids and grandkids need our thoughtful help.

FIVE WISE, EASY WAYS TO
SAVE BIG ON GASOLINE COSTS

1. **Shop efficiently.** Forget that second trip out to the post office to mail the forgotten letter or pick up the dry cleaning. Plan your driving like you plan your errands. Consolidate them and use a circular route that takes you from the nearest point to farthest and then back again at home base with as little zigzagging and backtracking as possible. Savings: up to 10% of gasoline consumption.

2. **Take turns with neighbors** doing common tasks like driving the kids to and from school. Or making in between trips to the supermarket for milk bread and so forth. If you have several friends with kids you could make the run as little as once or twice a week. Potential saving of up to 25% of your fuel bill plus time and wear and tear on the car.

3. **Be an easy rider.** Many drivers hit the brakes hard and hit the gas pedal the same way. When you start out from the light ease up to speed with a light touch on the pedal. Experts say we can improve our mpg by 15% or more with this one change alone.

4. **Avoid overfilling your gas tank.** When you fill up stop at the first click. One click only. Overfilling just makes gas slosh around and out of the tank. In the heat gasoline expands so much it can push quarts of fluid out of the fuel tank. So never fill to the top in summer heat.

5. **Change air filters and keep them clean.** Dirty or clogged filters reduce air flow and gas economy drops as much as 15% or more.

A **final way** that's just starting to catch on in both metro and suburban areas is using a power motor scooter like a Vespa. While still not a mainstream form of transportation, and I certainly wouldn't recommend it for most people, sales are mounting rapidly because they get 50 to 80 miles per gallon, cost in the range of $2000 to $5000 and that makes them efficient and affordable for the right applications—like urban deliveries and courier services. Seen a few gray flannel suits and dresses riding to work on them, too.

PAYING FOR EDUCATION COSTS OF CHILDREN AND GRANDCHILDREN

Rising Cost of Education Is Outrunning the Rising Cost of Energy

Over the past 10 years education costs have steadily been outrunning inflation costs by nearly two to one. Inflation has been running around 3% while education costs have soared by 6% per year.

Saving early is important.

The key to getting children or grandchildren through school without piling up a ton of debt is to begin to save from their early childhood years. If you start saving $1,000 per year for a child born now and that money were to compound at say 8% per year, when the child turns 18 they will have a college fund of $40,446.

Money Sense:

To put away $1000 per year, the easiest way to think of it is in monthly terms. $85 per month will do it. When you write out the monthly bills, write a check to the education fund.

Starting Later in the Child's Life Can Work, Too— Especially for Grandparents

Grandparents have several choices to help fund college. If retirement needs are met and assets are not a problem then annual gifting of $12,000 or up to $24,000 if both grandparents are in the picture can be done with no tax consequences to the donor. The most flexible way to do this is to set up a UGMA/UTMA mutual fund investment or savings account in the name of the child using their social security or taxpayer number. This is a good alternative if grandparents are starting a little later in the child's life. Of course, the increase in the value of the funds and any interest or capital gains is taxable to the child. The first $700 is tax free and the rest is taxable at the child's tax rate. The good news here is that the

47

money isn't restricted to being used for educational expenses. The bad news is the money isn't restricted to educational expenses only and the income is not tax deferred. Once the child reaches legal adulthood, they may withdraw the money and use it for tuition or educationally related expenses or whatever other purpose they desire—like a fire engine red convertible. So the gifts should be weighed against other vehicles. If there is a concern over use of the money then parents or grandparents may set up savings in their names to maintain control of the assets.

Money Sense:

See *www.savingforcollege.com* for straight, objective information on 529 plans and other ways to save or pay for college.

HOW MUCH WILL COLLEGE COST?

Too much compared to what you may have paid a generation ago. It's no secret that the cost of education is climbing faster yearly than most other major items in our budgets. College costs have risen 51% in the past 10 years. The real problem is that a lot of families fail to take advantage of the saving and investing plans available to help fund these costs. It's not a last minute undertaking unless you are among the upper middle class or better.

Do You Have $193,000 to $415,000?

According to the College Board, it will cost $193,000 for tuition room and board to educate a child born in 2004 at a public college. And a four-year private university is expected to run $415,000.

How to Ease the Burden of Future College Costs?

Start Saving Now! The most important step you can take is to start saving now. The younger the child is the better. At birth get the child their own social security number and make sure all family members are told about the education fund you are establishing. Cash, savings bonds and other all intrinsically valuable gifts should be put into the fund. The time factor and compounding will go a long way toward providing the funds needed for higher education.

Check into grants and programs that are available for schooling. Check your state for specially sponsored programs for in state residents. And think in-state schools if a private school seems out of reach. Encourage the child's grandparents to set up and contribute toward 529 plans and do the same yourself. This is the best thing going for accumulating education costs in tax favored and tax advantaged ways. If you work for a large company, visit the human resources department. Many companies offer tuition, grant and even scholarship plans for employee children.

Money Sense:

Fund early and fund often. The old school politicians used to urge voters to vote early and vote often. That's actually good advice for college funders. Fund early and fund often. Also look to sites like *www. savingforcollege.com* and if you want to know how much it will take in monthly savings to reach your college funding goal go to *http:// calculators.aol.com/tools/aol/college01/tool.fcs.* Another favorite college funding plan of mine is the Coverdell plan which used to be known as the Education IRA. It's owned by the students' parents, has a minimal restricting effect on other aid the student can apply for and they are a good way to get up to $2,000 a year into a child's education savings fund.

529S: THE HEAVY LIFTER EDUCATION FUNDING PLAN FOR STUDENTS OF ALL AGES

The 529 plan is the most advantageous of all education funding plans available, if you have the intent and the means and the need to get an education fund up to size quickly.

Reasons 529s are popular

1. Money in a 529 plan qualifies for tax deferred accumulation and comes out tax-free when used for educational purposes.

2. It's not only good for college tuition; it can also be used for additional fees, books, room and board or dormitory expenses.

3. The money can be used not only for college costs, but for secondary education, like private high schools or primary schools and even graduate school.

4. The money in 529s is not considered part of the students' assets. So if qualified they can apply for a scholarship and the money can be used as soon as it is received.

5. There are no exclusionary income provisions on donors in the 529 program like there are in IRAs or Coverdell Savings Plans. Whether you make $25,000 per year or $250,000 per year the same rules apply.

6. The plans qualify under the gifting provision of the tax law so you can put in as much as $12,000 annually in them without filing a gift tax return. Better yet, they can be front loaded with an initial deposit of up to 5 years of gift exclusion or $60,000 and $120,000 if married. That's why I refer to them as the heavy lifting vehicles for an education fund that needs to get beefy fast.

7. The plans are under the control of the donor, not the student. Whatever money is in there will be directed for educational

purposes by the individual setting it up. So it's just packed with benefits and few if any wrinkles.

Money Sense:

www.collegesavings.org provides detailed information about all 529 college savings plans and even helps you compare plans from all around the county. Remember, you can live in Nebraska and set up a New York 529 plan (just an example; not a recommendation.)

WHAT TO LOOK FOR IN 529 COLLEGE SAVINGS PLANS

Assets in 529 plans have grown rapidly because it is such a good way to pre-fund education costs. Every state now offers its own plan. That ought to make it an easy choice for consumers especially since many states offer a state tax deduction to residents investing locally.

However, the plans charge fees, just like there are with mutual funds. There are many fees such as enrollment charges, annual maintenance fees, sales loads, deferred sales charges paid when you withdraw your money, administration and management fees (often called the expense ratio), and underlying fund expenses. So just looking at the tax advantages may hide some of the higher costs that make another state's plan a better choice. Also some states may allow you to contribute higher limits and accumulate more money. It currently ranges from $100,000 to $300,000.

Comparing One Plan Against The Other

It's a good idea to compare several plans to find a reasonably priced one. You can go over this with a financial adviser or take a look at *www. savingforcollege.com* to do some comparison shopping. The Financial Industry Regulatory Authority (FINRA), which has regulatory authority over 529s set up its own consumer online help tool to help analyze how fees affect returns. It's called the "Expense Analyzer" and it can be found at the Smart Saving for College link: *http://apps.nasd.com/ investor_Information/Smart/529/000100.asp*. Another good comparison site is *www.collegesaving.org*

Money Sense:

You don't need to set up a 529 plan in your own state. So long as it's used for education expenses, the only expenses 529s were created to cover, you may live in Michigan and invest in the California State 529 plan. But consider 2 things: Some states offer a tax credit of their own for residents who set up plans within the state and the various and sundry expenses of the funds contribute to the overall cost of the plan or effect investment performance. So you'll want to factor in these or other benefits when deciding which 529 plan to invest in.

Money Minutes

MY MERCEDES EDUCATION PLAN FOR
FIGHTING BACK THE RISING COST OF EDUCATION

We all know the Mercedes Benz automobile emblem, the tri-part airplane propeller. My college plan is similar—breaking up the funding of college costs into three parts:

1. Children can work and earn money before and during their college years. It never hurts for a child to get a real sense of earning and saving money toward schooling. From the time they are legally old enough to work, in their teens, they can take a paper route or other part time job. If you own your own company you can put them on the payroll for tasks like stuffing envelopes, sorting, filing, typing and so forth. What's more, they can shelter any income they make up to the IRA limits each year by contributions to an IRA in their name. If it is a Roth IRA the money comes out tax free, provided it's been aged 5 years, just like an Education IRA. Only difference is the contribution going into a Roth is after tax money. However, right now even regular IRAs can be used by family members to fund education costs and early withdrawals—under the age of 59-1/2 are permissible without penalties, for education purposes. But the money is taxed as ordinary income.

2. Encourage students to perform well in school because good grades are worth real money—in the form of scholarships, grants and also better employment opportunities. There are many scholarships available in both the academic as well as athletic areas. A friend of mine has a son in his third year at a Northeastern University. He didn't qualify for any scholarships before entering college but just by maintaining a "B" average in college he is getting a grant of $2500 per semester. That's $5,000 per year for getting good grades. If his son, who was always smart but hadn't applied himself earlier, had done as well in junior high and high school he might have received a free ride to a good college. Again, encourage good study or strong sports participation if that is your child's strength. Both can be taken to the bank at college time.

3. Fund the currently available savings plans—and fund them early. the Coverdell Savings Account (CSA) with up to $2000 per year in savings possible up to age 18; gifting of up to $12,000 per year under the UGTMA; and my favorite, 529 plans, which are like mutual funds.

Money Sense:

It's amazing how many smart and educated people find themselves in a financial bind when it comes time to deal with college tuition payments. Of course, not every child can get a full "free" ride on either academic or sports ability. Most of us have had to pay for tuition one way or another. In my experience, from dealing with clients of all stripes, procrastination derails most college funding plans. So don't put off planning until tomorrow or next year. Let family know you will put all cash gifts into Johnnie and Katie's college fund, that there are ways they can make college funding possible with 529 plans, Coverdell plans, annual gifts and other savings plans—and everyone wins.

THE LOTTERY OR OTHER WINDFALLS
YOU INHERIT — WHAT TO DO ABOUT THEM

Okay, you might win the lottery and you might get struck by lightning. You could also inherit a surprise windfall from a well off relative. So what then?

Choices you'll face:

- Quit your Job
- Spend It
- Save It
- Give It Away

Don't Quit Your Day Job

First thing is if it is a lot of money, in the 7 figures, for instance, (that's a million or more), don't do anything rash like quitting your job—at least not right away and not unless you are nearly ready to retire. If you are 50 and have say 15 years or so to go though peak earning years, it would be a big mistake to forego all those years of earnings to live off, say, one million dollars. Life expectancy has an ironic way of working out in your favor under these conditions and you might end up out of money before you end up out of time—a nice but uncomfortable problem.

What If You Don't Like Your Job?

With a nice financial cushion to back you up, you could readily find a new job or retrain in a career you like. To start you might want to read a book like Marla Brill's "Windfall: Managing Unexpected Wealth So It Doesn't Manage You." Don't argue about the time because with your lump sum of cash you can suddenly afford the time to stop and read. Brill covers all the angles here, not just the financial but the emotional and psychological.

Find a reputable financial adviser

If you don't already have one and don't feel comfortable investing a large sum of money yourself, seek a professional advisor. Here's a situation where good advice could be invaluable to you for the rest of your life. Of course, friends could help but be certain their advice is objective.

Money Sense:

By the way, if you aren't sure at all what to do right away, you can simply deposit the money with your bank, into a money market fund. If you are concerned about insurance, like FDIC insurance, talk to your banker about multiple account options. If they can't cover enough accounts, go to multiple banks.

Windfalls are relative. If you inherit something like $20,000, then the first thing to do, before the trip to Disney World, is pay off any credit card debt. Clean the slate.

Don't laugh about giving it away. If you happen to get hit by Green Lightning and the winnings are in the mega millions category, before you even show up to collect on the ticket better get a high priced tax attorney/ tax adviser who'll show you how to spread the winnings around to a lot of people without significantly reducing the amount you get to keep. If you win say $100 Million, you could make a lot of family members rich, too and still be a multi-millionaire. This isn't the time to be selfish.

DO YOU NEED ESTATE PLANNING?

The Law of Unintended Consequences

It is estimated that over half the people in the U.S. die without leaving a will. That's known as dying "intestate". The truth is no matter how we die our estate has been planned for us—either by us and by our design or by the state and their design

Chances are we wouldn't be pleased with the plan the state has for our families. Nor will they. There are a lot of unintended consequences connected to going down that road. So if it is a choice, to just not deal with a will or living trust or do any estate planning, do yourself and your family one big favor; put them on notice. Perhaps it will lead to a useful discussion that will change an unwanted and unintended outcome.

Good News; Estate Planning Has Become Easier For Most of Us

Estate planning has become relatively simple for most of us because of more generous laws allowing us to leave sizable assets to our spouse and children. Annually there's the $12,000 gift you and your spouse can each make, to anybody. There is also a lifetime gift of 2 Million starting in 2008 that can be left to children without paying any gift tax. If married that doubles to 4 Million. So estate planning is becoming pretty basic for at least 90% of the population.

Easy Doesn't Mean Simple

Okay I can hear folks saying, Bob I don't plan to have more than a 4 Million dollar estate. So why do I need a will or an estate plan. Simple! If you understand your options, and what can happen if you don't make certain choices—naming beneficiaries and trustees or executors of your will—you are setting the stage for a bunch of very unhappy campers. Your surviving family will have to deal with the paperwork and legwork and prolonged delays in getting done what otherwise could happen automatically—or in a few weeks—and without much cost. I've seen the financial and emotional cost to families out of pure negligence or just plain ignorance of the law. It's not pretty. It's pretty awful.

Money Sense:

I'm quite serious about wills and basic estate planning to pay your bills and then distribute your assets in a way you intend. You'd spend more time picking a new kitchen stove than preparing a basic will and roughing out an estate plan. If you fill out a simple questionnaire it wouldn't take more than perhaps an hour and a half with an estate professional to explain your options, what you need to set forth in your will, and a roughed-out estate plan. And then if you all you need is a plain vanilla will, and you want to purchase that in a stationery store, so be it. Just don't leave it all to chance.

ESTATE PLANNING MINI BASICS—
FOR MULTI-MILLIONAIRES

A well designed estate plan provides peace of mind. Thanks to new changes in the tax and estate planning laws, it doesn't have to be that complicated either. There are a few easy ways to give away a sizable amount of assets while you are living and also some things you can direct be done with your estate that can save a gang of money in taxes. Starting with ...

Annual Gifting—Like Hogwart's Magic—An Ingenious Little Tool That Wipes Out a Lot Of Estate Taxes.

Each and every calendar year, you can give away $12,000 to any and as many individuals you wish, with no gift or estate tax consequences. If married, you can double that. So you can give up to $24,000 to each person you wish from you and your spouse. With 3 kids and 4 grandkids you could give away $168,000 per year in 2008 so long as you have the cash or liquid assets to cover it. No tax consequences whatsoever. As an added bonus, no estate taxes will be payable by anyone later on.

Gift Tax - The Mega Million Dollar Exemption

There is also a gift tax exemption allowing you to give away a cumulative total of up to $1 Million to whomever you desire while you are alive without owing any federal gift tax. Again, if married, this doubles to $1 Million each. This is not altered by the annual gifting but if you go over $12,000 per annual gift you have to file a gift tax return—Form 709—notifying the IRS, even though you won't have to shell out the gift tax now.

Finally there's the mammoth estate planning exemptions, the...

Estate Tax Exemption, the Titan of Estate Planning Tools

For 2008, you can bequest gifts of up to $2 Million to individuals, free of any estate tax. So can your spouse. And to ensure no loss of tax saving benefit in the event one spouse should pre-decease the other, a bypass trust can be used to automatically leave the first $2 million to the kids, bypassing the surviving spouse and then when they pass, they still have $2 Million to leave for a total of $4 Million passing to the kids without any estate taxes to be paid. Without this if the first spouse were to pass and there is a $4 million estate the entire $4 million would pass to the surviving spouse who could leave $2 Million to the kids but the remaining $2 Million would be subject to estate tax.

Money Sense:

Good news on the estate tax. The ET exemption is rising to $3.5 Million in 2009. So you'll want to have this escalation built in by your adviser.

ESTATE PLANNING ORGANIZATION AND HOUSEKEEPING

We Should All Have an Aunt Ronnie

An associate had a dying Aunt Ronnie. She was very organized. She summoned the family together, showed them where all her documents were, explained what she wanted for her funeral—down to the details of the post funeral reception—and got everyone's agreement about all of it. She even discussed who would get what. She was happy and while the family was sad, the funeral and subsequent estate planning matters went seamlessly. The peace of mind that comes from taking appropriate steps is something any and every family will be thankful for, especially when grieving and lowered emotional thresholds can lead to fuzzy thinking.

What Should Be Included In The Estate Plan?

Depending on your needs and the size of your estate, there could be many documents and agreements, such as: trusts; partnerships; corporations; limited liability companies; and for individuals, a fully funded revocable living trust agreement.

The revocable living trust has instructions for the individual's care while alive and in good health, poor health, and even after their death. If incapacitated, it provides for monitoring the estate as requested. Upon passing their estate is passed on to their loved ones—when, how, and to whom they want.

How Will The Family Know What To Do?

Take a cue from Aunt Ronnie and have everything well organized. A binder or portfolio that has all of your estate planning and financial planning information and important documents—trusts, life insurance policies—all in one place, will greatly benefit your family.

What other Necessaries Should be in the Estate Plan?

How to get and keep your estate or trust funded...A durable power of attorney—empowering others to act for you if need be...a durable health care power of attorney specifying what you want and don't want done medically...a living will...a trust transfer document...a life insurance summary...and, most important of all, a document location list. Especially important is a list of names, address and contact numbers of relatives, friends, clergy, and key advisers. If like many people you feel uncomfortable getting it all together but know you should do it right, it's well worth investing in a little consulting time—perhaps a couple of hours or so— with a professional to help you figure it all out.

DO SINGLE PEOPLE WITH NO CHILDREN NEED ESTATE PLANNING?

Five Reasons Why A Single Person Should Consider Estate Planning

Singles need to plan just as much as the married, maybe more. Why?

1. Without a proper will and estate plan there is less protection on the order of inheritance

2. A proper will and plan will distribute assets the way they want

3. If disabled or mentally incapacitated an estate plan will spell out whom and how the necessary care will be provided

4. Single people when they do get older and have greater needs can sometimes fall victim to caretakers who are after their money

5. Assets you care about or wanted to go to certain family members could end up being auctioned off for cash so the aggregate monies can be divided equally

Spelling It Out Prevents Unintended Outcomes

If you need further convincing, here's a sobering twist on what could happen without a will. Without a will your assets will probably go to next of kin such as surviving parents, siblings, and then nieces and nephews. Do you want your parents to inherit before a brother or sister?

Money Sense:

Often a single person wants to give their assets to a favorite charity and still take care of family members. A good way to do that is by purchasing

65

an insurance policy on their life naming the charitable foundation or community organization as beneficiary. That still leaves other assets available to be distributed to say brothers, sisters, nieces, nephews and so forth. Again, a well prepared estate plan can act to prevent a bad outcome. Even in the case of singles with no children some issues are too complex to figure out on your own. Seeking professional help is one sure way to see that your intended beneficiaries will ultimately receive your property and assets.

WHAT YOU NEED TO KNOW ABOUT NAMING BENEFICIARIES

Can't I Simply Name an Individual as Beneficiary of a Personal Asset and Be Done With It?

You could, if you knew all the things that might happen and have the background information or professional training to know what the consequences are should certain things change.

First of all the nature of the assets as well as the individuals you wish to benefit from the asset might change. Then what? Some assets you can change beneficiaries on. Others you can't.

Things like retirement accounts and life insurance policies can pass simply by naming a payable on death beneficiary. Here again there needs to be periodic review and perhaps changes made. Otherwise the law of unintended outcomes may trigger again. What if the payable on death beneficiary changes and you neglect to make the appropriate change? The issuer of the policy, annuity, or whatever assets is involved is not always obligated to determine what if anything has changed and if the named beneficiary is still the intended, or now accidental beneficiary.

Your state may not allow the type of beneficiary designation you want.

When you re-title an asset and add a beneficiary, say a bank account or a car, you may be making a taxable gift to them that has both income and estate tax consequences.

Adding another person's name to an asset might remove your ability to control or dispose of the asset.

Another hidden problem is that minors can't receive or control property that held in their names. You'd need to appoint a guardian to handle any property that is left to a minor.

Disabled or incompetent beneficiaries cannot receive property directly.

If the spouse is not the paternal parent of your children, there is always a possibility that unintended beneficiaries will ultimately receive property you intended for them.

Money Sense:

It all comes down to this: If you want your assets to end up with the right people get in there and do it yourself with an estate planning attorney. With capable advice and periodic review or changes when circumstances warrant it, the right people will benefit.

PRICING STOCKS YOU INHERIT

Stocks Are Nice To Inherit and Sell
But Keep A Record Of Price Right Away

A relative dies and leaves you some stocks. It could even be a friend or someone you' taken care of. You may hold the stocks or sell them after they are properly transferred, but what about taxes?

Get the Stock Price on the DOD

If you inherit from a relative be sure to establish or get a price for the stock on the day of death (DOD). As the old saw goes, do it right away. If several years pass before selling it takes more time and effort to establish the valuation.

Money Sense:

For the living with appreciated stock portfolios who are thinking of passing them on to relatives later, don't leave money on the table. If you have a long term capital loss carryover, or an excess of losses over gains that you have been accumulating because you are limited to taking up to $3000 a year against gains, and you have gains in your portfolio, it is best to use up the carry over losses by taking the offsetting profits. Otherwise, if you have say $10,000 in carry over losses and $15,000 in gains, only you get the benefit of the offsetting tax break on the gains. Your beneficiary inherits a stock but not the loss carryovers. The current value of the stock, whatever it is, at the date of death, becomes their cost when they sell. Naturally this all depends on your view of taxes. Many people feel a tax benefit not used is a real waste. Better to take at least the $10,000 loss in the above example tax free then let it be lost in the future. Pass the money or gift it tax free, instead.

Keep the Stock and Get a Tax Break Too

Here's a real way to get profitable stocks and pay no back taxes on appreciation. Let's say you are set financially, don't need the money and inherit stocks from a relative. You check it out and find these are heritage type holdings, blue chip stocks with a long and profitable history. You could just sit with the inherited stock and one day have it pass through your estate to say your children or grandchildren. Their basis or cost for tax purposes will be the closing price as of the date of your passing. So the total value the closing price times the number of shares on the date of your passing is their heritage cost for tax purposes - a nice treat on Uncle Sam that gets the tax burden to disappear.

THE PERSONAL SIDE OF ESTATE PLANNING

Estate Planning Isn't Just About Saving Taxes.

It's also about saving the family and relatives. A bad estate plan—or worse, none at all—can set the family up in a civil war that can last for years, destroy relationships, and erode estate value.

Many of my clients' survivors who have seen the benefits of a little forethought on the part of their parents have expressed their repeated appreciation for the pleasant outcomes. The work is worth the effort and very satisfying to the family in the long run.

Four Key Estate Planning Considerations:

- Who should inherit the assets, either general amounts or percentages
- Who should inherit specific assets and personal effects
- Should the assets be distributed outright or left in a trust (goes to how capable or money savvy the recipient is as well as how old they are)
- Over what period of time and in what manner should an inheritance be distributed, and who should be named as trustees or co-trustees (Remember: At some point, as time passes, these people are going to be dividing up the money)

Watershed issues?

Can't I let the children divide up the collectibles and jewelry? Yes, you can but do you really want to? Now the decision making process is in their hands. It can lead to fights among siblings and the rest of the family. Many families have broken up over insubstantial matters like who gets the cabbage slicer or the copper tub. Better to have it all specified according to the likes you know and the wishes expressed over a lifetime. Don't know what to leave to whom? Tell family members to make a list of possessions they would like—making sure they also know that some

71

trade-offs will have to be worked out.

Money Sense:

Does everyone have to be treated equally? Not at all. Everyone is different and has different needs. Some children you may rely on a lot in later years for care and other personal matters. Others who are distant or uninvolved may not have a reason to expect the same treatment. You may want to give some a lump sum and others a payout over time or perhaps do a combination of a lump sum up front and a residual payout. And remember, while you are alive, you are in control. You can change instructions as easily as changing a tie for dinner. It's your money.

WHAT TO DO WHEN A LOVED ONE DIES

We've talked about funeral pre plans but more often there are no pre plans, a loved one dies and we are faced with having to take care of essential details and arrangements quickly and while grieving for our lost loved one.

What's the first thing you have to do?

Enlist family help. Don't try to handle all the arrangements alone. This is a time to reach out to the rest of the individual's family and professionals who will helps with gathering values of investments, updating beneficiary information, checking for life insurance coverage and preparing forms for death claims. Funeral professionals will help set up and see that all funeral and burial arrangements are carried out. Their guidance is very valuable when making decisions during such a difficult time

Immediately contact your closest family members as well as your funeral, financial and insurance professional. Start gathering important information.

Information you'll need about the departed

- Date of birth
- Names of family members and loved ones' names and addresses
- Notable achievements during their lives
- Fraternal, community and church organizations they belonged to or supported
- Pictures and any articles or written information by or about the deceased

Both funeral professionals and the media will need this information.

Start Gathering information about bank accounts, property and investment accounts. See how they are titled and if beneficiary designations have been made. If there are IRAs or 401Ks are in the deceased name, begin to take steps necessary for the transfer of assets to the new owners. If the survivor is a spouse they may need to re-evaluate living expenses.

Money Sense:

Finally, and most important, allow time to pass before making any life-changing decisions. Avoid the urge to make any other substantive decisions quickly. Any changes involving finances, relocation or lifestyle should be discussed with both family and professional advisers to objectively get a better grasp of the big picture. For instance, if there are children from a previous marriage and they are to inherit half of a house from the surviving spouse, either offer a buyout or if that's not possible, have them agree to a transition period – perhaps as much as a couple of years – for the survivor to relocate and sell.

INVESTING: DO IT YOURSELF OR
USE A FINANCIAL ADVISOR

Do Like the "Rich" People Do—Get Professional Help

As a professional financial planner with many hundreds of clients, I'd have to admit I'm biased. However, I know a wealthy old friend of my uncle's used to say if you want to be rich do what the rich people do. As a general rule only around 25% of men use financial advisors. Among women it is 37%. But once you move up the financial food chain, the numbers change quite a bit. Among people with a net worth of $250,000 or more, two-thirds use financial advisors. As do virtually all of the top of the line entertainers, actors, and sports figures. So you have to ask yourself, what do these people know that the average person doesn't know. Could be not much, but financial advisers are doing what they do full time, every day. Their track record and your expectations are that your money will work harder and return more each year with their advice. If that's not the case you have an option. Fire the advisor and find one you like better.

Financial decision making and investing is not a part time job anymore than golf is part time for Tiger Woods or biking for Lance Armstrong. It takes full time effort to stay on top of the game. If you follow the well off and high net worth people and do like they do, chances are you'll be better off in the long run.

Here are just a few good Money Sense reasons to consider a financial adviser.

1. For Men only: Advisers are not likely to ever buy a stock or make an investment based on a "tip". Over half of the male investors surveyed admit they have bought stock based on a tip from a friend, relative or co-worker. If that hits home, get independent help.

2. They are not risk averse but don't like taking unnecessary financial risks where the chance of loss is statistically greater than the chance for a king size profit.

3. They'll analyze any interesting investments you come across or are unfamiliar with because they have expertise to draw upon in all areas.

4. They are not likely to roll the dice on a speculation. If you do it you apologize to your spouse and promise never to do it again. If an adviser sends your portfolio "south" it tarnishes their reputation, costs them clients and may be cause for legal recourse.

5. Professionals have a verifiable track record you can review, not just say-so.

6. There are so many choices of investment products to diversify your portfolio that are new and sophisticated it would be foolish not to take advantage of them because they are unfamiliar. It's an adviser's job to know about them and help you use them to maximize your returns.

WHAT'S THE VALUE OF SOUND INVESTMENT ADVICE?

Choosing the Right Adviser

A Big Apple—New York City, that is—financial firm runs a commercial that says it right: The phone call is free. The advice could be priceless.

Obviously, I have an economic interest in dispensing personal financial advice. And a real love of doing it for clients.

Money Sense:

The real value in the right advice could literally be worth hundreds to thousands of times the cost of the service. So if you have a substantial amount of money—meaning substantial by your definition—to invest don't be shy about checking out the price of advice.

How to Select the Right One—Qualifiers

So if you would be thinking of choosing a person to advise you, how do you select the right one? A good planner is first a good listener. They know their field and they are very good communicators. That's means they return all calls or e mails as soon as possible and they have a solid background in the financial services field. If you can't get the personal attention from your adviser that you deserve, you need to find another adviser. Among the other qualifying things you'll want to know:

- *Compensation.* Are they paid commissions or fee-based (hourly or a flat-fee for evaluations. Commission based advisers are more likely to generate more transactions in your portfolio.

- *Asset Portfolio Reviews.* How often. Annually may not be enough. Quarterly is the benchmark. This also opens the door to periodic rebalancing of your portfolio.

- *Risk.* How much you risk is related to how much of a return you want to accept on an annual basis. If 10% or less is satisfactory you don't need as much risk exposure. If you are looking to do more than 10%, you need an adviser who typically works more aggressive investments.

- **References.** Touchy subject but ask anyway. A good adviser should have several clients who would be willing to discuss why they like the adviser.

- **Track Record.** References aside a good adviser should have verifiable tracking on their returns of client invested capital.

Money Sense:

So how do you find a financial adviser? Sources of advisers are many. You can look them up in the local classified, find one in your area through online searches, check with one of the advisory organizations such as and also ask a well-off or wealthy friend who they use. But wherever you go make sure you do your due diligence and ask a lot of questions. Final Word: Check out how the other half is living and if any of them are friends, ask where they go for advice. It's not infallible but let's face it, do like the rich do works more than not.

GETTING READY FOR A FINANCIAL PLANNER

Sooner or later an adviser's questions will turn to you. In terms of giving an adviser what they need to get a sense about you and your requirements:

Identify your core money. This is money you need to have growing day in and day out. The adviser's job is to help you identify this money and also figure out how much money and growth you need to support your life plans.

Figure out your risk comfort level. Think it over and try to find a point on the grid where you feel you are getting the right amount of growth with a tolerable amount of risk. Here's one slightly smug clue: If you play Texas Hold 'Em regularly chances are you have a high tolerance for risk.

Evaluate your investing philosophy. Be honest with yourself. How much risk can you and should you be willing to accept to reach the return you want on your investments. If you aren't sure here is a quick test you can take privately, courtesy of Microsoft and CNBC: http://www.msnbc.msn.com/id/3304753/.

Decide how much time you want to spend shepherding your assets. Do you need periodic or full time advice? If you are retired and have a good track record, maybe you only want a periodic review just to see if you are on track, have a properly balanced portfolio, and what adjustments can be made to improve things a little. This doesn't require full time advice, maybe a periodic review and update. In this instance, fee based planning—or advice by the hour, no commissions on products you buy—may be the best program for you.

If you have a very demanding job and have a life after work that involves a spouse, kids or even grandkids you are quite active with, you may not have enough time to stay on top of the markets and make the portfolio adjustments required to keep your money working at optimum efficiency. Relying on your financial professional to provide insight and street smarts to keep you on track can be very important to you, especially over a longer period of time. This could be fee-based planning or a combination of both fee based plus commissions.

Money Sense:

Whatever makes you comfortable is the right way to go. But periodic or full time, the right advice could be priceless. And being honest with yourself about your portfolio performance versus what a dedicated adviser can show proof of.

SMALL BUSINESS PLANNING GUIDE FOR THE HOLIDAYS—START IN EARLY OCTOBER

Companies are no different than individuals. The ones who come off best are those who plan in advance. In early October think about and decide on what your company might want to consider for employees.

1. Office Party. Set a budget in advance so you'll know how much you can spend. Parties on campus cost less than an offsite catered affair. Really small companies ought to consider a meal at a nice restaurant, perhaps one that is usually too pricey for the staff. And consider inviting spouses or significant others if it doesn't add too many people. Pros: Employees appreciate it especially if there are no bonus traditions. It's still something nice and an opportunity to socialize. Con: If there is liquor served the company may have liability for personal actions that injure others on the premises.

2. Gifts. Some companies give premiums like pens and caps or turkeys. Con: Frankly these aren't highly valued or appreciated. Pro: Instead, think of giving a gift certificate to a store they all might use, like Amazon, or Target or if that seems inappropriate just do cash. Another possibility is to make a charitable donation on behalf of all employees. Or allow each one to designate a charity of their choice.

3. Time off. Pro: This is an all-around winner. During the holidays companies just slow down, especially the week right before New Year. Consider closing down for an extra day around the holidays. One really generous company I know closes between Christmas and New Year and the employees value this more than a bonus. Con: None. Sure, it costs the company money, but it is more than repaid in improved morale and performance.

4. Bonuses. Fewer companies offer this but it is still policy in many industries, like financial services. Decide if it's going to be one bonus for all or a performance based bonus. And know in advanced that any performance based system will leave some people

81

dissatisfied. The overall bonus can be based on a percentage of profits or sales with sales tending to be less irregular.

Money Sense:

If your company hasn't done any of these things before, and it is a good year for business, don't be afraid to initiate one or two perks as a thank you from management for a good year of business. It's not an all or nothing deal. And it makes for a heckuva good morale booster. About the only con here is I have to say it's a good idea to point out to people that this is not to be expected each and every year. It all depends on increased sales and sufficient profits to fund the largess.

PUTTING THE GO IN YOUR FINANCIAL GOALS

The saying goes that whether you bargain with life for a pint or a bushel, life will pay you what you ask. It's a well known secret that most successful people don't get to their goals by accident. They either have a vision or plan or expectation that the something wonderful will happen.

First Step in Setting Financial Goals

First decide what your dreams and objectives are.

- Retirement
- Children's Education Costs
- First Home Deposit for the Kids
- Retirement Home
- Luxury Car
- Travel to Exotic Locations
- Continuing Education
- Legacy to Charity or Community

Now the outcome of your expectations

- Retire at 65
- 6 Months of Expenses in Emergency Fund
- Number of Years of Expected Retirement and Living In Good Health

Remember, this isn't just an exercise. It's a map for your mind. Once you have your heart of hearts talk with yourself, and your spouse, and write these aspirations down, then, begin to set up your steps to get there.

A colleague of mine dreamed of owning a lake house. For years he thought about it and talked about it and he even took his family out to look at lakefront houses casually but regularly. Nothing happened. The right house or lake or time just didn't come together. Finally he took to heart the idea of writing it down on an index card and pasting it above the computer monitor on his desk. "I will live in a lakefront house." Within six months of that posting he found the house of his dreams on the lake of his choice and is moving his family there full time. And it is so beautiful has a hard time keeping his mind on work..

Money Sense:

Decide what your financial dreams are and write them down. Then make your investing plan to get there. Like getting to Neverland, first you have to believe.

WHAT TO DO WHEN YOUR INVESTMENT PORTFOLIO LOOKS LIKE HUMPTY DUMPTY AFTER THE BIG FALL

In a Big Market Downdraft, Sell, Buy or Stand Pat—What to Consider

Sooner or later there is going to be a time when the stock market takes what seems like a fall it might not recover from. Volatility has been magnified in recent years. A 100 point drop from 14,000 on the Dow is not the same as when it was trading at 9,000.

When trending in an unfavorable way for a short to intermediate period, in many cases investors just need to hold on, be patient, and do nothing. Allow the stock market to work through the unfavorable trend, move back up and values will be restored and eventually go higher again from there. However there are also other factors to consider in making decisions when you feel your portfolio has been hammered:

1. *Time.* How soon before you will need to begin drawing money from the portfolio. If it's a few years away chances are the best thing to do is stand pat.

2. *Risk.* How comfortable do you feel riding out the market? Is it a temporary downdraft or a more secular bear market that will take a good while to work through its drop, consolidate, and begin to start building an upward trend again? Again, you may not have to do anything except perhaps to consider adding to positions in companies that have presented unusually good buying opportunities.

3. *Goals.* There are different types of investment objectives just like there are different types of horses for different race tracks. One way to think of portfolios is in goal categories like capital preservation (income producing—70% or more in bonds and interest bearing cash equivalents) conservative (more money in cash and bonds than stock), balanced (a mix of income producing equities or bonds and stocks, capital growth (large cap growth stocks 85%, 15% bonds or cash) or aggressive (virtually no cash and a mix of

85

large, mid cap, and small cap stocks with an emphasis on high annual returns). Review your goals, look at the positions you hold and finally the market. You will have a better sense of the right thing to do.

4. *Adjustments.* Whatever you do don't think in terms of a total portfolio overhaul. Make small and intelligent adjustments.

Money Sense:

As investors, we go through several different scenarios in life. At age 50 you have a statistically good chance of riding out downtrends and coming back stronger than ever, especially if you take advantage of a temporary lower market situation to add to your legacy stocks at great prices. If you are currently living off the income from your portfolio, then you'd probably want to be in a more protected position so your portfolio isn't likely to go down with the market. You might have a plan to be on the sidelines or be fixed income securities or bonds that aren't negatively affected by overall equity market conditions. Having a capital preservation portfolio by its very nature will cushion you against precipitous market drops as bonds and fixed income instruments tend to hold up better in declining markets—and cash loses nothing.

WHEN DO YOU NEED FINANCIAL PLANNING?

Many people think that financial planning is for wealthy people. In actuality, many successful people who plan for wealth start financial planning with their first dollar.

Financial planning is really three disciplines: managing wealth, wealth planning and transferring wealth.

Managing wealth should start with your first dollar. The health of your wealth isn't much different from your general health. If you want to be in good physical shape you wouldn't wait to start working out, eating right, and keeping a healthy lifestyle until after you've had your first heart attack, would you? (Okay; don't answer that!)

The kickoff to wealth planning is fine-tuning an asset portfolio (regardless of size) for growth, income, taxable and non-taxable considerations. It looks at the development of a game plan from the time you are working and building up assets to the time you are retired and beginning to think about transferring wealth. Everyone is different. Some of us may need money sooner than others. Retirement or emergencies can intervene outside of the scope of the plan. But having the plan makes it easier to fine-tune for the unexpected.

Transferring wealth has to do with determining the most economical ways that your well earned wealth can be transferred to your loved ones while you are still living, disabled or ill. It's all about finding legal ways to get your money to those whom you wish to receive it in a way the Uncle Sam gets the least amount possible. After all, state and estate taxes can eat up a substantial portion of an investor's wealth.

Could You Expect to Benefit From The Services of a Financial Planner?

It depends on whether you have the time, the talent, and the experience to manage the financial part of your life. It's not necessarily an all or nothing decision.

Events that might prompt you to seek the services of a planner

The Financial Planning Association suggests the following specific events or needs may trigger the desire for professional financial planning guidance:

- Making sure your money will last during retirement/ rolling over a retirement plan
- Handling the inheritance of a large sum of money or unexpected financial windfall
- Preparing for a marriage or divorce
- Planning for the birth or adoption of a child
- Facing a financial crisis such as a serious illness, layoff or natural disaster
- Caring for aging parents or a disabled child
- Coping financially with the death of a spouse or close family member
- Funding higher education
- Buying, selling or passing on a family business

Money Sense:

These days many of us take satisfaction in the DIY or do it yourself approach to things. But financial planning is a complex strategy, often involving not only your lawyer, but your accountant and financial advisor working together as a team.

CAN YOU GET A WORTHWHILE SECOND OPINION ABOUT YOUR FINANCIAL STATUS WITHOUT GETTING YOUR INVESTMENT DOLLARS PLUCKED?

Those about to retire and those in retirement are often appreciative of an unbiased second opinion about their finances. But they are wary of sharing personal financial information with anyone they don't know and are especially fearful of someone unscrupulous trying to get their advisory hands on their investment dollars.

Most middle age and seniors have investment advisers of some sort whether it be accountants, lawyers, and tax or investment advisers. But chances are nobody knows the whole story. To get that second opinion on the big picture you have to find someone who feel has a sincere interest in just providing honest advice and not just trying to sell you something.

A couple of ideas on getting there:

1. Tell an advisor you feel comfortable enough to meet with and discuss your financial situation with that this is just an informational meeting not a selling interview. That clears the air of any expectation beyond meeting to go over your assets and perhaps make some general suggestions about changes that seem necessary. No obligations and no fees are attached to this kind of meeting.

2. Although they can be a hard sell the financial seminars run by large companies are less likely to be and they can provide you with a lot of general information that will give you a sense of where you stand relative to what's available in investment and tax vehicles that enhance income and minimize tax concerns. And then if you still feel you want to take up with your regular adviser, bring them the information and express your wishes.

Money Sense:

Recently a friend of mine had his IRA account analyzed by an investment adviser using a portfolio analyzer and optimizer. Using the same funds over the same period and allocating the same resources differently produced a 120% greater return on the invested funds than his current portfolio. Of course, the recommended investments were load funds but with that much of a differential in performance you'd have to give it a closer look. So take advantage of the tools and advisers you have out there and see if it can't enhance the performance of your assets. The cost of analysis should be nominal or free. The fees come in if you make the recommended changes.

WHO NEEDS TO KNOW YOUR PERSONAL FINANCIAL BUSINESS ANYWAY?

Secrecy is Not Usually a Smart Option

Generations ago our grandparents each did their discrete things. Grandpa went to work, brought home the paycheck, paid the bills, gave grandma spending money, and made the family investments. And he kept the money and its whereabouts to himself.

Of course, if grandpa died before grandma—a statistically likely event—all kinds of chaos broke loose. No one knew where anything was kept, if there was any insurance, bank accounts and who knows what other assets were around. And grandma often didn't have a clue about finances or making investment decisions. Just finding out about the assets in time was like a pirates' treasure hunt.

Fast Forward to a Better Day

Thank God, things have changed. Most couples share information and many both work. So a lot of the guesswork is gone. However, the simple truth is that most people aren't organized enough about what they have in the way of estate and financial assets and there is generally much more to know. Keep in mind, too that when a spouse dies it is a time of terrible emotional upheaval and the more organized and the more people in the know, the less stressful that time is going to be.

Create a Concise Personal Financial Asset Checklist

Organize and share your investment information. It's the smart thing to do. Include:

1. Names, addresses and phone numbers for accountants, attorneys, tax advisers and investment counselors.

2. Lists of all accounts – checking, savings, safety deposit boxes and brokerage accounts, 401Ks, CDs, stock certificates.

91

3. Amount and location of any other non-liquid assets like real estate, coin collections, private equity investments, limited partnerships, promissory notes and so forth.

4. Insurance policies issued and amounts.

5. Location of your will.

6. What you want done with certain assets—cars, for instance—and who should receive them after you die.

7. Anyone you want notified after you die who is not a family member or contact.

8. Who owes you money and who you owe money to.

Money Sense:

This list of your personal financial assets/secrets should be typed up and shared with your spouse, parents, children and trustees. If you are very bothered by sharing the information, put it in a sealed envelope and extract a promise it won't be opened until you die—from those you fell might just be interested in finding out what you are really worth. Just don't count on it being observed by all those you care about.

MAKE A BETTER PLACE FOR YOURSELF FINANCIALLY

Barbara Goodman, 89, a retired psychologist now living on the Upper West Side in Manhattan suffered the most precious loss a parent can experience. Her son Andrew was killed in 1964 while he and two other young civil rights workers were working in Mississippi to sign up Black American voters. She often speaks to young people and tells them "Your job is to make the world a better place."

What a worthy goal. I couldn't agree more. But I feel there is an important corollary to that goal in my field.

Sure, many of you are thinking "hey Bob, what chance have I got to make the world a better place? You can. Just stay with me on this.

To make the world a better place you first have to make a better place for yourself in this world. That's the challenge. Can you do it? Yes, you can.

Your Duty Call to Financial Self Sufficiency begins with these three shrewdly simple steps:

Intent. No step toward change, no path to transformation or reinforcement of good finance habits can begin without intent. All you need is intent to start with.

Know How. Step by step this book will guide you with simple, easy, manageable ways to keep on the self-sufficient track financially. Armed with intent and information the only other thing you need is—

Discipline. You've made up your mind, and sighted the target, now stick to your guns and hit the bull's eye.

Anything else, Bob?

Yes and here is our first **Money Sense** *thought.* Write down this phrase on a small piece of paper or 3 by 5 index card – I will be financially self-sufficient. Don't type it. Write or print it neatly in your own hand. And then put it in a prominent place on your desktop or computer where you will be sure to see it every day. Just trust me on this. Write it down. Put it up. See it every day.

YOU'RE IN CHARGE

An elderly couple got in their car and started back home after a trip to the store. At the first red light, Tom kept going. Luckily nobody else was around. They came to the next light and it was also red. Tom drove right through it, too, with no hesitation. Now Linda was getting real nervous. She wasn't planning on any ambulance ride. As she looked ahead she could see that there was another intersection coming up and sure enough the light was red. She turned to Tom and in as nice a way as she could manage, she said, "Tom, are you planning on stopping for this red light?"

Tom turned to her and said: "why, am I driving?"

Life is more than a month to month deal

So many people I have counseled have education and experience but when it comes to their finances, they are like Tom. Nobody's behind the wheel. The money comes in and it goes out but where it goes, nobody knows. How they even get from month to month, nobody knows. Look it doesn't matter who you are. Say you're a doctor. You got trained in medicine, right. Then you open up an office and pretty soon you are drowning, not in patients, but paperwork, insurance claims processing (no claims processing, no money coming in), malpractice insurance, rent, payroll—money, not medicine. Nobody trains you in how to manage your finances in med school.

So how do you get started planning and managing your finances?

Personal Finance 101. Do you know where you are on the financial road of life? Do you know what lies ahead of you? Are you prepared? The first step is knowing what's out there in front of you and then taking the necessary steps to be prepared for it.

Think small. Start with everyday things you can manage like expenses. Then monthly budget and savings. And then we'll move up to the big things like saving for education, retirement and even a little bit of tax talk. All in bite sized nuggets.

95

Money Sense:

You're in control. You are driving the financial car that's going to get you to your destination safely and securely. You didn't know how to drive, but you learned. If you can drive a car you can learn about handling your finances. It's not linear algebra or quantum physics. Most of it is simple arithmetic. When you get to a point of serious discomfort, or you can't find a solution anywhere in these pages, seek a professional adviser who gets paid for their advice, not the products they sell.

PAINLESS LIFETIME SAVINGS PLAN

Tony had a friend John who worked in the same company as he did for over 10 years. John had a couple of kids and his wife only worked part time. Tony had no kids and a wife who worked full time. John drove a nearly showroom quality maintained car around 10 years old and Tony had a new one every 3 years when the payments were finished on his old one.

One day John and Tony were having lunch. John mentioned he was moving to a new house, in a brand new house in a new development in the best section of the same town Tony lived in.

Another thing: John took his family vacations every year and paid cash. So Tony flat out asked him." How do you manage it?" John's secret was simple. From the time he was 16 with his first paper route, he saved enough money from each paycheck to purchase a U.S. Savings Bond each month. When he graduated high school and went off to college he continued the practice but dropped the amount of the bond a month because he was only working part time. Off to service after college he increased his bond a month plan and then after he got out and went to work he kept up the habit. Only each time John got a raise and that was every year in those days, John would increase the amount of his bond savings. If he got a 5% raise and that was $2,000 he took 25% of that or $500 more into his yearly savings plan. "I don't' miss it because it's money I haven't seen before and I still get more in my paycheck after the raise. Later on when his company started 401K plans he went in for the max.

How John paid for his vacations every year was also simple. He's cashed in his oldest savings bonds for whatever amount he and his wife decided they needed. And since he was continuing to save more money each year he considered it a better way to go and stay pretty much debt free.

Money Sense:

Saving, like the rent or mortgage, is best done monthly. Buying is simple. If you have a payroll savings deduction—less frequent today—you are set. If not, bond purchases can be made at your local bank. Finally you can purchase direct now at *www.treasurydirect.gov.*

YEAR END PLANNING CHECKLIST
TO PUT YOU ON THE FAST TRACK FOR NEXT YEAR

1. Start planning now for next year.
2. Know your expenses.
3. Budget your contribution to Traditional IRAs.
4. Take investment losses.
5. Meet with professionals, attorneys, CPAs and financial advisors.
6. Assess risk tolerance.
7. Establish investment time horizon.
8. Plan on getting out of debt.
9. Start a systematic investment program that continues into next year and thereon.
10. Set goals.
11. Donate to charities.
12. Cookie Jar Expense Checklist.
13. Forget the negative returns of this year.
14. Set aside a specific amount of money each month to invest.
15. Participate in company benefit plans, 401(k)s, ESOPs, pension IRAs, individual (non-IRA) savings, life insurance, etc. and try to put some away for emergency funds. If you get that type of balance and savings initiated, then the next year could be a great year for you and your investments.
16. Holiday spending – spend only what you can, develop a budget and stick to it.
17. Place as much money as possible into your company benefit plan. Maximize your contribution.
18. Gifting.
19. Ownership and beneficiary designations.

20. Medical bills.

21. If you are self-employed, business expenses should probably be taken this year.

22. Increase your participation in your 401(k) program.

23. If you donate money with a credit card, you can use it as a deduction even though you won't actually pay it until next year.

24. Take advantage of new education credits and other tax breaks and keep proper records.

25. If you itemize and don't pay a lot of state income tax, you can deduct state sales tax, including sales tax on any vehicles purchased.

26. Check to make sure you have made estimated tax payments.

Money Sense:

Following this checklist annually will put you on the right track and ease money/tax worries.

FINANCIAL AND SURVIVAL EMERGENCY PLANNING CHECKLIST

I've had so many calls from radio listeners who want to know what they could do to be better prepared in the event of another dire emergency like Hurricane Katrina I just had to include an emergency checklist for all

Survival favors the prepared

What would you do in an extreme emergency? What if you had to leave and perhaps abandon your home, or what if you would have to stay inside your home for a long period of time? What would you need in the way of money, food, emergency and medical supplies, and communications devices?

A financial reserve is vital. What would you do if you have no liquid assets other than credit cards to access and what if the nearest banks you can get to have no power and therefore no ATMs are working? Major grocery stores are all on point of sale electronic terminals at checkout and without power they can't ring up your groceries. So they would likely be closed. And if open they would only be able to deal with cash transactions. A few months ago I had to put my food back when the power went out and the super mart manager explained they just couldn't ring us up. Given what our neighbors have been through in New Orleans as well as several recent similar disasters in our area along the Mississippi here is a short but vital—

Disaster Emergency Checklist:

- Water Water Water. Gallon Jugs of it. Enough for a couple of weeks. Or, if you prefer, there are super quality water osmosis filtration systems that can delivers up to a gallon of water a day for 10 days. Why water? You can't last more than a few days without it.

- Cash—at least enough for a few weeks of supplies and food.

- Junk Silver Coin—you just never know when someone might not want paper money.

- Food—stuff that won't spoil or get waterlogged like cans of tuna, sardines, spaghetti and meatballs etc and power bars.

- Batteries. Lots and lots of batteries. In all the usual sizes—AA, AAA, C, D, 9V.

- Power Generators. Useful and necessary but of course you need gasoline to run them and it may not be convenient or safe to store around the house. More expensive but safer generators can be run on propane.

- Cell phone. With at least one backup battery. Limited use unless power comes back so make a short list of people to be in touch with.

- Call List. Who would you call if you had just a few calls to make to secure your family, let others know you are okay or come get your loved ones out of harms way.

- Johnny Bucket. You can turn a 5 gallon plastic container into a waste basket, put in a plastic liner and change it once a day— burying the used bag. It also works as a seat.

- Bleach. If you have wounds or need a disinfecting agent, Bleach works. Just be careful how you use it. It can burn skin, has toxic fumes and should be diluted with water.

- Antibiotics. Normally you need a prescription to buy them, but farmers and ranchers buy antibiotics over the counter at animal feed and supply stores. Check the Web for additional sources.

- Bandages and gauze for dressings.

- Honey. A good germicidal coater for bandages and dressings.

- QR powder. Available at many mass market retailers. Stops bleeding.

- Duct Tape and Blue Tarpaulin Sheets.

Sources on medical supplies courtesy of Dr David G. Williams publisher of an internet health newsletter.

QUICK PERSONAL FINANCE TIPS
FOR THE AMERICAN FAMILY

View the Financial Picture from 30,000 Feet.

- Inventory what's happening with the family.
- Examine the family's overall financial situation and create a clear set of financial goals.
- Check the progress chart to see if the ship's on course to meet family goals. Make course corrections, as needed, to stay on track.

Financial goals are important

For some, it's retirement, or planning for child's education costs. Others are concerned about a retirement home, a type of car or boat. Still others want to leave money to the community or certain charities. Without these goals there is nothing to reach for. Having a goal of providing a good education for a child is meaningless if no money has been saved. Discover the family's sincere needs and then act accordingly.

Look over the budget. Create a budget by recording expenses for one month. Complete the Cookie Jar Expense Checklist to see where there is a need to cut back or increase spending.

Cut debt to the Bone. If there is a $2,000 balance on a credit card that carries a 16% interest rate just making minimum, monthly payments will cost nearly $300 in finance charges and still leave a balance of more than $1800 at the end of a year. Consider lower interest cards or refinancing your home to pay back substantial high interest credit card debt.

Talk to the kids about money from an early age. Getting the family financially fit means educating the children about money. Providing an allowance for chores will also present opportunities to discuss budgeting, saving for one big thing or spending it all each week on little things, and saving in general for the future. Involve them in family decisions about car buying or taking a vacation. Older kids can take on the research end of obtaining auto insurance or college financing plans.

Plan with your parents. If family members haven't been a part of your parents' financial planning point out the value of being informed so you will be able to carry out their wishes in case of an emergency. Prepare a checklist of important information. Know the location of important legal documents, insurance policies and key contacts like legal and financial advisors. Express too who should be interested in certain belongings in an estate situation.

Money Sense:

Last but not least, plan for your own retirement, early, early, early. And the earlier the better, the easier, the least expensive in terms of how much to put away and the most rewarding in terms of how well you can enjoy your retirement years and how much easier it will be for the next generation not to have to worry for you.

PROTECTING YOUR MONEY WHEN DISASTERS OCCUR

Let's face it: If you would have talked to people down in Louisiana, Mississippi, and Alabama before Hurricane Katrina hit, chances are nine out of ten of them would have said that they really didn't believe a disaster would occur. Now we see what can happen.

Prime Concerns When a Disaster Strikes

- How to get to your investment dollars.
- Where to place your cash.
- What to do with your bank monies.
- How much and how to handle cash on hand to name a few.

For three days after 9-11, the nation's stock exchanges were closed. There was no way for an individual to get money in or out of the markets. That money was locked up. There was no liquidity whatsoever.

Disaster Preparation Lesson # 1: No one should have all of their liquid funds in investments or in any one area. What about emergency cash? Most seniors will probably tell you that they have a certain amount of cash stored in their safe deposit boxes. That's okay unless you can't get to your safe deposit box. The banks in New Orleans were flooded for days and there was no way to get to that emergency money.

Disaster Preparation Lesson # 2: Have liquid cash on hand in several different places, so when a disaster hits, you have somewhere to go for cash liquidity.
Aren't The Banks safe? Sure, banks are extremely safe; however, how do you get a check cashed or money from your account if your bank and their ATMs are underwater. In most cases, you are out of luck with no liquidity.

Disaster Preparation Lesson # 3: Have cash to have on hand? From a general financial planning standpoint, I always suggest putting aside emergency funds that will cover four to six months of expenses. For a disaster situation, I suggest having enough for at least one month of emergency expenses, in cash, somewhere that is extremely accessible to you. Note, this is over and above your general emergency funds. I don't mean have this cash in your pocket, but you should have emergency cash stored in several different places, possibly a savings account, a safe deposit box or hidden in a safe place in your home. Pick several different places that will be safe so you can get liquid cash in the case of an emergency.

Disaster Preparation Lesson # 4: Have a reliable friend or relative who can and will help you during a disaster, someone who can provide you with food, shelter, clothing, transportation and possibly an emergency fund to tide you over. You may even want to give them cash to hold just for such an extreme emergency. I realize there is risk in this but we are talking extremes here. Extreme times call for extreme measures.

Disaster Preparation Lesson # 5: Have bank accounts with at least 2 different banks. Perhaps one of them with a bank that's also near where that reliable friend lives.

Money Sense:

You need to have 3 to 6 months of expenses. The average person has less than 6 weeks of emergency funds. After that they are strapped. If you don't have at least 3 months of expenses, that's an area to work on.

FUNERAL PLANNING PROTECTS YOU AND YOUR FAMILY

One friend to another at the coffee shop: "I want to know when I am going to die. The other says, I don't want to know when, I want to know where. And then I plan on not being there." Since choice is not an option, let's deal with this puppy.

How Much Will it Cost?

If you are planning a cremation the cost will be somewhere between $500 and $2000. That's not including burial and transportation. The cost for a regular funeral, with casket, will run somewhere between $5000 and $15000 or possibly much more. A major portion of the regular funeral expense will be the casket. When the Pope of the Roman Catholic Church died recently, and costs were not a major consideration, it was especially noteworthy that he chose a pine box as a casket. These typically are the least expensive casket options. Mahogany is nice, and if you are very well off and have a lot of money to go around, go for it. However, no one will see it after it is interred—not even the neighbors.

What Information Do You Need When Making Funeral Arrangements?

- Date of Birth
- Maiden name
- Social security number
- Years lived at present address
- Place of birth
- Were you a service veteran
- Religious, fraternal or other service organizations affiliations
- Family members names and cities where they lived

Additional considerations: Closed or open casket, photographs, accepting gifts or charitable donations, number of limousines, after burial reception and food.   How many certified copies of the death certificate will be needed.

IF YOU ARE A PLAN-AHEAD PERSON, WHEN SHOULD YOU START THINKING ABOUT PLANNING FOR FUNERAL ARRANGEMENTS?

There are just two choices. For yourself, the only one you have a choice in is the pre-plan and that is becoming a popular option. You get to make your own choices and arrangements and avoid having the family struggle with all the information needed, guesswork decisions, and perhaps even emotional crises that can develop over the details while they are distraught with emotion.

Three Advantages to Having It Your Way

1. You get to control the costs. Once you sign the contract the price is locked in and inflation proofed. If you sign for a $5000 funeral today and are buried in 15 years, no doubt the cost of the arrangements will be a good bit higher. But your cost will still be $5000. Not a penny more.

2. You get to have the arrangements as you would prefer them. Without getting too personal you may want a closed casket and if those wishes are unknown, then the family has to choose. And this is a highly charged issue best not left to the choosing of others at such an emotional time.

3. You prevent family strife. The piece of mind knowing that family members won't have to deal with differing views or fight at such a highly emotional time is something they'll probably appreciate long after the burial is over. I recall my aunt calling us all together when I was just out of college and she was dying of cancer. She told us all that she had pre-planned her funeral and just what the arrangements were and in case everyone didn't understand certain aspects of the funeral she went over them—including who would get what, what was in the will, and what she was leaving to the option of family members. I recall it was very little of importance and we all remember that almost two generation later. Thanks to Aunt Ronnie for being such a thoughtful and tough minded trooper for the whole family.

Money Sense:

The vast tangible overriding benefit here is the cost saving. But perhaps the most sweeping benefit of all is the stress and emotional relief you provide before, during and long after the funeral is over.

WHAT IF YOU MOVE AND HAVE
A PRE-PLANNED FUNERAL?

Check with your funeral professionals. See if your program is through a nationwide provider. ServiceMaster International is one such organization and it works through or owns many of the local funeral service providers, at least in major metropolitan areas. If that's the case you are protected no matter where you move.

Just to be certain, before making a funeral pre plan, discuss potential moves with the service provider to make sure you are sufficiently covered for most if not all eventualities. Also there may be some provision for relief in the event that you are in an area not covered by the provider.

The emotional relief a pre plan provides your family and loved ones in time of bereavement is worth much more than the effort you put into setting it up.

Money Minutes

INVESTMENT GIFTS – GIVING EVERGREEN FOR THE HOLIDAYS

We try so hard to give gifts that will bring laughter, joy and amusement into the lives of our loved ones that sometimes we get to a point where it's over kill. In addition, some of us like to give something that has value longer than lettuce lasts in July. Here are some thoughtful and practical cash type gifts that will be appreciated over the long term.

1. *Give a piggy bank.* If you want to teach someone the saving habit, there was never a better way than the old-fashioned piggy bank. Buy one that has a removable cover so when it is full it's taken to the bank. With any luck the recipient will make a deposit of the contents into their savings account and you may have a convert in the capital preservation struggle. It will teach them to save and build up money for emergencies, or perhaps pay for a vacation instead of charging it. Of course, you'll put a nice wad of green in the piggy to start things off right.

2. *Give coins.* United States coins are very available from the mint and there are older U.S. and commemorative coins that are collectible. U.S. coins have value—the older ones have intrinsic value because of gold and sliver content—and they are also beautiful and considered works of art by collectors. They also have a history and many appreciate in value. Anyone can purchase coins with values ranging from one half cent to 20 dollars. It's not only a fun gift but it is a way of teaching family about money.

3. *Give investment books.* They make good gifts for those who are on the career trail and making more money each year. A few general books that I like to recommend are "The Millionaire Next Door" and "The Road to Wealth". Another is Ken Farmer's "Keep Pedaling". For anyone trying to gain a better understanding of how to invest or why it is so important, these books are a good start. And who knows you might launch an investment career.

4. *Savings bonds.* Even though most folks put them in the drawer

113

for years and years, the money keeps adding up. Not steeply but gradually. And all of us could use a nice safe, plain vanilla investment that is backed by the government and pays compound interest year in and year out.

5. *Make educational gifts to your kids and grandkids.* The Coverdell Education plan ($2,000 per year) or the newer 529 plans are a great way to jump start and keep a college fund growing big time.

6. *Donate Stock That's Appreciated in Value.* If you own stock that's gone up in value and you want to get double benefits, double in my opinion, donate that stock or a portion of it to a deserving family member. They get to pay the tax on any appreciation if they sell it but they also get a stepped up basis—meaning their basis (value for tax purposes) is considered to be the value as of the date they take ownership of the stock.

Money Sense:

Some folks will point out rightfully that the value of savings bonds may not be worth their giving because interest rates may fluctuate in the wrong direction. However, there are now inflation protected bonds or (TIPS) offering the best of both worlds—safety of principal and protection against rising inflation.

REAPING MAXIMUM REWARDS
FROM CHARITABLE GIVING

There are two rewards in making a charitable donation. There's the fact there are tax and financial benefits to you as the taxpayer in making the charitable contribution. And there's the feeling of well being you get from satisfying an impulse or inner need to help a church you attend, school or college you or the children or grandkids have attended, or a hospital that took special care of a loved one. This combination can make the financial sacrifice, if you can afford it, almost painless.

There are also times when your philanthropic impulse is stirred by extraordinary events like the Tsunami that hit Indonesia and Thailand in 2004 or Hurricane Katrina in the Gulf and Florida in 2005.

Easiest Way to Give to a Charity

The easiest way to give to a charity is by making an outright gift. Gifts can be made either in the current year or as part of an estate distribution.

Check Out New Charities Before You Give

In giving to a charity, in the case of a global tragedy, it is prudent to consider how well the charity manages its money and how much of what's donated is put to work for its stated purpose.

Money Sense:

Don't give cash contributions. Make sure it is a check. And don't feel pressured to give to the person at the door. Any reputable charity will be glad to provide you with their address and tax free status as well as give you time to check them out before giving.

Getting the Most for Your Donated Buck

There are very good rating services that can help the giver measure the efficiency of most charities. There's American Institute of Philanthropy,

3450 North Lake Shore Drive, Suite 2802E, P.O. Box 578460, Chicago, Illinois 60657. Phone: (773) 529-2300. Web: *http://www.charitywatch. org.* There's also The Better Business Bureau's Wise Giving Alliance, 4200 Wilson Boulevard, Suite 800, Arlington, VA 22203. Tel: (703) 276-0100. Website: *www.give.org.* And Charity Navigator, 1200 MacArthur Boulevard, Second Floor, Mahwah, New Jersey 07430. Tel. 201.818.1288. Web: *www.charitynavigator.org*

CHARITABLE REMAINDER TRUSTS –A GOOD WAY TO DO GOOD FOR ALL

Sell Your Profitable Assets and Pay No Taxes

A lot of people with substantial assets are sitting on large paper profits or capital gains. For instance stocks, real estate or a private company they own. They want to sell and take a profit but they are concerned about the taxes. The charitable remainder trust is a great way to accomplish the sale without paying any taxes.

Three Reasons to Like Charitable Remainder Trusts:

- Boost retirement income
- Lower your estate tax
- Help your favorite charities

Setting up the Trust: Since there are decisions to be made and proper paperwork you'll want to meet with an attorney who will set up the trust and help you decide about trustees. With stocks if a husband and wife are involved, they can be trustees. But if it concerns real estate or a private company they there must be an independent trustee to make the sale. Other decisions involve the rate of interest, the income beneficiary, and what charities are going to be the beneficiaries of the trust. The charities can be changed any time. There's even a provision that prevents creditors from getting to the money—called a spendthrift provision.

The money in a CRT is invested like any other fund only the trust is the owner of the investments. The funds could be in tax-free investments so the income is tax free or in taxables.

The pluses, many

- You get all of your money from the sale of the assets without paying any taxes
- You also get a tax deduction that can be carried out for several years

117

• You can invest in any "prudent man" investment, take the income for life and the charity gets the money upon your passing

Money Sense:

A CRT can be set up so a life insurance policy is also purchased naming a family member(s) as beneficiary. When the trust pays out the insurance policy pays out an equal amount to the family member.

The drawbacks, few. You can't spend down the principal after the sale since you've given away the assets to the trust beneficiary. And, of course, the charitable organization gets the proceeds at your death. But the insurance kicker mentioned above could be added to get you a tax free double dip. So check with your adviser to see if CRTs are something you should incorporate into your planning.

SELL, GET RID OF, OR DONATE YOUR USED CAR

To Trade or Not To Trade

It's time to retire the old car that has given you so many years of faithful service. Dealers aren't fond of taking old or high mileage cars in trade. They have too many late model cars coming back in trade or off leases. So whatever is offered to you in trade value toward a new car probably factors in the hassle of getting rid of your car; it may not be worth trading it in for the perceived value you'd get instead of going for a straight cash deal with no trade.

Best bet: Check it both ways with dealers. Compare the cash to the trade deal to see how much you are really getting for your "baby" and their "clunker."

To Sell or Not To Sell

Money Sense:

You could sell your old car or give it to a needy relative. The question to ask yourself is: How reliable is the car at this point and do you want or are you willing to put up with the possibility of follow up phone calls about problems that may have been pre-existing. Even worse, what if the car suddenly decides to go to the auto grave yard— seizing up or dropping the transmission making repairs so expensive they cost more than the vehicle is worth. Now just who do you think they'll call?

A Third, Easier, And Better Way

If the car is drivable and you don't want the headache of dealing with a trade or selling it yourself, a lot of charities who will take it off your hands. How easy is this?

• You donate your car to a charity—making sure it is a Tax Code approved 501 (c) 3 charitable organization

119

- They come pick it up
- You a receipt for the vehicle

- You get a charitable deduction based on the price they sell it for at auction

All's well. The charity gets the money from the sale, you get a tax deduction and the buyer gets a vehicle that won't come back to haunt you if it doesn't work out.

Money Sense:

Take the proper deduction when you donate. The IRS is cracking down on auto deductions because some organizations overestimate the value of these gifts to encourage your donation. So make sure you are dealing with a properly qualified charitable organization. If you aren't using the actual sale price the vehicle brings at auction, double check the value being stated on your receipt or the letter from the charity to make sure it is in line with the value you would find for the vehicle at Edmunds. com or in the Kelly Blue Book where car values are established. If the value is overstated, you'd best consider using the stated wholesale price. Over $500 be sure to fill out IRS form 8283 and file it with your return. Finally, if you want to make a big difference in a needy family's life, check out 1-800-Charity Cars (1-800-242-7489), *www.800charitycars.org.* Key thing to remember in order not to get yourself in trouble after the fact with an auto donation is to make sure the amount of the deduction you take for the car is the amount the charity gets for the car or the so-called value for usage if the car is not sold.

BE GENEROUS WHILE YOU'RE ALIVE

Giving Is A Luxury That Rewards
The Giver More Than The Recipient.

"Kindness in giving creates love" said the 6th Century pre-Christian era Chinese philosopher, Lao-Tzu. I always say, take care of yourself first. But once there and you find your accumulated assets are more than adequate—if in doubt, check with a financial adviser—then you ought to consider giving or gifting to those you love while you are around if for no other reason than to see the joy in their faces when they receive the gifts.

Money Sense:

Uncle Sam allows you to give $12,000 per year to as many people as you wish. You file no return, explain nothing to no one, do no paperwork and create no tax consequences at all for the recipient. If married you can double that to $24,000. Makes it a nice thing to do all around.

You Can Give Other Things Besides Money

If you have real estate or stocks or a company you can donate a percentage of these. You can gift real estate, a car or other valuables.

If Able, You Can Give More—And In More Ways

- Another way you could put a large chunk of money in the hands of an heir with little up front is by purchasing a life insurance policy on your life. Just be sure it is all done in the right way. You donate money tax free to the loved one. They purchase a life insurance policy on you—making certain to name themselves as both owner and beneficiary of the policy—and make the premium payments while you are living. Even if they are using the annual gift from you to make premium payments, it's okay. When you pass, the proceeds of the policy or the death benefit passes to the

121

heir, tax free. It could be a substantial sum that you wouldn't be able to leave any other way.

- 529 plans allow you to give large sums to money to pay for college and educational expenses of your grandchildren and initial funding can be as high as $60,000 over a five year period.
- You can also pay for medical expenses of loved ones.

These are just a few ways to express your caring to loved ones while still alive. If you've got it, don't flaunt it, Give it instead—without strings; why make them wait. That's my opinion and I'm sticking with it.

TIPS: THE TRIPLE-A-#2 LOW RISK INVESTMENT WITH INFLATION PROTECTION

Treasury Inflation Protected Securities

Another way to diversify your holdings and add a low risk investment that adds income to your retirement funds is through treasury inflation-protected securities or TIPS as they are called.

As with I Bonds, you may purchase TIPS direct through the Treasury by mail or by going on line at *www.treasurydirect.gov* .

TIPS are issued in multiples of $1,000 and in your choice of 5, 10, and 20 year holding periods. However, unlike I Bonds they can be cashed in any time. Interest is paid every 6 months and added to the principal. So no two interest payments will be the same and so long as there is inflation your interest payments will go up and so too will your principal. If there is deflation the interest payment might be the same or possibly be less. Sales can be made direct through the treasury or through your broker or bank for an additional charge.

Interest is tax free at the state and local level, but you do have to pay federal taxes.

Money Sense:

If you are the conservative type, older, and you like to sleep like a hibernating bear in winter consider keeping a fair amount of your liquid funds in TIPS.

Money Minutes

WHO GETS HURT WHEN INTEREST RATES GO DOWN?

We've had such a historical low cost of borrowing money in recent years you almost have to go back two generations to match it. It's good for borrowers but is it good for everyone?

One group of people who get especially hurt by lower interest rates is retirees and those living on fixed incomes. Or for that matter anyone living on the income from their investments. When interest rates go down, so do returns earned on assets. Where earnings of 6 or 8 per cent were common not too long ago they might be around 4 or 5 per cent or even less today. On a $200,000 savings account, 8 per cent yields 16,000 per year; $1333.33 per month. At 5 per cent it is 10,000 per year or $833.33 per month. $500 a month is a big difference. If there is no other income coming in it may mean an adjustment downward in lifestyle.

What Can Be Done to Protect Against Declining Interest Rates?

Interest rates move in cycles and once a trend is set in motion, it tends to follow along for awhile. We had over a dozen cuts in interest rates several years back followed by about 14 increases in a row when the Federal Reserve was looking to prevent inflation from re-appearing. Still there are a few things that could provide some cushion against a sharp drop in income when interest rates decline.

Diversify into a number of different investments so that your income stream isn't coming from one or two sources that are interest rate sensitive. Some investments will guarantee you a preferred rate of return for a number of years. This might make sense for a portion of your assets.

Sometimes reshuffling your portfolio is necessary to improve income streams. A fund, for example, with an income element, like bonds, preferred stocks or high yielding common stocks will tend to hold up better in declining interest rate markets. The same is true of junk bond funds that invest in zero coupon bonds of lesser quality issuers. Their face rates are high and when market rates fall their underlying values increase, allowing you to benefit from an increase in asset value, which presumably you could draw off to keep up the income stream. Real estate investment trusts are also less subject to short and intermediate fluctuations in interest rates.

If you have any uncertainty about your portfolio income level think about diversifying streams of income and protecting against being overweight in just one area. Do your own research or seek out an adviser but don't just stay in place when interest rates start their down cycle unless you have a lot of principal to spend down. IF you are living on a fixed portfolio income you need to cushion against erosion. Long term bonds tend to decline less than short maturity ones. Laddering or staggering bond maturities also helps reduce risk and so do lesser quality bonds that have higher coupon rates or yields.

INFLATION AND TRANSPORTATION

No doubt about it. The cost of getting into your car and going somewhere just keeps going up. Back in 1999 on the radio I talked about the price of gas being at its highest level since 1990 when the U.S. was preparing for Operation Desert Storm. The national average for a gallon of regular unleaded gas was more than $1.29. That was then.

The last time around in the oil profit opportunity cycle the average price got up to well over $3.00 for a gallon of unleaded. In some places like New York City it reached $4.00. Isolated gougers were charging as much as $7 in a few places. The next crisis they'll take us to $100 per barrel oil and $5 per gallon for regular. It could shackle the economy.

The point is no matter how bad the oil gougers and pirates stick it to us we don't yet seem to have learned our lesson. Look at the number of V-8 hemi pick up trucks and Navigators being driven by people with 1 or 2 kids. This oil ransom money isn't going away. It's like trying to pay off a blackmailer.

The only way to bring down the cost of your transportation is to get proactive. It's time to make miles per gallon (MPG) the bulls eye in your driving target. If everyone drove a smaller more fuel efficient car, getting say 25 to 28 miles per gallon, then the pirates would have something to scratch their chins about. So would the oil companies. If you have the money think hybrid. It's not quite there yet but it's on the 90 yard line. And with a few other intelligent tactics you already know, you could cut your gasoline costs by 30% or more. Over the long term it's energy conservation and investment in alternative energy sources and development that will help moderate costs. But the price spikers are out there waiting for the next opportunity to stick it to us. Let's get mad. Let's not take this any more.

Money Minutes

WHAT IS LONG TERM CARE?

Simply put, it is the care and caring for an individual who can no longer accomplish the essential daily activities around taking care of themselves—eating, drinking, sleeping, toileting, getting out of bed or walking, concentrating, paying bills and communicating with family friends and service providers. If these are too difficult to perform it's time for long term care.

When is it needed? Terry Shiavo needed it at age 26. You, your parents or other aging family member may need it tomorrow or some day. But that some day will come.

What Choices of care are there?

Assisted Living Facilities. A step between living completely on your own and living in a nursing home, ALFs are best suited for those who need some help with daily living but who want to live on their own as much as possible.

Money Sense:

Choosing assisted living when you are still pretty healthy, may enable you to postpone going to a nursing home much longer and also stretch your care dollars.

Continuing Care Communities. CCCs resemble little towns containing different kinds of facilities—housing, apartments, small houses, assisted living homes, and nursing homes—for different needs. Move in when you are healthy and active and you can stay for the rest of your life. As your health changes, you transition to the most appropriate facility and care you will need.

Money Sense:

If you are the do it yourself, plan ahead type working with adequate but not unlimited funds, this can be a good value.

129

Home Care. These are services that external agencies provide within recipients' homes.

Money Sense:

It's hard to put this on an economic scale because home care may be a choice that has a great deal of psychic value for aging loved ones and provides some relief and piece of mind for those caring for their family member directly. It takes a special person and family to provide home care.

Nursing Homes are for those who need more nursing care than they normally would receive at home. A nursing home may be the right choice if you are leaving a hospital following an illness such as a heart attack, stroke or broken bone and your doctor feels you need therapy and more time to recover—perhaps with managing stairs and other activities requiring physical therapy—before you go home.

Personal Care/Rest Home. Personal Care or rest homes as they were more commonly known are for those who need some help but who can still do some things for themselves. For example, you can still dress yourself but you may need help with meals. A rest home is not for those needing skilled nursing care or help with everything. Not all personal care homes provide the same services. It depends on the size of the facility.

Money Sense:

It's best to candidly discuss needs with the Director of a Personal Care home so there is a mutual understanding of what they can and will and are staffed to provide. They are not nursing homes at a discount, nor are they staffed to provide professional nursing care.

Hospice Care. For those who are not expected to live more than six months, Hospice services will help make the aging family member and the family as comfortable as possible. This type of care may be provided in a private home, nursing home, hospital, or assisted living center.

PLANNING, COST AND FUNDING OF LONG TERM CARE

According to the 2003 MetLife Market Survey of Nursing Home and Home Care Costs the average daily rate for a private room in a nursing home was $181 per day or $66,065 annually. The hourly rate in 2003 for a home health aide was $18. Of course, both the daily and hourly rate are much higher today. And rates vary in different regions of the country with Alaska being highest and Louisiana lowest. The average stay in a nursing home is 2.4 years making the average cost of a nursing home stay approximately $168,192. A resource for checking local costs is at *www. myziva.net.*

Six sources of funds most people use to meet their long term care expenses are:

1. Personal Assets and savings
2. Veterans Administration benefits
3. Medicare
4. Medigap Insurance
5. Medicaid
6. Long Term Care Insurance

Planning for long term care is the most difficult part of financial planning. While most of us know there will probably be a need for this many just keep putting it off. It's important to discuss and to know and understand long term care needs for the individual getting ready to retire, who is currently retired and whose parents are in these situations.

The problem is only going to get bigger as the baby boomers begin retiring.

Money Sense:

There are some simple steps to take to ease the burden of long term care yourself:

131

- Take care of yourself. Eat right, exercise and read or play cards or things that engage your mind as well as your body. Healthy longer means postponing care needs, and saves money for fun things.

- Get your financial house in order. Here comes that word adviser again. It's worth getting professional advice on a matter that may seriously effect your assets, your desire to leave a legacy to your spouse and other family members and

- Check out long term care insurance. These plans can be structured to pay all expenses involved. They have inflation provisions and pay for care as long as needed.

FINDING VALUE IN HEALTH CARE INSURANCE

Once a year, with little warning and not enough information, consumers have been hauled into what's known as the annual choose your health care coverage derby.

Employers used to cover about 80% of their employees with low cost and near unlimited health insurance. That was before the cost of insuring an employee and family mounted to around $10,000 per year. The new trend is toward plans with much higher deductibles. These can run up to $2,000 per year for the family. However, there are hidden traps in the event of long term or chronic illnesses where the annual costs can mount so high that it could bankrupt a household. So you need to carefully weigh the choices you make when choosing or changing your plan.

The new plans take into account the health savings or flexible spending accounts that allow consumers to deduct pre tax money from their pay and put it into an account used to pay for out of pocket and uncovered health expenses including deductibles, drugs, and co-payments to doctors.

To find real value there are some guidelines to consider:

1. How healthy are you?

2. How healthy is your family?

3. Do you take any prescription drugs on a regular basis?

4. Do you use the emergency room a lot?

5. Are there any health problems that tend to run in the family?

6. Do you have an adequate emergency fund for the unexpected medical expense or are do you plan to use a flexible spending account to cover the next year's expenses?

Once you have a fix on these issues—using the past couple of years' experience as a guide— then think about how you will tailor your health insurance. Medical care is so advanced we have options that were pure fantasy a generation ago. But these options come at a price ranging from normal to exorbitant. So the least expensive plan may offer you a payroll cost savings only if you aren't going to be using medical services regularly.

Healthy or not consumers also need to look at long term care and disability insurance if not provided by an employer.

If you do run into exceptionally high bills in a current year and don't expect it to be a permanent situation, before using your credit card which may carry up to 20% annual interest rates, see if you can work out a payment plan with the medical provider.

For do it yourselfers seeking more help than the insurance company brochures may provide, take a look at *www.planforyourhealth.com* or *www.fpanet.org/public.*

LIFE INSURANCE — WHY AND HOW MUCH?

Like the announcer who clears out the room when he announces the record jackpot for the mega-gazillion lottery, the reception room at the country club cocktail party grows stone silent as soon as the insurance sales rep enters the room.

Face it, who wants to think about death and dying. That's what people think about when they think life insurance. That and a pushy sales person, mind numbing charts and contracts written by attorneys who didn't have the personality to go into accounting or financial planning (smiles please).

Sure, the main reason to purchase life insurance is for the death benefit which the individual hopes the beneficiaries won't collect on for a long, long time. However, there is more to life insurance than just the grim reaper. There are short and long term benefits as well as estate planning aspects to life insurance that make it an essential part of every complete financial plan.

Essential Uses for Life Insurance Benefits:

- Creation of an Estate (if there isn't one or one that's insufficient)
- Pay Potentially Costly Estate Taxes
- Liquid Cash to Pay Expenses and Debts of the Estate
- Income Replacement and Protection Benefits for Survivor's Lifetime
- Permanent Death Protection so you can Spend Down Other Assets and Enjoy You Retirement

How Much Is Enough?

If your family or other people depend on your income you need life insurance to help them live without your support if you pass away. A quick rule of thumb is to take your income and figure out what you clear after taxes and before expenses. How many years do you want your loved one to continue to live like they do now, without you around to

135

provide the money. That's a great place to start.

Money Sense:

The traditional life insurance rule of thumb was you need 7 to 10 years of income to adequately cover your family in the vent of your early demise. The right amound depends upon what other assets you have available.

CHOOSING THE RIGHT INSURANCE COMPANY

So many insurance companies to choose from.

Which Insurance Company Is Best For You?

Most insurance companies are rated and have to pass crucial testing requirements to pass the ratings scale. That makes it a little easier to pick one.

There are five major services that rate insurance companies:

- A.M. Best—ratings in the "secure" category are B+, good, A-&A, excellent, & A+ being superior
- Moody's Life Insurance
- Duff and Phelps Credit Rating Company
- Standard and Poor's—ratings from AAA-, extremely strong to R. Stick with A rated or better
- Weiss Research—Ratings BBB and up are the strongest

Each one has a slightly different way of measuring an insurance company's strength. The first three provide comprehensive ratings based on interviews with the insurance company. And they charge the carriers a subscription fee. Weiss Research and Standard and Poor's provide statistical ratings but don't charge a subscription fee to the carriers.

Comparing One Rating Company Against the Other

The ratings services do that for you but *things to look at include:*

- Is the company's surplus (net worth) adequate for its obligations?
- Is the company's liquidity sufficient to meet its ongoing income needs?

- Are the company's riskier investments of high quality and sufficiently diversified?

- Has the company shown consistent annual earnings?

Money Sense:

There are about 1800 life insurance companies in North America to choose from. Working with a financial advisor or independent insurance agent will certainly help you speed up the selection process and could ease you mind in picking the best insurance company for you. Don't just use price as an indicator because you might regret it later one. You'll be fine if you stick with the strong and better rankings of the rating services. If you are the do it yourself type, choose a website like http://www. insure.com, www.selectquote.com or www.intelliQuote.com Pricing and research ratings will be displayed there as well. They only deal with the highest rated companies. But don't rule out your local advisor as they will offer reasonably competitive rates too. And they will advise you about certain options that you may not be aware of and want in your policy.

LIFE INSURANCE – WHICH KIND IS RIGHT?

There are so many kinds of life insurance policies available today. What do you need to know.

Know the Basics

There are two basic types of life insurance: temporary and permanent. Each has many variations. But let's just stick with the two major groups above.

Temporary coverage, better known as term insurance is aimed at providing a specified amount of coverage for a stated period of time or term. The premium or cost for tem insurance increases with the age of the insured, as chances of dying get greater, but it can be bought with a level or fixed premium for a certain number of years—5, 10,15 or 20 years. It pays a death benefit but builds no equity or cash value. You are paying strictly for protection.

Permanent coverage is insurance that can be continued, so long as premium payments are made, for the lifetime of the insured, regardless of age. It pays a death benefit and also builds up equity or cash value.

What's Best?

No one policy is the absolute best. The best policy is the one that fits your personal situation and risk tolerance. Whether you chose whole life, universal life, variable life, or term life is irrelevant. In going over your situation the right combination or policy will surface or it may be that using a variety of policies and even from different companies will give you the best most flexible portfolio.

Are there Tax Advantages to Life Insurance?

Yes. Permanent life has significant tax advantages such as an income tax –free death benefit, tax-deferred accumulation of cash. You also have access to cash funds by borrowing or withdrawing the cash value of the policy.

Money Sense:

Sometimes a mix of term and permanent or whole life is a nice hybrid choice to give you the best of both worlds. If you are 40 when you buy life insurance you'll likely have family obligations and other things that require more than someone say 70 years old will have. But if you buy at 40 and live to 100 you'll have paid a lot of premiums on temporary or term coverage that are gone out the window but right to have at the time to provide adequate coverage at the most affordable price. And bear in mind that term has to be renewed at higher premiums or dropped in which case there is no longer any coverage. The permanent insurance, even for a small portion of your needs will have cash value and a death benefit and you'll also have access to those cash funds via borrowing or withdrawing the cash value of the policy.

LIFE INSURANCE – A VERSATILE WAY TO REWARD EMPLOYEES

Employers with as few as 3 or more employees have a bigger challenge than their larger competitors to make it attractive for good employees to stay with the company. One way to promote long term retention is with what I call a Sears "good" to "better" benefits package if not the Sears "best".

The traditional benefits that are pretty much expected by employees today are social security, employer-sponsored qualified plan, either a defined benefit—pays you so much a month at retirement—or defined contribution—employee contributes but the benefit isn't defined —such as a 401 (K), individual savings. There are other rewards that are appreciated. One is life insurance.

Why Life Insurance is a Valuable Benefit

First there is the death benefit. If the employee dies, salary stops and the family could be in a squeeze financially. A death benefit can keep the income stream coming while the family reorients itself. Also tax favored low interest rate loans and withdrawals can be taken from the case value of a policy, unless it is term insurance.

Second is the retirement income. Years go by and cash value builds. By the time the employee retires, they can receive a steady retirement income. Later, when death occurs, there could also be a payable death benefit.

Third there is the psychic income. With or without a cash value buildup, life insurance is a valued benefit to key employees who care about their families. Also policies may be offered to cover the employee's spouse and minor children at the same reduced group rates at very little extra cost to the employer. But the value to the employee may be great indeed.

Money Sense:

These days, employers are hard pressed to stay competitive with wages and benefits and many ask me if the expense of something like life insurance is worth it? Obviously, benefits do cost the employer. But since they also tend to keep employee turnover lower, most employers figure the added cost of training or retraining exceeds the cost of providing the wanted or needed benefits in the first place.

NO LOTTERY TICKETS IN THE GAME OF LIFE—
THINK SMALL, WIN BIG

A major state lottery has as its marketing theme something like ...."You can't live the dream if you don't play the game. Buy your lottery ticket today."

Of course we Americans are master marketers and I certainly appreciate the value of a well thought out marketing campaign. But can you understand how it pains me to think that of those who would need some kind of reliable return on their money—most of all in this life's lottery—so many will waste their hard earned money and all too scarce disposable dollars buying lottery tickets in the hopes of getting struck by "green lightning".

If you want to win the lottery of life take a dollar or 5 or 10 or so dollars a week – whatever you have decided to take an impossibly high risk gamble with and instead of buying that lotto ticket, put it into your 401K or Roth IRA (individual retirement account) or even a CD (as in certificate of deposit, not compact disc) at your local savings bank.

The kind of discipline that it takes to do this and the kind of reward it pays will never be equaled by systematically blowing your money on a lotto ticket—except for the one in a million or so lucky stiffs who happen to get struck by the fairy godmother of chance like Cinderella.

Money Sense - Challenge Yourself For a Year:

If you doubt the logic here I challenge you to take half your lotto wager money each week and put it into any one of the savings vehicles mentioned above for 1 year, keeping careful track of just how much you spent on tickets—or just throw each ticket into a cigar box and count them up at the end of the year—and how much you put in savings. At the end of the year take a look and see how much you've "won" with saving versus how much is gone up in smoke in the cigar box.

Money Minutes

LIVING YOUR FINANCIAL LIFE WELL

As Robert Fulghum says in the intro to his best selling book on living well, *"I already know most of what is needed to lead a meaningful life. It isn't that complicated. Living it—WELL—that is another matter."*
The same can be said of our financial life. For most of us, it really isn't that complicated, but it is tough to live it in a way that will work out. And so my purpose is to bring you some of the simple tools I have discovered that work for most of the people most of the time. Many topics have been covered in books about personal finance, many times over. The problem is getting the message out in the simply put, engaging way you learned about things when you were in grade school. This book will present scores of simple and key principles in that simple one-room schoolhouse way so you'll get friendlier with your money. Money has been so maligned that it still isn't talked about much in school. Many people who have it figure they don't deserve it, that it is perhaps "evil" or can't be held on to. To many people money is just something for spending Becoming friendly with money and living well with it takes a little backing up and understanding just what the essentials are in a clear, plain and real simple way.

Fortunately, in St. Louis, where I have spent the past 40 odd years advising clients, there tends to be a more conservative approach to making, investing and spending money. Like Warren Buffet, I like being away from the high roller finance centers in New York, San Francisco, Chicago, and Dallas. It is a way to tune out the static and the frenzy of Wall Street and concentrate instead on Main Street principles and needs of mainstream clients. While providing readers with literally hundreds of shrewdly simple money principles here, my hope is to help regular folks, like most of us, to truly master the fundamental tools that will make you a financial success in life. Perhaps not rich, but not financially stressed or worried either.

Money Sense:

Try keeping away from the noise, chatter and rumor around investing. Underneath it all there's a lot of simple common sense you can understand and fell comfortable with. And now with the advent of the 'pump and dump' bulletin boards and email list servers never invest in a stock touted in an email or on a message board. Do your own homework and make up your own mind. That includes investments recommended by your adviser.

DOLLAR COST AVERAGING—THE SMART WAY TO GET THE LOWEST PRICE PER SHARE

Whenever anyone asks me "Bob, what's the best way to invest?" my first response is always, "Simple; the way that makes the most money." I can hear you saying, sure Bob. Easy to say; hard to do. True, but there is one way that helps take most of the guesswork out of the situation.

Let's say you have a solid company—growth, real profits, solid management and a good industry. You really like this company and you want to buy shares. But you aren't sure when or if it is the best time to buy. Is the stock price low, too high or just right? That's one issue. Another consideration is what does the company's industry look like, Is it high growth, or a mature industry. A third issue is what stage the market cycle is at: trending up, down, or sideways? Fortunately there is a way to take the guesswork out of the timing or when to buy. It's a proven technique known as dollar cost averaging. The way it works is simple:

How it Works:

Each month you put an equal amount of money—say $25, 50 or $100 or a number you are comfortable with—into buying as many shares of the company as the money allows.

Will it buy the same number of shares each month? No because the price of the company will fluctuate with the market and you'll be buying at a different price each month. Here's an example of how it works out with a $50 per month investment:

DOLLAR COST AVERAGING

Month	Jan	Fed	Mar	Apr	May	Jun	Jul	Au	Sep	Oct	Nov	Dec	Total
Money Invested	$50	$50	$50	$50	$50	$50	$50	$50	$50	$50	$50	$50	$600
Share Price	$10	$11	$13	$14	$15	$13	$12	$11	$10	$9	$11	$12	$11.75
No. of Shares Bought	5	4.5	3.8	3.6	3.3	3.8	4.2	4.6	5	5.6	4.6	4.2	52.1

At the end of a year you put $600 into Company "B" stock and purchased a total of 52.12 shares. The average price per share over the year is 11.75. However, your dollar cost average per share ($600 divided by the number of shares bought) is just $11.51. So by putting in a fixed amount of money each month you are able to reduce your average cost per share to a price below the average price of the stock over the same period, eliminating the guesswork over when to buy.

Money Sense:

While Dollar Cost Average doesn't assure a profit and can't protect against loss, Dollar Cost Averaging can be a great way to buy solid growth investment at the best possible price—by investing the same dollar amounts every month.

MONEY AND EMOTION—WHAT YOU CAN
LEARN FROM POKER

For those of you who have been in the stock market during and since the time the Dow Jones Industrial Averages and the NASDAQ hit 15,000 and 5,000 respectively it has been like a long game of Texas Hold 'Em. Maybe you haven't been to the losers lounge yet but you are often feeling like you have the short stack of chips in the game.

The roller coaster ride that many call investing is just made all the more dramatic by the fact it is hard not to get emotional when your money is at stake.

Strangely enough there are some pretty good rules in poker that we make good sense when investing, too. Not that I'm equating poker with investing. I'm not even advocating you play poker unless it is the free kind at places like www.ultimatebet.com or www.partypoker.com. And if you go there you promise me you'll remember that I said play the free games. (Yeah, right, Bob).

Okay, back to the market and collateral poker rules because you don't even have to pretend to be interested in poker to get the universal common sense in these rules. Kenny Rogers hit song The Gambler said it all.

Never count your money at the table. If you have so little to risk that you can't afford to lose it all without it changing your life, don't play. I mean, don't invest. Putting up say $5,000 or even $1000 and then watching your stock go up and down everyday is sure to give you vertigo or acid reflux. If you are the kind of investor who has to stay glued to CNBC all day counting your pennies, you need a more well-rounded life.

Know When To Hold 'Em and Know When To Fold 'Em. When you make a bet, make sure your eyes don't give you away. Keep your poker face or step away. Better to fold early when the cost is slight—say an 8 to 10% loss—than to ride it out hoping for a miracle recovery.

Know when to walk away. If you can't read the other people at the table you are the weak link. Others are reading you.

Know when to run. Know the odds. If the stakes are too high and odds are you lose, you lose. Know the odds and don't buck them unless you are sitting on a big stack of money and luck is running with you.

DEFINING STOCK INVESTMENTS

Stocks come in two basic types, common and preferred stock.

Both represent shares of ownership in the company. Common stock is unsecured ownership so it isn't backed by any assets of the company. Shares are originally issued by the company and then freely trade among investors on public securities exchanges. There are certain rights shareholders receive such as voting for the board of directors and approving other major decisions that are put before the shareholders, participating in profits through dividends declared by the company and appreciation in the price of their share value on the exchange. Common shareholders have a subordinated or lesser claim than other creditors, bondholders, or preferred shareholders to any assets of the company in the event of say a liquidation or bankruptcy. After everybody else gets paid then the common shareholders are entitled to whatever assets may be left. That's the risk that balances off the shot at a higher return on capital than for instance bondholders would receive if the company is highly successful.

Preferred shareholders have more security in the event of a corporate liquidation. They are ahead of common shareholders in claims to the company's assets or in this case next to last in line common stockholders. In addition, preferred shares often pay a dividend that's higher than the dividend, in any, on common stock.

Are Stock Investments Guaranteed?

Stocks offer no guarantees but history shows stocks have outperformed bonds or treasury bills 80 % of the time in 10 year holding periods, over 90% of the time in 20 year holding periods and except for one period, and 100% of the time in 30 year holding periods. Over shorter periods stocks have been riskier than bonds outperforming them only 60% of the time. (source: Jeremy Siegel's Stocks for the Long Run, McGraw Hill, 1998.)

Money Sense:

Except for short term periods, stocks are the premier investment vehicle for your capital, in my opinion. They outperform bonds in most 10 and 20 year periods and in all 30 year holding periods. As Jeremy Siegel says in his books it is "Stocks for the long run."

Links to more information: *http://www.dowjonesmarketwatch.com/*, *http://www.thestreet.com* , and *http://www.finance.yahoo.com* are all good websites for learning the basics of equity and bond investing. And they are free.

INVESTMENT TECHNIQUES/RETURNS
– BUYING STOCKS

Risks and Returns in Stock Portfolios

Should you invest in a portfolio or a handful of stocks or stick with just one or two? You play the risk game with a highly concentrated portfolio. It's great to have one or two big winners but who knows what individual stocks are going to do when we buy them?

Gauge Your Risk

I've seen employees of local companies make a lot of money placing all of their company benefit money into their company's stock. I have also seen them lose a lot of money. The sky's the limit with one or two investments. And the downside is potentially high, too. Look at Enron, Global Crossing, MCI and so many others.

Can You Lose More in One Stock
Than a Group of Stocks?

You can lose a lot in both. One of the sages said put all your eggs in one basket and watch that basket closely. You could put it all in one stock and watch that stock closely or put it into a lot of handpicked companies and watch them closely. But decide how many you can watch. The larger the number of stocks in a portfolio, the more time you will have to spend doing research and keeping abreast of developments. How much time do you have and how much of it do you want to spend doing investment research and follow up.

Two Mistakes That Can Torpedo Your Investment Boat

Thinking short term is probably produces the highest mortality rate among investors. Sure, you'll hear gurus like Cramer "diss" the "graybeards" for buying and holding, but how many investors can do what he does and do it consistently, month after month and year after year. How many professionals can do it? Just look

153

at the mutual fund leader boards and the greatest advancers list of stocks each year. How many are repeaters?

Getting swept away by "hot" trends is the second mistake. It was dot com in the 90s and these past few years there was Taser and maybe it's China today or Google and tomorrow it will be another big thing. Just because it is making money today for someone doesn't mean it will be making it for you tomorrow.

Money Sense:

Start out with a few stocks and build as you gain experience and confidence and have the time and commitment to develop your own diversified portfolio.

DRIPS—THE SMALL INVESTOR SECRET

Not often but once in awhile there's more than just leftovers on the investment table for small investors. The Dividend Reinvestment Plan (DRIP) is or can be an investment goldmine.

DRIPS are set up by around 1000 public companies so that investors can reinvest their stock dividends to purchase additional shares of the company without commission. This is a way to have your portfolio grow automatically even in you don't invest any further new money.

Most DRIPS are totally free of brokerage commissions and other charges because the company offering the plan wants to encourage shareholders to use it.

DRIPS+. About 100 companies offer a sweetened version of the DRIP known as a "Discount DRIP". To promote shareholder participation they give a discount of up to 5% on reinvested dividends so the shareholder buys at the market price less 5%. On a $50 market value stock that's $2.50 per share.

Money Sense:

To invest in a company's DRIP you must first buy a share of stock and have it registered in your name. Once that's done you are in on one of the best but not so heavily used insider stock discount purchase plans. To get more information or get say a young earner off on the right foot, Charles Carlson has a good book titled "Free Lunch on Wall Street" which discusses DRIP programs and the companies that offer them in greater detail. Or check *www.dripcentral.com/*.

Money Minutes

DRIPS AND DSPS! THERE'S A DIFFERENCE

Building your portfolio, one share at a time!

DSP or direct sales plans will allow you to buy share(s) of stock directly from the publicly traded company. Once you have the single share you can then participate in the direct re-investment of future dividends through the company DRIP explained earlier.

The biggest step in setting up a direct investment plan is the purchase of that first share. It's difficult and often expensive to do through a brokerage house and you have to get the share registered in your own name. So sure enough a few good services have developed to help new shareholders get that first certificate of ownership at the lowest cost.

DSP Resources

The Money Paper, 555 Theodore Fremd Ave., Suite B-103, Rye, NY 10580 publishes a newsletter for investors interested in direct investing (*www.directinvesting.com*). Their Temper of the Times service helps non-subscribers makes their first DSP investment. And Vita Nelson, the publisher of the Money paper has a DRIP mutual fund she co-manages. First Share (*www.firstshare.com*) is a similar service. A list of public companies with share purchase plans can be found at *www.firstshare. com/ColistAE.htm#colistAE*. The National Investors Association Corporation's "Own a Share of America" program also helps individual investors get going.

Money Sense:

The main thing is to get going. Once you own your first share you are on your base step in the wealth building pyramid. Once you get the dividend reinvesting started you'll receive a quarterly statement from the company showing you how many shares your reinvested dividends have purchased and how many shares you now own.

157

Money Minutes

IPOS — COMING OUT PARTIES FOR COMPANIES

When a company's shares are sold to the public for the first time we say it goes public or has an initial public offering. It first trades on one of the exchanges or in the pink sheets. The offering is usually managed by an underwriter who handles the deal by buying the shares from the company and in turn selling them to the public. The underwriter may stabilize or make a market in the stock for a limited time afterward. However, once the issue is "public" or freely trading, its fate is in the hands of investors and the market which will decide the value or price to place on the shares of the company.

New issues tend to follow the general direction of the market and for that reason they are brought to market when the industry they are in is in favor with investors. A good example is the 2007 IPOs of two private equity companies Blackstone Group and KKR who made a fortune for their private investors and then for their execs by going public to raise even more money.

IPOs are usually very speculative and they are also hard to get. They may be unsuitable for most investors and if the issue is considered "hot" or highly desirable because of the advance "buzz" or information floating out there about the company's prospects, the demand will exceed the supply of shares.

The underwriter then allocates shares to members of the underwriting syndicate and they in turn will allocate them to their individual clients. The hotter the issue the more likely they will be allocated to the most valued and well heeled clients. All of this combines to make new issues or IPOs very hard to get.

Money Sense:

If you suddenly find that your account exec is offering you shares as part of an initial public offering and the offer is for as much as you would like, buyer beware. This is probably not a hot issue. In fact, it may be a meal of cold turkey. The hotter the issue the harder it is to get. Nothing easy in the IPO market is HOT.

159

Money Minutes

INVESTMENT TECHNIQUES/RETURNS –
CARDINAL RULES FOR MAKING INVESTMENTS WORK

Okay I admit it's going to be a little difficult to give you instant distilled wisdom on a subject that more books have been written about than just about any other topic. But I will give you some cardinal rules. Each of these will make money sense on its own. Remember the movie the Dresser? It starred Albert Finney playing an aging actor doing abbreviated versions of Shakespeare plays. This section reminds me of his Highlights from Hamlet only we'll be doing Highlights from the likes of Warren Buffet, Peter Lynch, Charlie Munger – and more:

Can any investor beat the stock market today?

Yes, in my humble opinion. But it isn't easy because you need to do a few "simple" things consistently. Even good handicapping systems have a long term record of success, but most people who follow them just don't stick to them. They monkey it and then it won't work. The investor gets disillusioned, blames the system, and tosses off investing as not for them. Here are some sensible rules to follow:

1. *Stay away from stock tips.* Remember: If it's a good stock it's not a tip because other brain cells have discovered it. You just need to get in before the story is played out and there is still upside. What I said about tips goes for the stock du jour—stock of the moment—on shows like CNBC. A study several years ago on Barron's weekly recommended stocks showed that they had a brief flurry of interest and prices went up and then – you guessed it –went down again. This goes triple for those pump and dump e mail and junk mail recommendations. By the time you get the hot news look at the stock and see where it's been and how far it's come already. That should be enough of a clue as to what time it is on the investment clock. The worst of the bunch are so called penny stocks. These are subject to promotion by extreme hucksters and will cost you the shirt off your investment back.

2. *Do your homework.* There's no substitute for good background

161

research and today it is so readily available. From Value Line, available at many libraries to Yahoo Finance, Market Watch, Zachs, Motley Fool and so many, many more mainstream resources you can piece together a good research picture on the stock you are studying. With all the information available you'd think Warren Buffett would have an inside track. Yet he is a big believer in reading company annual reports. And if you want a real inexpensive education on how to do research and read annual reports and do your investment homework properly then——

3. **Join an investment club.** The National Association of Investment Clubs has many thousands of local clubs who meet regularly to engage in an established discipline of assigning members to research new investment candidates, reviewing those candidates with the club members, making buy or no buy decisions and also reviewing holdings to determine if any further action is warranted. They also produce a magazine called Better Investing that's a real treasure of information and can be purchased even if you don't belong to an investment club. For more information write: Better Investing Magazine, 711, W 13 Mile Road, Madison Heights, MI 48071, call toll free (877) 275-6242 or www.betterinvesting.org. Don't forget though that this is consensus thinking and the club's goals, risk tolerance and timelines for selling may not match your own.

4. **Work with a support team.** This includes your own efforts coupled with the synergy you can get from other professionals. Today you can assemble a pretty broad and deep well of information about most companies you might think of investing in. This includes doing your own investigative homework, checking investment websites, reading any research reports you can lay your hands on, doing some competitive analysis—your target company versus the rest of the companies in the same industry.

5. **Diversify but don't overload your portfolio.** Don't own a lot of stocks. Don't own a lot of funds. And don't chase the most popular funds of the year or stocks either. With funds it is rare to find repeaters among the top 10 performers in any one year or in any one category year after year. If you do happen to find the Lance Armstrong or Wayne Gretsky or Tiger Woods or Chris Evert

Lloyd of stocks, like Berkshire Hathaway, stay with a winner. If you diversify you can comfortably own around eight funds. Eight funds with the right managers can give you all the diversification you need no matter what the size of your portfolio. And with the information available today you can check to make sure you actually have diversification. No point in having your money in two or three funds with the same top ten stocks in their portfolio. That's phantom diversification.

6. **Rely on your instincts.** Peter Lynch is one of the savviest investors and one of the 20th Century's most profitable portfolio managers. At Fidelity Investments, he consistently beat the market for over 13 years running. Lynch suggested investing by walking around, at for instance the shopping malls, listening and paying attention to what's around you. Even listening to what your kids were into at the mall. You don't need a research analyst to tell you that Starbucks or Wal-Mart or Target is a good company to invest in. For instance, when your teenage kids or grandkids were all asking for iPODs that was a good hint to reconsider Apple. It had much more than a dead cat bounce. At its low a few years ago it was under $5 and at this writing it's over $200 a share.

7. **Take a long term approach.** If you are thinking you can make a living at this, day by day or week by week, put down my book and read the books with the titles like How I Made A Million Dollars In The Stock Market. Often it's by writing a book entitled How I Made a Million Dollars…. Plan to be in the market for at least five years or more. Plan on making new investments in up and down markets. You are buying stocks, not buying the market. This is a get rich slowly plan. Patience has its rewards: If you had invested $1,000 in Berkshire Hathaway, a small textile company, when Warren Buffett took over management in 1965, and held onto it until today, it would be worth over $5 Million. Of course, if you are 85 and glad to see the sun shine every day, you might have a different view of long term. And if you are 85 you are unlikely to be invested very heavily in the stock market anyway. And speaking of plans….

8. **Have a plan and stick to it.** Stay in the market and buy more when you can, and buy more especially when you can buy a

163

solid stock and it's at a low price. Many people lost in the market drops of 1987, 1994,1998, 2000, 2001 and 2002. But the ones who lost the most are the ones who got out and stayed out. Those who bought in 1987 after the drop are pretty much in clover today. Just one example, Berkshire Hathaway stock was down to $2,000 per share after the market crash in '87. Today it is around $25,000. So stay and play. IF you stay in and buy when it's high and buy when it's low when it is high again—and history proves the market will make new highs again—you'll be even on your purchase made at the highs and a good bit ahead on the purchases you made during the lows.

9. **Buy at low cost.** If you aren't taking full advantage of the services of the full service brokerage or investment firm consider opening an account at a discount firm like Schwab or Siebert, Options Xpress or Scottrade. See www.hotstocks.com/brokers/ for a more complete list. Of course you'll get little or no advice but you won't be paying very high commissions to amortize against your purchase price. If you are paying $99 commissions on a ticket to buy say 50 shares of a 15.00 stock that's a full point or 16.00 on the stock you need just to break even. And another $99 on the way out will cost you another point. If you were to purchase the 15.00 stock at say Muriel Siebert which charges 14.95 for an unassisted trade or 37.50 for a broker assisted trade (so you can have it your way) you are still paying a lot less to get in and out of a stock than with a full service firm. Another way to decease your investment cost is to buy shares in companies that have dividend reinvestment plans or DRIPs. They allow you to reinvest your dividend payments in additional shares which are purchased commission free. In addition to DRIPS there are also DSP or direct sales plans where companies allow you to buy their shares direct with little or no commissions. For more information check out www.sharebuilder.com. A note to retirement fund builders. DRIPS and DSPs are generally not the place to be building retirement funds. You are best off maxing out your 401Ks and IRAs first and then with any extra private investment money you'll be directing into stocks, consider these low cost vehicles.

10. **Don't watch the market or watch your stock(s) everyday.** There's almost a cardinal rule that when you buy a stock, no matter how

good the underlying company is, the stock goes down right after you buy it. Pay no attention. It's just a momentary distraction designed to thwart your long term objective of capital gains from above the average growth in company sales and earnings that is sooner or later going to be rewarded in the market by higher values. It's also a way to get the scared money off the table.

11. **Don't be in a hurry to sell.** If you have done your homework and know the company you are buying and enough about the business it is in you have no reason to sell unless something fundamental has changed. And I don't mean a sagging market. The overall market condition may have little to do with the company you've purchased. Oh sure, if it's in a cyclical business there might be times when business slows and sales and earnings do the same, but if the fundamentals, earnings and growth relative to industry peers, profit margins and cash flow hold up, don't be in any rush to sell. Over the long term you'll probably be better off most of the time by hanging on.

12. **Consider All Printed and Internet Information Carefully.** If you do a lot of reading or cyber-researching, you can easily find out what the top investment clubs are buying. That's not always a guarantee you'll buy and be a winner. Take for instance mutual funds. If you pick up a fund   report you'll be able to learn what their top 10 holdings are, and what positions they either put on or sold off in the past 6 months. Sounds good but what are you getting. You know what the fund bought, but not when they bought it and when they intend to sell it and maybe not when they sold it either—at least until the next 6 month report. The same goes for following the investing masters. Okay this is certainly better than picking stocks using a dart board but if you buy what Warren Buffet buys the same applies. You don't know why he bought it or what he intends doing with the holding and when he plans to sell. Nobody is telling you when to sell. That part of the game you have to learn on your own.

13. **Know your investment objectives — be realistic.** What kind of returns are you expecting? These past 15 years or so a lot of the benchmarks have been out of whack. Are you expecting double digit returns on your investments, every six months? History

shows that isn't sustainable over the long term. Seeking significant returns involves significant risk and more volatility or price swings than you may be prepared for. Meet with your financial advisor, establish your long term goals and set your expectations realistically.

14. *Study price earnings ratios.* Look at price earnings ratios, the number of times that a company's stock sells for times its earnings per share. Lately the ration has been over 20 and historically that's high, though not so high compared to where it was say in 1996, when Alan Greenspan was talking about irrational exuberance in the markets. Study ratios of other companies in the same industry as the one you are considering buying. Is its ratio higher lower or the same? Does that ratio have a high and low band throughout the year? When is it high; when is it low? Also what is its ratio relative to the market? This gives you some indication as to whether the stock is highly valued or not so highly valued on a relative basis.

Money Sense:

There is a book in just these investing rules so pay them serious attention and they will serve you well. Not every stock will come up perfect but if it gets good marks based on the appropriate benchmark rules above, chances are you've done your homework right and will reap the appropriate rewards—all in good time.

CASHING OUT OF THE STOCK MARKET

Sounds Good But ....

It's easier to get out than get back in. A lot of money has been made in the stock market these past several years. It naturally leads to the idea of "cashing out", taking profits, waiting for the market to go down and then getting back in again by buying at lower prices.

It sure sounds good. The question, of course, if you aren't a natural born trader, is when to get back in. The easiest thing to do is to get out. We can do it anytime because the market is so liquid. But market history shows that most people who get out don't get back in until the market is higher, often a lot higher.

The emotional factors around when to get back in influences investors so much that they wait too long to make the move.

The difference in results between people staying in or buying and holding investments versus getting out and getting back into the market comes down to a tiny window; sometimes just a day. And what a difference a day makes.

Do-Nothings Can Win — Big

From January 1st, 1988 to January 1st, 1998 the Standard & Poors Index of Stocks had a cumulative total return of 426%. That's if the investor stayed in the market and did nothing at all.

If a person was out of the market during that same period and only missed the ten biggest days during those 10 years their returns would only be 98%! That's 300% less for being out of the market for just 40 days. Of course, that's previous history and there are no guarantees on future returns but it points out the mystery of the market. No one knows how much the market is going up or down on a given day. Some days it goes up, some down and some sideways. Miss those up days and chances are you are not going to have a good year.

Money Sense:

Long term, the winners are in it long term When one of the greatest minds on Wall Street was asked "What's the market going to do today?" he replied, "It will fluctuate." If you are thinking about cashing out, think of the weather in London. When it's raining, stick around for 5 minutes and it will clear. The market may be down today and for several days or even weeks or a few months but before you know it, it will be right back up.

FOUR GOOD REASONS TO SELL STOCKS IN YOUR PORTFOLIO

Even if you remain fully invested in the market there are times when you need to make changes in your portfolio.

Here are four times to consider selling:

1. ***Profit taking.*** If you sell a winner and take a profit it is usually a good move. Also be aware of the tax consequences and the overall effect it can have on your results.

2. ***Your investment objectives change*** and the stock no longer fits. If you are using a broker or advisor this is a good one to check. For instance, if holding a speculative stock that pays no dividends and you are now looking at having a portfolio that produces a dividend check every quarter or perhaps even each month, then the speculative stock looks good to sell.

3. ***Taking losses to offset gains.*** If you have a good year with lots of ordinary income and capital gains and a paper trade loss – a stock that's worth less than you paid but are still holding – a sale here would offset or reduce the amount of profits you show and therefore the taxes you'll pay. The best situation is when you have ordinary gains and long term losses. The loss is worth more tax saving as an offset to an ordinary gain on which you'd have to pay ordinary (usually higher) income taxes.

4. ***Something has changed with the company or management.*** Serious investors have a number of criteria they follow in selecting a company to buy for their portfolio. Two criteria are management and growth—not just intrinsic growth but growth relative to peers or comparable companies in its industry. If growth momentum goes lower you'll want to assess whether it's a one time or one quarter event or has something fundamental changed in the company's long term plan. If there are top level management changes, you'll want to seriously assess why. Top management

exiting the company is often a harbinger of more bad news down the line.

Money Sense:

Often the market has a sixth sense though it can be overdone a lot. Watch price action when management changes or earnings announcements are made. It is sometimes possible to take advantage of a temporary warp in market reaction to news and, provided your investigation of fundamentals and reasons for buying hasn't been altered, increase your position in an otherwise sound company that's been irrationally beat up by the media. And this is also one of those times when it might make good sense to double-check with your professional advisor.

THREE MORE GOOD REASONS TO
SELL STOCKS IN YOUR PORTFOLIO

1. *To Rebalance a portfolio.* When one investment has increased in value so that it represents a significantly larger portion of your portfolio's value, you may want to look at rebalancing. Let's say you own a stock that has risen so much it went from 15% to 50% of your portfolio's value. Half your portfolio in a single investment is increasing your risk. Selling off part of the position and reinvesting in another stock is a good way to re-diversify. You'll see mutual funds do this when on of their top 10 positions has an extraordinary run-up and skews the portfolio too heavily. They will sell off a block even if the fundamentals haven't changed. And that's another reason why you can't blindly follow what a fund does with their investments. You may not know the real reason for a change.

2. *The investment is underperforming.* If a company you own for the long term hoping it will reach a certain goal disappoints you for several quarters, watch it closely. And if you lose confidence in their ability to meet stated objectives, then you may want to liquidate all or a substantial portion of the investment. Here is a case where following your "hunches" as Doctor Joyce Brothers has advocated, is probably a good idea.

3. *The stock goes down.* Okay. This one I threw in as a ringer. Why? Because it is almost an absolute investment rule—at least it seems that way— that when you first buy a stock it goes down—temporarily. Maybe it's a test of strength of conviction by the market gods to see how much faith you have in your research ability.

Money Sense:

Don't just "cut and run" when a stock goes down until you are sure that the reasons you got in are no longer valid. And don't let a temporary market drop shake you out of an otherwise sound investment. Just make

171

sure the reasons you invested in the first place are still valid. And if they are, maybe it's a chance to buy more.

INVESTING IN PRIVATE EQUITY – RISKY BUSINESS

Several years ago I was watching a high stakes thoroughbred horse race on television. I saw one of the favorites stumble and fall in the final quarter mile stretch. The horse broke a leg and had to be put down. When the reporter asked the owner how he felt he simply stated, with an expressionless face, that "You have to have long pants on when you play this game." It's a risky business.

The same can be said of PE investing. Private equity involves investing in the untraded securities of or taking an ownership position in a private company. Think stocks without the stock market or the regulation. Of course rewards can be sky high, but only if—emphasis on if—the company stays in business long enough and is successful enough to go public. There were PE investors in Google and in Microsoft before they went public. Some of them are Billionaires today. Even Martha Stewart is in that club.

Private equity investing is generally restricted to accredited investors, those high net worth people having at least $100,000 or more of income at least 2 years running and with a net worth of over 1 Million dollars. The ante for private equity fund investing, sort of a mutual fund of private company investments, is usually $250,000 and up. Lately some of the funds have dropped the ante to as little as $25,000.

You can also invest in the shares of a single company as an accredited investor. If you are the type who does their due diligence or research homework well, you might consider private equity investing with a very small portion of your funds—2 to 5% maximum. Private equity funds look for returns of at least 15% annually to as much as 5 or even 10 times your investment. The flip side is they could lose all your money.

High potential returns for very high risk.

Many of these private companies are still emerging, without sales or profits and often in highly competitive fields with no market share. In the current crop of companies you'll find leading edge startups in voice over internet protocol (VOIP), hybrid engine technologies, energy recovery and similar bleeding edge fields.

For those wanting to take a chance on a pooled fund the Blackstone

Group recently went public allowing investors to play on their expertise at making private equity investments in other companies, enhancing the value and then selling them off. Once again, because of the lure of this type of investing and potentially high returns, the price of the stock may exceed the underlying value of its assets. In other words, you are paying for future return or performance on the stock that you didn't get yet.

Money Sense:

Three Things to Remember with Private Equity Investing:

- Check with your financial advisor
- Make sure you can afford to lose it all
- Wear long pants

The lure is the high, possibly extraordinary, once in a lifetime returns. The reality is we are talking high potential returns for extremely high investment risk.

COFFEE TALK ABOUT WOMEN'S INVESTMENT CONCERNS

Women's Financials

Yours may be a different very different household but here are verifiable facts about women's financials and why they generally have different financial concerns than men.

They make less money

Women make around 71cents for every dollar a man makes doing the same work

They live longer

Making less money is one thing but the big gap between men and women doing the same work if significant because women tend to live six years longer than men—around 80 years versus an average 74 for men. (Please, no jokes about who is putting who in their grave first.)

Fewer have pensions—fewer still have as much pension income

Women provide the child care in many families, and interrupt their careers to raise children. They also tend to be the caregivers for elderly parents. All this adds up to less time in the workforce and less accumulated retirement funds. That's reflected in pensions. Only 30% of women versus 48% of men received pensions and the average pension income for men is twice the $4800 women receive.

But The Bad News Isn't All Bad.

Times are changing! Back in 1992 a survey showed only half of women were involved in the family's investment decisions. Some suffered mightily when spouses made risky unilateral financial decisions with retirement funds that didn't work out. That complacency has faded. Today forty three percent of all individuals with over $500,000 in net worth today are women. Nearly seventy percent of all new businesses are owned by women. Half of law school grads are female as are nearly 47% of med school grads. So women's incomes will be going up steadily. One study shows that by 2019, two thirds of the wealth in America will be controlled by women.

Money Sense for Women:

Take a page from your high net worth counterparts. Work with a professional financial advisor you are comfortable with, someone you can share personal visions and financial dreams with and who'll work together with you to make those dreams come true. *Talk about savings.* Women have less money put away for retirement than men. It's even more important for women to save than men because of the probability that they will live alone at some point in their elder years. *Some risk is prudent.* Women used to be risk averse but they have moved into the ranks of sensible or moderate risk investors. Unlike men, they still tend to be "sensible" and less of a "gambler". With retirement funds and savings, gambling rarely pays off. *Final word:* Even if you don't think you are ready or have sufficient assets to discuss with a financial adviser, most of us will be happy to provide some initial consultation at no cost and no obligation.

EIGHT SHREWD MONEY SMART THINGS
TO DO IF YOU HIT THE JACKPOT

Let's say you didn't take my advice and put your lottery ticket money in a cigar box every day. And then through some miraculous turn of events, you have the mega millions winning ticket or hit the big slot jackpot in Vegas.

What do you do with "jackpot" type money?

1. First double and triple check to make sure it is real and not a scam—like the Nigerian and other European e mail stings.

2. Resist the urge or instinct to just spend it because you have had your 15 minutes of fame or one big hit in life. The reality is you aren't used to the kind of money that's been dropped into your lap and it could permanently change your life in a good way if you deal with it common-sensibly.

3. Contact a CPA, attorney and investment advisor – you can afford all three now – and get advice about the legal, tax and estate consequences—and the number of people it makes sense to have share in the winning ticket (since most are bearer tickets and unassigned until presented)—and where the best place might be to invest the money.

4. Make sure that the professionals you seek are qualified or recommended by qualified people. You wouldn't ask a poor person how to handle a million dollars. Ask the most successful or wealthiest people you know for adviser recommendations.

5. You will have to report your winnings and pay the taxes the year the winnings are received. With a bearer (unnamed owner) on a lottery ticket the more family members or partners in the ticket, it is possible the tax consequences could go down enough so that more people sharing means more money for each. With a lottery ticket if you chose cash payment all taxes are taken out

177

up front. Over the 20 year period of installment payments you would likely end up with more money since it is similar to an annuity payment.

6. Don't quit your job, at least not for awhile. It may be a central part of your life and provide meaning as well as satisfaction.

7. Before you reward yourself, family or friends with a spending spree, pay off every single debt you have, including big items like a car loan, home mortgage or education loans.

8. If it is truly a sum of money beyond your wildest dreams, after you have covered your family and deserving friends, think about giving to those charities you always wished you could help more. There is a joy and satisfaction to giving that will reward you many times over.

KIDS AND MONEY

If you think your kids are too old to teach them about money—they might not be—then let's think about the refresher course below as being for the next generation.

My recommendation is to give your kids allowances.

Give them an allowance for making their beds, for cleaning the kitchen floor or for picking up in their rooms. If you're from the school that says you shouldn't pay kids an allowance for things they ought to do anyway around the house, that's okay. Then give them an allowance for every book they read. Who knows, you might help promote reading into a popular category of juvenile activity again.

Set Ground Rules

But if you give kids/grandkids an allowance set some ground rules. Make them agree to put a certain percentage of the money in a savings account, so they will also learn how and what it means to save. And the balance is the part they can do anything they want with.

Maybe Susie wants to spend all of her allowance on candy. Or perhaps she would like to save it up for awhile to purchase a big ticket special item she's had her eye on for a long time. Here's where the creativity and the teaching come in. Not feeling very creative, then here's some online help.

Money Sense:

Since kids are so computer literate today, here are a few online resources to put into your information bank. The Money Camp (*www.themoneycamp.com*) is a non profit organization of free personal finance lessons for kids, adults and home schooling purposes. Parents Money School, accessed from *www.monedbox.com.* is a 60 minute video of refresher help for parents and those who want to teach their kids about smart money management? And finally, Money Instructor at *www.moneyinstructor.com* is a good personal money and finance resource for K through 12 levels and especially useful for grandkids.

SAVING OR INVESTING—WHAT'S THE DIFFERENCE?

This has to be one of the top ten questions I get asked over and over.

Yes there is a difference between saving and investing.

Saving. It's pretty straightforward. When you are saving you are putting money into a vehicle like a passbook savings account, a CD—certificate of deposit with a fixed maturity date set sometime in the future (30, 60, 180 days or up to 5 years), or a government bond. In other words it is something you put your money into where you can't lose it. Yield or interest rate paid to you for the use of your money is low to moderately high. But the risk is very low to non-existent. Your money won't grow very much but you'll get a guaranteed return on your money and a guarantee that you'll always get the principal amount of money you put in plus the interest. In addition, saving is money you have around to have readily available for specific short-term goals. It could also be emergency type money.

Investing. Here you put your money into a vehicle where it could grow. It might even grow substantially. But you also could lose some or potentially, even all of your money or initial investment. Pick right you are in clover. Pick wrong and you'll be wiser but a lot broker. For instance buying a stock like Google, that's investing. While today it might be $300 per share, it could be $500 a year from now. It could also be $100. One way you are smiling. Or the other sleeping like a baby—waking up every 3 hours and crying yourself back to sleep. That's investing. Of course with proper planning, money you are investing will grow and it's where you put your money when you are looking down the road at a future expenditure—anything from a substantial purchase like a home or even retirement. Nothing short term.

Money Sense:

Don't use a long term mentality for a short term goal. If you are invested in the stock market, that's probably a longer term purpose. Don't think about putting money into the market and selling in six months.

Likely as not the stock will be down at the time you need the money and that, my friends, makes for a bitter taste in the mouth.

REALISTIC WAYS TO SAVE DURING
THE BIG HOLIDAY SPENDING SEASON

There's one time of year it is really hard to turn off the spending spigot, from Thanksgiving to Christmas and then right through New Year's. Why? Many retailer's make their entire year. Obviously we are all contributing to that perennial success story.

Aside from cutting your gift list and spending less per person, here are some ideas that may help ease the stress and strain of giving to all those you care about.

1. ***Try to buy sale items.*** If you are buying popular items, compare prices on the same items at several major retailers. And remember to shop early. Hot items will be gone if sales are good.

2. ***Set up a budget and stick to it.*** List those you'll be buying for and the amount you plan to spend on them. And here's a little trick that works very well. If you won't see the person until after the holidays you might even wait to purchase their gift until the holiday rush is over. There are usually terrific sales in early January on electronic items and big sale items that have come back in stock.

3. ***Look for sales with zero interest rates or no payments for 30, 60 or 90 days.*** And don't forget to ask the salesperson politely if they know of any way to get a lower price on an item. Sometimes they have extra sale coupons or they know an item you are shopping for will go on sale in the next few days.

4. ***Use coupons.*** One of the things that is different between us and the rich is that the rich clip coupons. Many middle class people just don't make the time to tear a coupon out of the paper they read everyday.

5. ***Take advantage of opening up a credit card to get an additional discount on top of the sale price—but then cancel it.*** Recently while shopping at a major department store, I purchased much needed wardrobe updates. I purchased on sale with additional coupons that took about 50% off the retail prices. At the register I was offered an instant approval credit card that would give me

another 15% off the already discounted items. It amounted to another $50. However, if you take advantage of this savings do two things: First pay down the entire balance immediately upon receiving the bill. And second, if you aren't going to use the card, make sure you cancel it.

Money Sense:

Finally, remember that every dollar you save you can use to invest, put in your emergency fund or pay down debt.

DAY TRADING – NOT FOR INVESTORS

A Tempting Pastime

What a tempting pastime. You've seen the TV commercials with ordinary people making wads of cash trading stocks with a few clicks on the computer between bites of their sandwich. Yeah, right.

Day trading is the purchasing and sale of a security or position in the market where the investor closes out the position at the end of the day. One or more positions can be put on or established and then taken off or closed out during the "trading" day when the market is open. The idea here is to profit from the daily price movement in a stock.

Remember, Trading is Not Investing

Sometimes you have a little help, like the folks did recently who were listening in on the trading squawk box at a major brokerage house. They heard when institutional buyers were going to establish or purchase a block position of 10,000 shares or more. You could, theoretically at least, run in front of the institution—which is why they call it "front running"—and put on a position ahead of them. Then when the institution makes their large buy you take advantage of the inevitable price increase by selling out the position. It could be hours or even minutes later.

Normally the way it works is that a day trader is following a price and volume action in a stock looking for a signal that indicates the stock will move enough for them to put on a position and see enough fluctuation up or down for them to close it out at a profit. Or they have news feeds coming in to their desktops and when then see something they think will have an effect on the markets or a particular stock reporting good or bad news, they immediately try to trade on that information.

Money Sense:

Yes, you guessed it. I am not a fan of day trading, at least not for investors. This is a very risky and tricky way to play the market. You have limited time to trade. This is not investing. You have to be perfect in your decision about what you're going to buy, what price you're going to pay and when you're going to sell. Margin account costs and day trading rules add to the difficulties. And your execution has to be near perfect.

185

Time is not on the investor's side and quick decision-making is the rule, even when it's a loss.

ARE THERE WAYS TO DAY TRADE PROFITABLY?

Rolling the Dice

In my opinion, there isn't a way to day trade profitably and with consistency. But I realize there are people who will want to try day trading, just like there are people who will want to try the casino on their vacation. I don't recommend it. Don't do it with retirement or emergency funds; stick to mad money. But if you insist on giving day trading a try, here are some facts and suggestions to consider.

1. *Accept the fact you may lose all of your money.* Over 70% of day traders in any given year will lose money trading stocks. This is fact. You may be smarter than 90% of the people and still lose your money. It's not about intelligence. If you are willing to accept that up front, you have cleared the first hurdle.

2. *Understand that day trading is not investing.* You aren't purchasing a company based on good earnings, strong management, solid business fundamentals, their pre-eminent position in a strong industry or the likelihood their success will be even better this year than last year. You are purchasing a stock purely on a technical basis or expectation of a good or bad news announcement or the momentum of the market carrying it in a certain direction or even taking advantage of the spread between the bid and ask price. It's very much like gambling. Do you feel unbelievably lucky today? If so you have cleared the second hurdle.

3. *Leverage can work for or against you.* Some day traders use margin. On margin you only have to put up half the money in order to establish a position in a stock. So long as you clear out the position at the end of the day you don't have to come up with any additional money or borrow it from your broker at the "call" interest rate. If you should sell out at a loss at the end of the day, you will have lost twice as much money as if you had purchased the stock for 100% cash. Further, if the stock were to drop enough you might lose so much you have to come up with additional money to maintain the 50% margin on your account, or be forced to sell out the stock at a huge loss.

187

4. **Get some training.** And I don't mean just buy a book—and there are many good ones out there. There are many online trading academies and even firms who will work with you. Obviously if the training is free it probably is offered with the expectation you will be trading funds through or with the host firm. You need a feel for trading and how to trade under the gun. Print resources for nascent traders can be found at www.investorhome.com.

5. **If you roll the dice, figure your losses right.** You have a $75,000 job and not many financial worries or dependents. You decide to quit your day job and put a $50,000 stake to work day trading. At the end of the year your stake is worth $100,000. You made 100% on your money; right? Wrong. You lost money. Your job would have paid $75,000. Your $50,000 stake would have earned, conservatively, around $2,500. You are out at least 75,000 plus interest for a total of 77,500 less the 50,000 profit you made. Bottom line: You have around $27,500 less at the end of the year than you would have had if you kept your day job.

6. **Apologize to your wife or significant other, in advance.** Chances are you'll be sorry about the experience and apologizing to someone.

Money Sense:

Phil Feigin of the National Association of Securities Administrators put in better words than most: **For the typical retail investor, day trading isn't investing, it's gambling. If you want to gamble, go to Las Vegas; the food is better.** (Source: Philip A. Feigin, "Day Trading Craze Should Give Investors Pause", NSAA). For many people, day trading is a lot like on line poker. Once in it can be so habit forming that it is difficult to break away from. The action, the emotional swings, and the day-to-day trading decisions become additive. Be aware and beware.

RIDING OUT INVESTMENT STORMS
HAS BEEN WORTH IT

Staying In The Market Is A Surprisingly Good Strategy

Whether you are an optimist or a pessimist, it works. Being an optimist I usually see the good news and outcomes in most of my activities. And so do the pessimists. I have always had a long term positive view of the stock market. In his seminal work "Stocks For The Long Run", called one of the best investment books of all time by the Washington Post, Jeremy Siegel, celebrity Wharton professor and bull market guru makes the case that stocks are not only the highest earning asset class but their returns become less risky with longer holding periods compared to fixed income investments like bonds.

Stormy Markets Always Pass

Getting back to stormy markets, they go up and down every year. During the 1990s the market had many years when it was down 10% or more. Declines of 5% or more occurred 332 times during the 1900s. 10% declines occurred 108 times, 15% drops 51 times and 20% or greater declines 29 times.

Declines of 5% last about 40 days on average, 10% about 108 days, 15% or more, 223 days and 210 declines last around 1 year. While every decline has a unique drop and recovery time, the market has always gone higher after pullbacks.

Markets Go Up More Than They Go Down

While riding out the storm has always been worth it in the past because the market has a perennial pattern of going up more than it goes down, that's no guarantee the future will bring the same results.

Siegel's newest book ,The Future For Investors, Siegel points to evidence that seeking above average yields and coupling that with value based prices produces above average returns, a little like the Dogs of the Dow Theory—buying the highest yielding stocks at the lowest relative price.

Money Sense:

In Midwestern lingo, if you buy good dividend paying stocks in companies with solid financials behind them and buy them at attractive prices—near or at the lower third of their price range for the year—you'll probably continue making better returns on your money than the average stock jockey. And so long as nothing fundamental has changed at the companies you are into, stay the course during rocky markets. You'll end up with better long term returns than the second-guessers.

REBALANCING INVESTMENTS – SHEPHERDING YOUR PORTFOLIO TO THE GOAL

Rebalancing is a proven way of making sure your investment portfolio stays on track by keeping various asset percentages in line with investment goals and risk tolerances.

For instance, at the start of the year investments may be equally divided between variable investments such as stocks, mutual funds, and variable annuities and the other 50% in fixed investments such as CDs, treasuries and fixed annuities. That's the benchmark. Now, let's say at the end of the year your variable investments do so well that you now have 80% portfolio valuation in the variable investments and 20% in fixed. Unless your master strategy has changed, it's necessary to rebalance to get back to 50% in each area.

Why is rebalancing important?

It's important to stick with your game plan or you could end up having too much portfolio exposure in one area. If that investment gets hit and goes down you could lose your gains and even original principal quickly. Rebalancing is designed to prevent having too much riding on one type investment.

When to do it?

Rebalancing may be necessary once a year or once a quarter. It all depends on what happens to percentages in the portfolio. For most investors once a year may be sufficient. Professional planners will usually do a quarterly review.

What are the benefits?

In up markets it helps you add value. In neutral markets where there may be a lot of ups and downs, if helps you maintain value. In down markets it helps you minimize losses.

Money Sense:

Do it yourself (DIY) types need to examine their portfolio at least once a year. Tax time is good because you are already involved in the financials of your business and personal income, doing investment profit and loss statements and so forth. If you are concerned about doing it yourself, have a professional planner do it for you for a flat fee, including recommendations. And if you'd like online help check out *www. retiredinvestor.com* for a great value in DIY portfolio management.

ISN'T STOCK MARKET INVESTING JUST ANOTHER FORM OF GAMBLING?

No, Stocks Are Not a Get Rich Quick Scheme

Some people treat buying stocks like it is a lottery ticket. It's not a get rich quick scheme. There certainly can be high risk in an investment in the stock market, especially if you are inclined to listen to so-called stock "tips" or aren't comfortable doing due diligence—a fancy word for homework—about a stock or public company after it has been recommended to you by a friend—or even a stock broker.

An investor could lose some or all of their money in a stock. The key is to get good advice, do good research on your own, especially if you have the time and like the process, and most important, to think longer term. If you don't have the time or like the process but feel that investing is a good way to put your money to work for the long term, think about getting an adviser to work with, one you feel comfortable with, perhaps through a recommendation from trusted friends.

By The Book Before You Buy The Stock

There's a favorite expression among coin enthusiasts, buy the book before you buy the coin. The same applies to stocks. There are a number of classic works worth reading and getting educated is the best play in the investment casino if you want to be a winner.

Money Sense:

There are simply too many good books to mention them all here so I suggest going to *www.Amazon.com* for a list of their current top recommendations. Some classic favorites of mine are: The Intelligent Investor by Benjamin Graham, a perennial favorite about value investing, One Up On Wall Street by Peter Lynch, a good book for the beginning investor with a simple but effective approach to stock detecting, and Reminiscences of a Stock Operator by Edwin LeFevre, fictional reminiscences of the legendary speculator Jesse Livermore. Sorry for leaving out anyone's personal favorites—and I am sure there are many—but the above three books will set your cap for successful long term investment thinking. A final recommendation because it refutes the thinking on speculation over investing is Jeremy Siegel's Stocks For The Long Run which uses a lot of statistical data that show how good stocks can be as an investment vehicle—you guessed it, for the long term. Good investment websites are Yahoo Finance, MSN, MarketWatch.com, to name just a few.

A final word about investing (quality stocks) v. speculation (penny stocks or stock tips): The main difference between gambling and investing is that the gambler is trying to win at really great odds. In the long term or long run there is no way the gambler can win consistently against the house. In long term investing the investor still has a good chance to win. This never happens for the gambler.

STOCK MARKET INDICATORS

Stock market indicators are like elbows. Everybody has a set. We'll just run down a few of them for you with some comment.

The Super Bowl Indicator says that if the winner is one of the old American Football League teams, the market will go down. If one of the old NFL teams wins, the market will go up. While nothing is infallible, this indicator has about an 85% accuracy rate. Problem here is that some of the AFC teams are former NFL franchises and vice versa so the indicator is getting a little murky.

The January Barometer predicts the market for the entire year. If stocks are up in January, the market will be up for the year. Since 1950 the January Barometer has worked 45 out of 50 times making it 90% accurate.

On the Street, there's also a hemline indicator. The higher the hemlines on skirts for the season, the higher the market will go. Long skirts on the fashion runway signal a down market.

And the Boston Snow Indicator says that if it's a White Christmas the market will go up the next year. Yeah right. It's also called the BS indicator.

Finally, and this is but a small sample, there is the Soccer Mom indicator. It's a lagging indicator meaning that if parents at the kids' games are talking about say computer chip companies then chances are the trend is about over.

So where does this leave us? Well professionals look at a lot of indicators and take a consensus. The best main-street type advice I can offer is don't bet the farm on any one indicator. If you have money to invest, don't invest more than you can afford to lose. Invest in companies not the market and don't invest in any companies that are, like the Boston Snow indicator, more S than B.

Money Minutes

INVESTMENT TIPS FOR A DOWN MARKET – GUTS AND COOL

A Leak In The Dam Lowers All Boats

Maybe this hasn't happened to you yet, but it will, sooner or later, if you are a long term investor. The market will go down and take everything you own with it. It's a little like a sinkhole in a reservoir. The water goes out the sinkhole and the whole reservoir goes down taking all boats with it. Time passes, the dam gets fixed, the water level rises again and your stocks go back up, too. You have two choices. You can get depressed, or you can think positive. On the positive side, you can make some changes that could prove highly beneficial down the road.

Nine Things to consider in a down market:

Down Market Tip #1: First and foremost, don't get emotional. Bring up your game plan and stick to it. Don't' be in the market unless you have a 5 year plan. Don't deviate from the plan for any reason. And keep your game face on. Be cool. Be calm.

Down Market Tip #2: Your pocketbook isn't affected by paper losses. You have a stock with solid fundamentals, good industry position, and future prospects. It's down along with everything else. You have no loss if you don't sell the stock. And unless something's changed about your overall assessment, don't sell. But see #3.

Down Market Tip #3: Sell if it may offset ordinary gains. You have a good year going with significant profits. You might want to offset some of those profits and save yourself some taxes by selling for some losses. Check with your accountant or advisor.

Down Market Tip #4: Buy more. If you have a rock solid investment that's temporarily gone South with the whole stock market, remember it's not a stock market. It's a market of stocks. Yours may be on the bargain table right now. If so, use the discount days to stock up and lower your cost.

Down Market Tip #5: The annual gifting exclusion is now $12,000. Consider giving any temporarily depressed stock to a loved one. Over time it could produce a big win for them and you'll be giving them more shares for the money. Everyone wins.

Down Market Tip #6: If the market has topped and fallen away from you, here's a really uncomplicated way to deal with it. You only have a few choices. If you are out of the market, you can stay out or get in. If you are in the market you can stay in or get out. If you choose getting out or staying out once again, your options are limited. You can head for the safety of fixed income investments. Their returns typically yield anywhere from 2% to 6%. Not bad, but you can do better if you are willing to consider a hybrid choice. Have some of the guaranteed investments but as long as reasonably possible, stay in the market and buy yourself some more shares.

Down Market Tip #7: It takes guts to win. Guts beats genius in the long run. In really depressed markets if you stayed in, buy more. In poker they call it "guts", and in the market it really applies. Those who had the guts to buy in the market drops of 1987, 1994 and 1998, 2000, 2001 and 2002 looked like geniuses. In retrospect, when the markets headed back to their former highs, those who stayed in and bought more recouped their original investment on old purchases and had new highs on their new purchases.

Down Market Tip #8: Play "catch up" in you IRAs. If you are over 50 you have an opportunity to take advantage of the catch up provisions of your Roth or Traditional IRA and your 401(K) program. With IRAS you can put a maximum of $4000 plus $1000 catch up for tax year 2007 (April 15, 2008 cut-off date) for a total of $5000. In tax year 2008 it's $5000 plus $1000 in catch up for $6000. That's more money now and over time it could grow into a lot more money.

Down Market Tip #9: Convert part or all your traditional IRA to a Roth IRA. With tradition IRAs down in value taxed paid on the conversion will be lower. So you'll save because you'll be paying less in taxes. That's the cake. The icing on the cake is when you take money out of your ROTH IRA you'll be taking the money, and profits out, tax free! Thanks, Uncle Sam...Thanks again, Uncle Sam. And did I forget to say thanks, Uncle Sam!

Money Minutes

KEEPING INVESTING SIMPLE IN A COMPLEX WORLD OF INFORMATION

With the quantity and accessibility of investment information available today, you'd need twice the speed of thought to absorb it all. As famed author Lewis Carroll once wrote in the voice of the Red Queen responding to Alice in wonderland who complained, "I am running as fast as I can but I don't seem to be getting anywhere." The queen replied "now here, you see, it takes all the running you can do, to keep in the same place. If you want to get somewhere, you must run at least twice as fast as that. (Lewis Carroll (1832 - 1898) English author.)

A "Real Simple" Style Investing Formula

Given the load that is on most plates of life today, let's try and lay out a simple recipe for investing that doesn't involve busting your brain every day.

- *Save early and often.* Let the magic of compounding over time reward you. A dollar put away today is worth twice or three times as much as a dollar saved 10 years from now. Or you better have at least 3 dollars to put away then, whenever "then" is..

- *Imagine what you want your retirement to be when you get there.* And start thinking about a plan to get there now while you can put away money and have it grow for years and years.

- *Strive for balance in your portfolio.* Having all your money in what's hot now is great but it is better to balance out your portfolio into areas that in combination will give you good long term results.

- *Rebalance your portfolio* at least once a year or when you see it is overloaded from trading or profit in a particular area.

- *Sell losers when you have gains* and are looking for tax losses.

- ***Stick with winners.***

- ***Trade sparingly.*** Buy quality and hang on for the long term.

THE RISKY BUSINESS OF MARGIN ACCOUNTS—STOCKS ON BORROWED MONEY

Leverage at a Price

A margin account is a brokerage account allowing customers to buy securities using money that is borrowed from the broker they have their account with. Usually an investor has to have at least 50% of the value of the securities purchased on deposit and have a minimum of $2000 in equity in their account. Once the trades are done the account value –the total dollar value of the shares owned times the current market value—cannot fall below 35% of the original cost.

If the account falls below 35% in value the broker issues a maintenance call to the investor. This is like the dreaded "blue screen of death" in Computerland. Nobody wants to get a maintenance margin call. A maintenance call requires the investor to come up with enough money to get the account value back up to 50%. If the maintenance margin call isn't met then the client's securities can be sold to make up the difference. And if there's any shortfall after the sale, the client is still responsible to the broker for the amount originally borrowed.

Is this risky?

You bet! It's always been risky. Many margin traders and investors were completely wiped out in 1929. But none of us reading this—me either—are old enough to have gone through that financial catastrophe. The big difference is back then the margin was 10% so there was 10 to one leverage. Today it's 50% so you can buy twice as much stock as you have free trading equity. What that means is for every point the stock goes up you stand to make double the profit, if it is a long (buy) position. If the stock goes down—unless you have a short position—it's like a 2 point drop in dollars for every 1 point drop in the stock price.

Is the Risk Manageable?

It depends. Though the idea of leveraging your profits sounds irresistible, most investors do not trade on margin today. A good thing, too. Anytime the investor doesn't have 100% of the value of the securities in their account there is more risk involved. When the wind and undercurrents in the market change it's tough enough to make necessary adjustments in a portfolio. If there is also negative leverage in the mix, there's little time to react and make necessary adjustments. Better to have 100% equity, and peace-of-mind.

Money Sense:

Margin buying is a perfectly acceptable way to leverage your money and increase the worth of your investments. It's just not for everyone. Generally I don't recommend it for clients close to retirement unless their equity portfolio is a small part of their overall assets; let's say they have a lot of income and investment property and that forms the bulk of their assets. And equities are a piece of the portfolio they can afford to leverage without any major effect on their income. For young clients who are still feeding a portion of their earnings into a portfolio of stocks over and above their retirement accounts, that's different. They can afford the risk and can also replenish funds because they are still in prime earning years. Don't risk principal that isn't replenish-able.

INVESTING IN PRECIOUS METALS

To complete their portfolio picture, some investors will weave gold into their investment cloak. Unlike other investments gold is seen as more of a shield against periods when either the economy suffers, when interest rates or inflation may soar or when grave international incidents erupt. The bottom line is gold is a hedge against bad times.

In recent years, we haven't had high inflation or high interest rates. There has been non-stop international tension. Gold has been trading between $250 and $600 for the past two decades, but broke its all time high in the first week of 2008 by spikng at over $850. Not much of a preformance record until recently. However, investors in this alternative sector are aiming to have their assets simply hold their value. And, as can be seen by its recent spike, gold is looking to break out into higher priced territory.

Ways To Own Gold

- Bullion bars—33-1/3rd ounces (1 kilo) to 100 ounce bars of pure metal.

- Gold Coins—quarter ounce, half ounce and 1 ounce Gold Eagles (U.S.), Pandas (China), 1/10th, quarter, half and 1 ounce Gold Maple Leafs (Canadian) to name a few.

- Mining Shares—purchasing stock in gold mining companies like Bemis Gold, Newmont Mining and other shares listed on the exchanges. Here you are adding the risk of upward and downward movement in the stock price tied to earnings performance or political and economic or currency risk if a foreign company.

- Gold Options and Futures. Extremely risky and generally not recommended.

- Gold Mutual Funds. Not much selection here and not much of a track record either but out there as a way to put gold into the mix with indirect investments mostly in mining shares. Often not limited just to gold but other precious and semi precious or strategic metals as well. Check the track record of any of these funds against others of a similar type before deciding to invest.

Money Sense:

Since direct gold investments—gold coins, bullion or gold certificates—pay no income and may even cost money to store—they should be placed in the high risk part of the investment pyramid representing around 5 to 10 per cent of assets. If owning bullion bars or gold coins is your choice I recommend the services of a reputable coin and bullion dealer. Readers may contact me for a longstanding recommended dealer.

ALTERNATIVE INVESTMENTS – TREAD CAREFULLY

Just like wellness visits to the doctor, keeping a portfolio fiscally fit means annual checkups. A part of that checkup involves rebalancing. Today's dynamic and more interdependent global economy has had an effect on the rules for balancing portfolios and has also led to consideration of investments in the mix that were once considered too dicey. The old saw, a medium risk portfolio ratio of 60% stocks and 40% fixed income—such as bonds, real estate investment trusts, convertible preferred stocks—was pretty standard. Now it's broadened to encompass what's known as alternative investments formerly used by only the very rich and the high risk investor.

Alternative Investment Menu

Alternative investments can range from:

- Participation in foreign markets and equities.

- Hedge funds—pools of capital run by professional managers for wealthy investors; they engage in long and short trading, options, currency and even commodities trading—managed futures funds—specializing in commodities and currency trading.

- Private equity—investment in privately held startups or development stage companies.

- Hard assets like precious metals or stamps and coins (to a moderate degree). In the boutique advisory firms even fine art and collectibles are considered alternative investment territory. In short, the search for above average returns has broadened the scope of the investment landscape to include many of the vehicles once used by only the more sophisticated investor.

- Commodities—it's not so much that commodities are such poor investments for the right people—like a farmer who is around crops all his life investing in say corn futures—but the leverage will kill you. Typically bought on 10% margin, a 10 per cent

207

decline and your capital is wiped out. You have to put up more money or lose everything.

* Oil and gas investments. Usually in the form of limited partnerships, these energy focused investments focus on oil and gas wells. "Quality" programs are best identified by a financial planner who uses a broker dealer network to pick only the best of the best.

Money Sense:

In Summer 2007, The Wall Street Journal quoted a household name investment banking firm as saying two of their hedge funds were "worthless". So don't expect a lot of links and references and moral support in an area I feel is too risky to consider for the majority of investors reading this book. Before you consider the yield enhancing benefits of alternative investments, know that the people who play in this arena are high rollers. They can tolerate high risk and even potential loss of substantial—possibly even all—of their capital. So if you are even casually thinking this might be for you, be sure to seek advice from a professional adviser. The cost is worth it and the potential for loss on these investments is huge compared to the cost of good advice. And good as their records might make them sound, without serious professional guidance, and a serious income behind you, these investments are generally to be avoided. Otherwise just go to the casino. At least you'll have fun while if /when you lose your money.

LIQUIDATING ART COLLECTIONS: PLEASING TO THE EYE, ENHANCING TO ASSETS, A BEAR IN ESTATES

"There are painters who transform the sun to a yellow spot, but there are others who with the help of their art and their intelligence transform a yellow spot into the sun." Pablo Picasso.

Perhaps no better definition of art exists. However, fine art can become an obsession to collectors with the means to purchase the works.

Christie's and Sotheby's auction records of the past 30 years or so have shown just how dramatic price increases have been for celebrity artists whose works have sold and then been resold even a few years later.

However, buying art is one thing and selling it is quite another. For one, collectors often become so attached to art they don't want to give it up or sell it. Another problem is that often children or other family members have no interest in the art, valuable or not.

So the issue becomes how to divest one's collection if both blessed and perhaps cursed by the gods for having one.

Here's what you don't do: don't just have a family member take it off the wall and go home with it. The IRS gets pretty upset about investment art winding up unaccounted for in a large estate.

The second worst thing is to just leave it to the kids in the estate. Chances are they'll have to dump it at fire sale prices to pay the estate taxes. Net cash leaves them much better memories.

That leaves the possibility of a partial donation. You can apportion say a 50% donation to a willing museum. That means the art gets to be displayed for 6 months at your place and 6 months at the museum. 50% of the value of the art can be taken as an income tax deduction while you are still alive. If the work is truly A list or B list art with value in the millions, you must consult professionals on it's value and more importantly to hue to the stringent IRS Rules surrounding fractional giving. Establishing the value of the art has to be done by a professional art appraiser. Consult your adviser or try one of the professional appraisal associations for a recommendation.

Other possibilities for liquidating art are gifting to your heirs while alive. Here you may have to file a gift tax return and pay the taxes. And there is also the option of a charitable remainder trust where you benefit from the income while living and the beneficiary gets the art upon death.

THE OTHER ABSOLUTE SAFE HAVENS FOR CASH — TREASURY BILLS AND BONDS

Looking for absolute security in your investments? Many investors do at least for a good portion of a large portfolio and liquid or emergency funds, and their choice of investments is either treasury bills or treasury bonds.

T Bills and T Bonds are backed by the full faith and credit of the United States Government as to payment of principal and interest. They carry virtually no risk of default. At maturity, they pay their face value plus their interest yield as income.

T Bills

T Bills are short term securities bought in maturities of up to 26 weeks. And they are sold at a discount to face value. So if you purchase a $1000 bond maturing in 6 months you might pay around $940 to $970 for it. At maturity you receive $1000. You can also sell them at any time before maturity through a bank or broker.

T Bonds

T Bonds are long term securities issued in terms of 30 years. You purchase them at face value and interest is paid every six months at the fixed or stated rate at purchase for the life of the bond. You can also buy and sell already issued T Bonds in the market through a broker.

Money Sense:

How to Buy T Bills and Bonds; Best bet is go to your nearest Federal Reserve Bank, with checkbook in hand and make a direct purchase, commission free. Or do it by mail at the Bureau of Public Debt at the Treasury Department in Washington, D.C. Have questions about treasury bills, notes or bonds or need help in figuring out what to do, call 800-722-2678 toll free for a 24/7 recorded message or a live person from 8am to 8pm Eastern Time, Monday through Friday except holidays. For you online fans go to *www.treasurydirect.gov* . Use T Bond and T

Bills for portfolio diversification, a risk free segment of your investments, education and for liquid funds.

TREASURY BILLS, NOTES, BONDS...
WHAT'S THE DIFFERENCE

The main difference is the time period it takes for the securities to mature. T Bills are short term and mature from days to four, 13, or 26 weeks. They are discounted meaning a $1000 Bill is purchased for say $950. Upon maturity you receive $1000, the face amount, the $50 being interest. T-Bills are issued in $1,000 increments.

T-Notes are issued in 2,3,5 and 10 year intervals, pay a fixed rate of interest every 6 months and are issued in units of $1000 multiples.

T-Bonds were issued in longer terms up to 30 years. The government stopped selling them in 2001 but started again in the fall of 2006. You can still purchase or sell older bonds that were issued but not yet matured through a broker. Interest is paid twice a year.

Yields, that's the current coupon or stated rate divided by the principal expressed as a percentage, vary on treasuries but you can easily find out the current yield through your bank or broker. Or call the government direct at (800) 722-2678.

Money Sense:

A word of advice to small investors. Think twice about investing in long term bonds because they tend to lose more of their value when interest rates turn up. Bonds with shorter maturities aren't so volatile.

Money Minutes

BONDS: ALTERNATIVES TO STOCK INVESTING

Bonds are like loans. They are interest-bearing or discounted (you pay $950 for a $1000 bond and get paid $1000 at maturity) securities that pay the bondholder a specific sum of money, usually at regular intervals, say quarterly or semiannually. Bonds carry a promise to pay back the principal money back on the part of the issuer, either a company or the government.

Kinds of bonds

There are treasury bonds issued by the government for short to longer periods of time, corporate bonds issued by corporations, high-yield bonds and municipal bonds.

Treasuries are the safest and most liquid (easily sold) bonds and are among US and international investors favorite havens for cash. Since treasuries are backed by the full faith and credit of the U.S. government they carry very little real risk of default. Full face value is repaid upon maturity and their income is exempt from state and local taxes. But federal tax must be paid.

Corporate bonds are issued by public and private corporations and are fully taxable. Municipal bonds are issued by a state or local government and may be exempt from federal and sometimes state income taxes. There are also triple tax free bonds issued by municipalities. They are exempt from local, state and federal income taxes. However, their returns are usually very low and only make sense for high net worth and highly taxed investors. Municipal bonds are issued to raise funds for special projects and general government operation needs.

Money Sense:

For the past few years, stocks have been the best returning investment vehicles for investors of all ages, but bonds are an investment vehicle that deserve a place or mindshare in many well diversified and wealthy client portfolios.

215

Money Minutes

I BONDS, THE TRIPLE "A", -#1, LOW RISK INVESTMENT WITH BUILT-IN INFLATION PROTECTION

Let's say you are feeling like you are an old 87. Hint: You probably aren't buying green bananas anymore (smiles).

The stock market is out and you don't want to lose principal. Is there a place to put your money where it will earn a modest return and where there's no chance of losing purchasing power due to inflation.

Yes; and the government has them both. There are two types of inflation protected securities. You can even buy them both directly from the government at www.treasurydirect.gov .

I Bonds

The I stands for inflation. Purchase can be made through the Treasury direct or your local bank in denominations of $50, $75, $100, $200, $500, $1,000, $5,000, and $10,000. You buy them at face value—you pay $100 for a $100 bond. You may purchase up to $30,000 worth a year.

Interest has two components. When you purchase the bond a fixed rate is applied and every six months—May and November—a variable rate is applied that's tied to the Consumer Price Index (CPI). Interest is paid when the bond is redeemed and you have to hold it for six months before selling. After holding the bonds for 12 months you may sell them at any time. But in the first 5 years there's a 3 month interest penalty due upon sale because "I bonds are meant as a longer term holding and can be held for up to 30 years. Interest is free from state and local taxes.

Money Sense:

Interest earned on bonds used for education expenses is at least partially and may possibly be all deductible. All the interest is exempt from state and local taxes. Your principal is protected form inflation by the semi-annual CPI adjustment. It's a good deal for conservative risk averse investors who really need to know their money will be there without having to watch it every day.

Money Minutes

U.S. COINS: COLLECTING METALLIC ART FOR FUN, CAPITAL PRESERVATION & PROFIT OPPORTUNITY

Coin collecting is such a fascinating hobby. First off it's real money. And who doesn't like to collect money. Second, coins have intrinsic value, if you are collecting older coins minted before the mid 1960s. After that time except for certain special issues directly from the U.S. Mint, all the silver was taken out of coinage and the treasury started using clad copper blanks. The intrinsic value in coinage comes from the underlying or meltdown value of the precious metals—usually silver or gold and rarely platinum—in the metal blanks that the coins are stamped from.

Coin collecting is a hobby that has also produced great returns for individuals here and around the world.

There are three classes of coin collecting. One is the junk silver coin collector. They collect and may even horde large quantities of common date coins in any condition as a hedge against either a fall in the value of the dollar or other catastrophic world events that would make the silver or gold content of their horde worth more. However, the main reason for holding junk silver is as a store of value, and not as an investment that will appreciate on an annual basis. It's a place holder or dead zone in a portfolio that is not expected to either rise or fall but maintain its approximate asset value from year to year.

The second class of collector is a hobbyist who enjoys assembling sets of say pennies, nickels, dimes, quarters, half dollars or dollars and many times the object is to complete a type set of coins by filling as many year dates or all if possible regardless of the condition or mint state of the coins. It's a fun activity, there are many clubs for coin collectors and there's a large body of knowledge around coin collecting that is shared an available to enhance the joy of the activity.

The third class of collector is the one interested in coins as an investment. Coin investing requires a more focused knowledge of grading, rarity and scarcity of particular coins, price history and demand for certain types and issues and most important, working with a reputable dealer. If all the criteria for appropriately balancing a portfolio are in place rare coin investing can make up a portion of your assets somewhere between 5 and 10%. You'll want to work with a professional numismatic dealer to make sure you are getting recommendations for the right coins for your purpose, budget and portfolio.

HEDGE FUNDS – THE "THIN ICE" INVESTMENT

Hedge funds, unlike the regular pools of investor money that usually are long positions and hold 'em affairs, are free to exploit temporary inefficiencies in the market. They will short stocks and usually do very well when the markets are falling. So it's easy to see why in the years following the Spring 2000 market break, hedge funds sure looked good against their peers. Markets were declining, there were international incidents—the bombing of the World Trade Center, war in Afghanistan and then Iraq, tumbling interest rates and more.

Another area where hedge funds shine in making money is by positioning themselves in interest rate disparities by borrowing money at short term rates in the short term market and then investing the funds in longer term higher yielding securities. Now that the Fed is steadily ratcheting up short term money rates, the easy money has been made and for the near term future it's not a recommended strategy. Here's why:

Taking Advantage of Market Disparities
And "Niche" Opportunities

As with most complex and sophisticated investment vehicles, hedge funds, once they multiply, start attracting a lot of money from across the net worth spectrum. Eventually the markets find their balance again and the options or opportunities become much more limited. Then the funds—ever seeking fresh needed opportunities—get involved in increasingly complex trading strategies, the real "thin ice" of speculating. Areas like aircraft finance, lending to distressed companies, and even playing the mortality tables by buying coops and condos occupied by elderly tenants, waiting for the inevitable end, redecorating or remodeling, and then marketing the apartments at current much higher market rates. The object is to make money or get a positive return on investment capital in any market climate. Good in theory but difficult to achieve with regularity.

Money Sense:

Stay away. This is for *speculative investors only.*

When asked about hedge funds I immediately picture those muscle sports car commercials where the caption under the gravity defying show reads, closed circuit, professional drivers, do not attempt.... In other words don't try this on your own. For a better choice in a tough market, look to the new long/short funds. A final alert, several hedge fund and buyout companies are considering going public. Whenever a market niche has about run its best course is the time the public is let in. Also bear in mind that recently some hedge funds have actually had to cease operations due to extraordinary losses. Now what does that tell the thoughtful investor? Enough said.

STANDARD LOANS FOR HOMEBUYERS

Mortgages or loans for homebuyers come in a variety of flavors. Let's start with the basic ones.

Standard or Conventional Loans? Typically they are based on each person's credit standing or FICO score as well as income guidelines. They do not require mortgage loan insurance, and only use the underlying property as security for the loan. A down payment of from 5% up to 20% or more may be required as well as documentation of the applicant's or family's income. The loan to value ratio (percentage value of the loan compared to the market value of the property as determined by the lender) is usually conservative. So a $150,000 house may have an outstanding mortgage ranging from $105,000 to $140,000 or a loan to value ration of 70 to 90%. Conventional is another way of saying standard mortgage. These carry the most favorable interest rates because they represent the lowest risk category of mortgage for the lender.

FHA Loan. This loan is insured by the Federal Housing Administration, a federal government agency. Started during the Depression it was designed to provide insurance to lenders against defaults. It's available for qualified buyers nearly everywhere in the U.S. and is tailored for lower income people who might not qualify for mortgage insurance or be able to make a conventional loan down payment. FHA loans require a smaller down payment than conventional mortgages.

VA Loan. This loan is available to the veterans of United States Military Forces and qualifying survivors who have not remarried. They are provided by banks and other mortgage lenders. A portion of the loan—up to $60,000—is guaranteed against default by the Veteran's Administration. If a mortgagee does default on VA loans the VA will make good up the amount of the entitlement but may then go after the borrower for the money. The down payments on VA loans are very low.

Farmers Home Administration Loan. Loans for rural families that are administered by the US Dept of Agriculture. Payment periods are up to 40 years. No down payment is required. The mortgage is insured and applicants must meet income requirements.

Money Sense:

If you qualify for one of the entitlement mortgages, say as a farmer or veteran, go for it. However, if you have enough for a down payment of 10% or more consider the rates being offered on the special program versus a conventional loan.

NON-STANDARD LOANS FOR HOMEBUYERS

The current boom cycle in real estate has produced an unusually high rise in housing prices, especially in certain high demand areas of the country. To make it easier for buyers who might be shut out of the market due to high payments, banks and independent mortgage bankers have developed scores of new types of real estate loans, such as:

- Adjustable rate mortgages
- Shared appreciation mortgages
- Balloon mortgages
- Open end mortgages
- Hybrid mortgages
- Buy Downs
- Zero Point mortgages
- and my least favorite of all, Interest Only Mortgages

The Interest Only Mortgage Bandit

In places like California where real estate prices have gone up the most in the country, the interest only mortgage has become fairly popular as a way to getting into the richly priced market. However, this is a very high risk type of financing vehicle designed only for very special situations. Just like it sounds, with an interest only mortgage you only make payments on the interest portion of the loan. There is no amortization or reduction in the principal. At the end of say 5 years, a $300,000 mortgage with 6% interest and a monthly payment of $1,500 would still have a mortgage balance of $300,000. Your hope here is that the price of the house will have gone up enough so that if you sell, price inflation will pay off the mortgage and leave you with a little cash.

Extended Term Mortgages

Like the bigger and bigger SUVs, a new super sized 40 year mortgage is starting to appear in a few places on a trial basis. It's another way of cutting down the monthly payments so more people can afford the

American Dream. The price of course is much higher interest payments over the course of the loan.

Money Sense:

If you are considering any of these creative financing approaches or the new longer term mortgage, you need to discuss them with your loan officer, mortgage banker, real estate professional and accounting or financial advisor. Finally, ask yourself what might happen if things don't work out and say higher price inflation doesn't bail you out?

WHAT TYPE HOME MORTGAGE IS BEST FOR YOU?

When interest rates are moving higher, adjustable rate mortgages tend to be more popular than fixed rates. High appreciation in home prices in certain parts of the country has spawned creative financing and new more exotic mortgages. With interest rates at or near historic lows for most of this first decade of the millennium, we have had a long run of good real estate times and are experiencing a correction especially in speculative markets like Florida, California and Arizona to name a few. So in the midst of all the economic and interest rate fluctuation —

What Should You Think About
When Choosing A Mortgage?

Earning power. If your earnings are on the rise and you anticipate a pretty good increase in income over time, a graduated payment mortgage—one where the payments gradually rise over the course of say 5 years and then remain fixed at a higher rate of interest—may be a good choice instead of a fixed rate. Major Advantage: You'll be able to qualify for a larger mortgage with graduated payments.

Length of Time in the Home. Staying 5 years or more? You may want to know your payment is going to remain the same for the long term and in fact be easier to pay each month as your income rises and so a fixed rate mortgage may be the right choice here. Expecting to move in 3 to 4 years? An adjustable rate mortgage could serve you better. After all, you don't care if rates rise. You'll be out before the bulk of any increase hits—most adjustables can be had with fixed rates for 1 2 or 3 years and even up to 5 and then float to new market rates with a "cap"—upper rate fix over the base rate—after that. Added benefit: You would probably qualify for a bigger mortgage with an adjustable rate feature. In a fixed rate scenario the banks will be more conservative with the guidelines and probably want points as well to give them some hedge against possible rising rates while the rate they charge you is fixed. And one more advantage here is, in the event interest rates do decline, you'll end up with lower payments in the event that you decide to stay past the initial fixed period.

Market expectation: If you are rock sure the prices of median homes in your area will continue upward in the next 5 years—say you are moving into the "A" list neighborhood or right in the path of development, you might consider rolling the dice with a balloon mortgage. Here you get a mortgage with low rates and 30 year payment terms, so the payment is locked and lower than on a fixed rate mortgage. Of course in 5 years the entire balance of the loan comes due and you'll either pay it off or have to refinance. Money Sense: IF you choose this riskier option make sure you get an automatic refinance option or you'll end up with having to go through the entire mortgage closing process again, including title search, lawyer's fees, maybe points, and all the other higher associated closing costs. You also need to be pretty certain the market will play out you way. Obviously the money pros are betting the other way.

Risk Factor. You take on more risk with an adjustable rate mortgage. Long term it may or may not turn out better. The fixed rate would turn out better if rates end up going a lot higher and you stay in your home a long time—longer than 5 years. If interest rates are at or near their historic lows, like they were in 2004 and 2005, and you do plan to stay in your home more than 5 years, odds are that the fixed rate mortgage would be the best choice. Here again, a discussion with a real estate or mortgage person will help clarify your own thinking and help you make the choice that's most comfortable for you.

Final Money Sense Note:

Whatever you decide, if it turns out the choice no longer works due to a change in circumstances, the loan can always be paid off and replaced with a new loan before it matures, and usually without any pre-payment penalty (however, there may be fees and costs associated with the new loan). There are exceptions such as yield maintenance loans but they are much more specialized and used mostly in commercial real estate.

MORTGAGE IN LAW

Helping the Family Buy a Home

Many of us find ourselves at a point in life where we'd like to be helpful to family. Call it passing around the blessings. Life is good and it's really nice to be able to help when needed. So your son(s) or daughter(s) come calling when it's time to make that home buying decision. Maybe they found, like many of us did, that the home buying transaction can make, as Ross Perot once said, a "giant sucking" sound that takes every dollar out of our pockets, and then some.

At the risk of sparking a family feud here, consider a few things carefully before committing money to your kids for a home.

First, Make Sure They Are On Sound Financial Footing.

If there's only one income, a real rarity today, make sure there is enough income to cover the mortgage, not just a hope and a prayer. The old-fashioned 25% rule—meaning 25% of your income should cover the monthly expense of your living space—is out the window. But if it's over 40% of income for the mortgage and one pay-check, there's trouble ahead.

Second, Figure Out How Much House They Can Afford.

There is so much help available these days in the form of calculators to figure this out. A good site for first time buyers is at *http://www. fanniemae.com/homebuyers*. Quick example: With a monthly income of $5,000, monthly additional debt of $1100 and $10,000 in available funds, the results show a monthly affordable payment of $1400 which will fund a $148,000 loan at 7% interest. Based on a purchase price of $164,940 the estimated down payment and closing costs come to $18,143.00 So there is a shortfall in available funds of $8,143 (18,143 minus the 10K available) the buyer has to make up to close the deal.

229

Third, Ask What Kind Of Mortgage They Plan On Getting.

This tells you a lot. If it's a 30 year fixed rate mortgage, no cautionary flags. The lender will have qualified them using pretty conservative guidelines. Should be okay. If a 5 year fixed with a balloon and you are contributing say ten or fifteen thousand dollars to the initial transaction, ask what they plan to do about saving up for that eventuality (and how good have they been at saving up to now). Proceed with caution here as you may very well have to come up with another 10 or 15 thousand when the balloon comes due. And if it's an interest only loan, think black flag. At least you want to encourage going back to the drawing board here to structure a more sensible transaction or maybe waiting a few years. Unless of course you are in your 60s or 70s with several million in net worth and not figuring there's any likelihood you'll outlive your money.

Money Sense:

If the kids don't know how much mortgage they can afford, it is easy to find out by going to one of the mortgage calculators, for instance, at *www.bankrate.com*, *www.lendingtree.com* or *www.money.msn.com*.

THE HIDDEN COSTS OF MORTGAGE FINANCING & REFINANCING

With so much refinancing and interest costs at rates not seen this low in 40 years or more, it is possible for people to refinance, take built up equity out of their houses and do a lot of things with the excess cash while—at the same time—reducing their monthly payments. But consider all the costs associated with the refinance and whether it is worth it. And beware of dealing with a funding operation instead of your local bank. Many times you get lulled into a cheaper rate situation only to find out in the end that when all the associated costs or things you didn't know about get figured in—even though you will receive an estimate of the costs—you may not end up with what you thought you were getting Here's some of the need-to-know in order to make sure you have enough cash or enough grossed up in the mortgage to avoid problems at the closing or help you decide if it is the right choice..

Mortgage Cost Checklist

- How much are you planning to put down (for a first time mortgage only)?

- Is there an application fee?

- Is there a processing fee?

- Is there a charge for your credit report?

- Are there any points. These are up front interest payments designed to buy down the rate on the loan. This is mortgage speak and it sounds like you are getting a better rate but if fact you are paying a chunk of interest today for a lower interest rate. However, points up front really raise the overall interest rate.

- Is there an origination fee or an underwriting review fee?

- Is there a commitment fee? Is there any mortgage tax, or mortgage

231

transfer fee? How much?

- Is there a rate lock fee ? This is what you get charged to hold the rate for a certain number of days after it is approved. It's like mortgage points. It's money out of your pocket.

- How much is the attorney fee? If you have no personal attorney make sure you shop around for the services. In a high cost area a fee of $750 may be completely unrealistic. But if you have a legal plan, here's where the payoff comes.

- Does the bank charge an attorney fee? The bank may charge you for their attorney.

- What about title insurance? How much is the survey?

- Does the lender require lender's as well as owner's title insurance (they get a free ride on this but you pay extra for it)?

- How much is the appraisal fee?

- Is mortgage insurance required? This can be a significant charge on a large mortgage.

- Is there a rate lock fee—a fee to hold the interest rate once commitment is received? More mortgages speak for money you have to lay out before the closing.

- What are the estimated settlement charges to be paid at closing?

- Can the mortgage be paid-down and will the payments be reduced? On conventional mortgages you pay down principal but the payment remains the same. On interest only loans, the monthly payment floats with the amount of remaining principal. So if you pay down $25,000 of principal, the monthly payment declines.

- Are there penalties for paying off the mortgage within 1 to 5 years?

MORTGAGE PREPARATION – WHAT YOU'LL NEED TO SPEED THE PROCESS

Okay, you have done your homework and you want or need financing for a new home. Or you want to refinance an existing mortgage to reduce payments and free up equity.

What will you need to have ready for the mortgage lender to complete the application process and assure it goes smoothly.

Pre Application Mortgage Checklist

1. Photo of your social security card and driver's license.

2. Addresses of your primary residences for the past 5 years. If rentals also list names, addresses and phone numbers of landlords.

3. Name and address of your employer(s) for the past 5 years.

4. Gross monthly salaries.

5. Tax returns for the past two years including W2s and 1099s (if self employed).

6. Last pay stub.

7. Names, addresses, account numbers of all banking accounts—checking, savings, CDs, money markets.

8. A copy of your last six months of checking account statements.

9. List of all assets and locations and account numbers of personal securities, IRAs, 401Ks or other liquid assets.

10. List of open loans and credit card balances with names and addresses of companies, outstanding balances and monthly payments.

233

11. If self employed: current P & L and financial statements or balance sheet for past 2 years; also a letter from a CPA or other professional stating you have been self employed for the period of years stated on the application.

12. If a refinance, a copy of your survey and your deed and your latest mortgage statement showing the payment figure and the balance outstanding.

Money Sense:

This is quite a paper chase but it will save you endless hours of toil and delays or worse yet running into expiration or extensions of rate locks—all of which cost you money. If you have these documents available you'll have 95% of the requirements in the bag. And if need be you'll have material at the ready to shop your needs with alternate sources of funding.

BALLOON MORTGAGES—ARE THEY A GOOD WAY TO FINANCE?

The real estate market in the past ten years has been very rewarding. People buying new and resale homes have made out quite well both in terms of equity build up and increase in the market value of what they purchased. When making a home purchase there are several different types of mortgages to consider.

Lower Interest, Now, But Refinance May Cost You Later

A newer more popular type of loan is called a balloon mortgage; it usually carries a lower interest rate. The payments are set up like a 30 year mortgage, with a 360 month (30 and 12) payment schedule but they mature and have to be paid off in 3, 5, 7 or 10 years—instead of the conventional 30 year mortgage which matures in thirty years.

The downside is that when the mortgage matures you have the entire principal to pay. With balloon mortgages you don't amortize (pay down) as much principal each month so more is owed after say 5 years than with a conventional mortgage. If for some reason you couldn't refinance you'd possibly be in jeopardy of losing your home and the money you have invested in it.

Money Sense:

A balloon mortgage works best for those who either don't plan to be in their homes for more than a few to several years. For instance if it is a first home, you are planning a large family and know you'll have to move into a more spacious house a few years down the road. It would also make sense if you think that interest rates are going down. Then when the note matures you would refinance at a lower fixed interest rate—f you are right about rates. And a final word: If you are thinking of a balloon mortgage as a way of stretching your buying power to the limit, buying a more expensive home and counting on inflation and price hikes to increase your wealth, you'd be like so many other cockeyed optimists lured by the easy policies of lenders in a gray or sub-prime area. The real estate decline beginning in 2005 was due in large part to such loans.

To educate yourself more fully on mortgage and financing issues see *www.mortgageprofessor.com*

REVERSE MORTGAGE – PUTTING YOUR HOME TO WORK FOR YOU WHEN YOU RETIRE

About half of the people who retire do some type of advance planning for their retirement. And like all plans, realities will often affect the outcomes of the plans.
When that happens, you may need to make adjustments.

Cashing In On Home Value Without Moving

One of the harsher realities is that expenses can rise more than expected and some people can find their expenses coming uncomfortably close to or even outrunning their income. If that's a situation you find yourself in, and your major asset is your home, a reverse mortgage can save your bacon. This government insured mortgage option may be the right way to boost your income and your standard of living.

When Do You Qualify For a Reverse Mortgage?

You need to be past the age of 62.

What About Credit History?

Credit scores and income don't matter.

The reverse mortgage loan is based on:

- Age of the house
- Age of the youngest borrower
- Location and value of the home
- Current interest rates

The major benefits of the reverse mortgage loan are:

- No matter how long you live, the built up equity in your home

237

will provide an income. It will never run out.

- You'll have converted that built up equity into current income when you need it.
- There are no monthly payments to worry about.
- No loan repayment is required, so long as you live.

Money Sense:

Reverse mortgages are a good source of income especially if you have a lot of built up equity in your home and it represents the bulk of your retirement assets. If you need more retirement income and you don't want to give up your home, a reverse mortgage could provide you with a supplemental income for life. Just understand that this is a rising debt and falling equity loan that undoes the equity build-up in the home over time. Think of it as cashing in on your home's appreciation without having to move. A good choice for those without immediate heirs or beneficiaries we wish to inherit based on needs of their own. However, never use a reverse mortgage or home equity loan to invest. Further resource: *http://www.aarp.org/money/revmort/*

SHOULD I RENT? SHOULD I BUY? HOW TO DECIDE WHAT IS BEST.

The rent versus buy decision is more than just a money issue. It is a lifestyle, control and labor issue as well. Let's look at the softer issues first.

Renting? It appears easy. There is no risk of ownership. If the value of the property declines it has no effect on your investment. The property owner fixes the pipes, changes out the thermostat, upgrades the HVAC, and takes care of all mechanical or structural repairs. All you do is mow the lawn and pay the utilities in most cases. It is simple, it is temporary, it is stress free, you can relocate fairly quickly if need be, and it can be the best solution in many cases for housing options. However, rent goes up, and up, and up. You cannot lock in a fixed rate on rent. Renting could be the best option for some, if employment is not stable, if ultimate housing needs aren't clear, if you are single, if you are not certain where you will settle down, if you are looking to save toward a down payment or establish a better or longer period of credit history to qualify for a standard or conforming loan at better interest rates.

Owning? It takes more money and effort than renting that is for sure. There are up front expenses to buy a home—appraisal, survey, title insurance, homeowners insurance, credit report, mortgage application fee, attorney fee, funding of escrow accounts if established just to name a few. However, there are terrific new loan programs especially for first time owners, loans with zero down payment or interest only for the first several years, which we will examine separately and sometimes sellers will help with the closing costs. So the overall effect of owning can be cushioned financially. Also there are new responsibilities. You will be the one calling contractors to fix the things that break, to put in the things you need, and to get the bids for the work that's needed. You can, of course, pretty much fix your payment when owning. Real estate, school and municipal taxes as well as home insurance are almost certain to rise. So your monthly cost will go up some on an annual basis but you will have the increased value of the home working for you plus the equity build as the mortgage gets paid off. Finally there is the psychic income that comes from "pride of ownership."

Over 60% of families own their own homes. Added responsibilities aside, there is a clear trend toward owning rather than renting.

THE NUMBERS BEHIND RENTING VERSUS OWNING YOUR HOME

To give us a look at a typical example of owning versus buying we'll take the case of a family of four wanting a 3-bedroom property. They locate a home for rent in the area they like for $1200 a month. They also have the option to buy that same exact house for $160,000. I am using St. Louis, Missouri as a model here. While this comparison could vary depending on the area, and that in turn could affect your decision, the idea is to show you a realistic example you can analyze to help decide what's best for you.

Renting in the same Property for 5 years:

Moving costs (same as owning, so no value placed here):	$0
Closing costs (you pay the deposit + first month's rent, but those are not "costs," they are deposits)	$0
Total rent ($1200 / month to start, then presuming 3% annual increase)	$76,450
Total contents insurance paid	$1250
Total extra cost of auto ins. w/out the home discount (2 cars)	$500
Total repair expenses	$0
Total tax deduction earned on the rent paid	$0
Total appreciation earned on the property increasing in value 3% a year (presumption)	$0
Total Net Cost:	**$78,200**

Owning for 5 Years Starting with a 10% Down Payment:

Moving costs (same as renting, so no value placed here): $0

Closing costs (appraisal, credit, flood letter, title, survey, inspections, recording, and other approx. fees – you can eliminate or reduce by negotiating with the seller to pay at closing!) $2500

Interest lost over 5 years on 10% down payment at 4% (presumption, less taxes paid on interest at 30% bracket) $2475

Total payments P&I at 6.25% fixed rate + MI $56,941

Less tax deduction net received from interest paid (same bracket) $13,081

Less equity paid down on loan over 5 years $9594

Total taxes paid (presuming 1.1% of new est. value each year) $9342

Less tax deduction net received from taxes paid (same bracket) $2802

Total repair expenses (this of course can vary widely) $6000

Less total appreciation earned on the property assuming a 3% a year increase in value (presumption) $20,081

Realtor expense to sell property in 5 years at 5.75% $10,354

Total Net Cost: **$42,054**

Total Net Savings Owning VS Renting: $36,146
($7229 net saved per year, which is $602 per month!)

Let's face it. There are a lot of variables here. However, whichever way you look at it owning tends to come out ahead of renting.

REAL ESTATE – STILL THE AMERICAN DREAM

There's scene in the 1967 movie the Graduate where Dustin Hoffman, the fresh out of school not too sure what he wants to do with his life kid is reluctantly attending a cocktail party celebrating his college graduation. A friend of the family comes up to him and says: "I've got just one word for you...are you listening? (long pause) "Yes." "Plastics." Of course by that time the industry was already on a tear and plastics were fast becoming a mainstream product. Fast forward and we see them everywhere today. Then came uranium—by God, it's back—computers, the Information age, the Internet. And now investment in China.

A Long, Long Term Record of Good Return on Investment

Almost from the dawn of American History, real estate has been golden. The dream of ownership has sparked settlement, expansion, wars, and produced wealth beyond the dreams of avarice for over 200 years. The recent downturn was pretty much caused by creative mortgage products that involved no interest payments for certain periods of time and the normalization of internal up and down market movements but the reality is that even this real estate market cycle has had a long run on the upside and was due for a correction.

Today real estate ownership is at its highest rate in history with well over 60% of families owning their own homes. It's the keystone in many family fortunes and many more families own homes than directly own stocks and bonds.

When radio listeners ask me, Bob, is now a good time to buy real estate I say, the American dream is alive and well. Interest rates are low; near their lowest point in nearly 40 years and home prices have been stable to increasing steadily depending on what part of the country you live in. So consider carefully whether you should be making a real estate ownership decision but do consider it.

Small wonder that Will Rogers once said: In a real estate man's eyes, the most exclusive part of the city is wherever he has a house to sell.

243

Money Sense:

No good thing goes up forever, real estate included. Currently the real estate market is in a period of adjustment due to over-speculation in hot markets like California, Florida and Arizona. There's been fallout from what's called sub prime lending, a practice that encouraged many families to buy property and homes with interest only loans, artificially low "come-on" interest rates and other unsound financing vehicles. The upshot is an increase in late payments and foreclosures. The bottom line here is figure out how much you can lay out every month to make a mortgage payment. Times that by twelve. Divide it by the stated mortgage rate to get a lump sum mortgage amount and you'll know how much house or property you can shop for. You'll also have to adjust for amortization of principal, generally 1 to 1.25% per year.

BUYING VERSUS RENTING A HOME

Is it better to buy or rent a home? There are advantages and disadvantages to both. Real estate runs in cycles. In the 1970s and early 1980s, home purchases were almost sure to have a profit at resale time. Then, in the late 1980s, real estate prices started to sag and many homes were considered overpriced. You almost have to have a crystal ball to see what's best for you. One thing is certain; you need a long term view.

The advantages of buying a home are:

- You build equity or ownership in your home. It is almost a form of forced savings. Chances are very likely and well supported by decades of history that over the longer term a resale will result in good capital appreciation—more money than you paid.

- You can remodel your home any time you wish to suit changing needs or tastes.

- As a homeowner you are entitled to significant tax deductions.

The advantages of renting are:

- Renters don't have to be concerned about real estate prices dropping.

- Renters can invest the money saved by renting.

- Renters don't have to worry about refinancing or interest rate hikes.

- Finally, renters are not locked into one location. You may move any time you wish.

Money Sense:

If a person has the money, wouldn't it be better to own than rent?

Darn good question but there's no pat answer. The buy versus rent decision isn't just based on finances and financial success, though that's certainly an important element in the consideration. A person who is going through a lifestyle change may find that being tied down to a home purchase is really not what they wish.

Is there something in between owning or renting?

There is. It's the rent with option to purchase. Think of it as try before you buy. After you live in a place for awhile and decide you like your apartment or rental home you may want to buy it. In a lease with option to buy you typically will receive a credit for a percentage of the rent paid as either a down payment or a credit toward the purchase price of the home or apartment.

The bottom line here is talk it through with a professional real estate agent. They can help you make the right choice for your situation. And if you have no past experience owning, talk to friends or relatives who do and they'll be able to clue you in on the hidden expenses that real estate ownership entails.

FIRST TIME HOMEBUYERS

You've decided to take the plunge and go for your first home. Where do you start?

Go a qualified lender and get pre-approved for a loan. Some realtors call this a qualifying letter and may require it before taking you out to see listings. Don't let that affect your disposition at all because it has three advantages:

- It gives the buyer more buying and bargaining power since the seller knows that the individual is already qualified and if interested in the house, could make a purchase and be accepted immediately.

- It helps the buyer target their price range accurately since they know how much loan they are qualified for.

- It gets you prime attention with the realtor. After all, they know you are serious and not just kicking tires, and have a realistic price target.

Next, seek out a buyer' agent to help you with purchase decision. A home purchase is often the largest purchase in a person's lifetime and it involves among other things, negotiation with the seller. Having a professional representative in your corner can make a big difference, and save you hundreds or even thousands of dollars.

Money Sense:

One reason for using a "buyer's agent is that their loyalty by signed agreement is to you, the buyer. The listing broker or agent is working for — being paid – by the seller via the commission fee, a percentage ranging from a flat fee on up to 6% or more of the selling price of the property. Their loyalty obviously has to lie where their money is coming from. Buyer's agents don't necessarily have to charge you a fee because they do in fact get a portion of the real estate commission paid by the seller to the seller's broker and agent. But you might pay a flat fee for

247

services or a commission if you purchase a for sale by owner property.

CLOSING COSTS ON HOME
PURCHASES & REFINANCING

What's the difference between closing costs on a refinance or a purchase?

Sometimes with teaser promotional rates on refinancing there is very little or even no closing cost in the loan process. However, if you are retaining legal counsel the refinance costs could run $750, $1000, or more. On a purchase expect to pay approximately double that or more, say $1500 and up. The main reason for the price difference is the cost of title insurance.

On any purchase the lender will require title insurance which is simply meant to protect the lender or borrower in the event a dispute arises over the ownership of the property. The cost of title insurance is directly related to the value of the property being insured. So, the higher the value of the home, the more expensive the insurance.

A separate part of closing costs can be points or extra interest that is charged on a loan. Points used to be 100% deductible when closing on a purchase but now they are amortized over the life of the loan. In other words if you borrow $200,000 from the bank to purchase your home and there is a surcharge of 1 point or 1 percent of the borrowed amount you would pay an additional $ 2,000 – and it can be paid directly to the bank out of the proceeds of the loan. So your loan would gross up to 202,000. That $2000, if you have a new 40 year mortgage, would be deducted at $50 per year. But check with your accountant as these tax issues have a habit of changing over time.

Closing costs, title insurance, legal, mortgage points and so forth are typically paid by the purchaser or buyer.

Money Sense:

You can request in your purchase contract that the seller pay part or all of the closing costs and even the points for the buyer. If the seller pays the buyer's point, the buyer will still get the tax deduction. Can you get a loan with no points? That would reduce the amount of money you need for closing. Yes, but the interest rates are higher on zero point mortgages. In the long run that makes the overall loan more expensive. You'll pay less money each month in interest by amortizing or reducing the cost of

249

the loan upfront with points. If you stay in your house for even 10 years that's a long time to pay extra interest.

BUYING A HOUSE – WHEN NOT TO

It's The American Dream, But Not An Entitlement. Live in your own space. Own your own space. It's practically an entitlement. But it could also turn out to be a nightmare. When should you think twice and postpone the decision?

Single Income with Kids. Think twice. If you are the sole earner with kids making the move to a house, what happens if the job ends or your income is interrupted? How much in emergency fund have you stockpiled—6 months (bare minimum), 9 months (much better but few have it), 12 months (you should be fine, but the reality is it's easier to find a diamond at the beach than someone with 12 months of expenses put away).

Less than Excellent Credit. Credit worthiness determines the interest rate you'll pay on the mortgage loan or what kind of loan you qualify for. The difference can mean tens to hundreds of dollars more per month in payments, even when the interest rate is less than a full point more. Think twice especially if you are offered what are called "no doc" loans where you don't have to provide verified income information. They automatically have much higher interest rates built in. Mortgage company takes a bigger risk, they take a bigger bite. Result: You pay a higher price.

100% Financing. Yes, even conventional banking and mortgage companies now offer mortgages up to the full value of the prospective house you are buying. Once again, think twice. If you haven't been able to save enough money for a down payment of at least 10% what are you going to do about all of the things that crop up once you are in a house? Things that require cash to deal with—repairs and routine maintenance, emergencies like a hot water heater or boiler failure, and all the other things that you may even know about but never thought you would need to keep up a house.

Interest Only Mortgage. Don't think. Forget about it. Unless you have a crystal ball and can see ahead 5 years when the I/O feature stops and regular interest included payments begin, why have a troubled mind about the roof over your head?

Hybrid Mortgage. Fixed rate up front and then an adjustable or new rate after say 3 or 5 years at the prevailing market rate. One to think about but not necessarily a go. If you feel you'll be situated well enough to make a switch to a fixed rate mortgage and that rate isn't much higher, go for it. Otherwise you are probably going to play a shell game with a variable rate or another balloon type mortgage where you gamble on rates being lower in a few years.

Money Sense:

The bottom line is if you have to gamble on your finances being better tomorrow than they are today, maybe you should wait for tomorrow to borrow.

SELLING YOUR HOME—BROKER OR BY OWNER???

For every buyer there has to be a seller. Sooner or later if you own a home you will probably be a seller. What should you do?

It would be great if you could just put a sign on the front lawn announcing your house is for sale and then sell it immediately. Unfortunately, that is not what usually happens.

Market and location make a difference.

If you are undecided here are a few centering thought on whether to go "for sale by owner" or FSBO or Regular v. Discount Broker. In a blistering hot area where houses are generally sold within a few weeks to a month or so of listing you could take a shot at a FSBO. Or if your home is in peak condition in a desirable area, has no major flaws, including poor decorating (something most of us aren't good at seeing ourselves) or poor mechanicals (plumbing, heating, A/C and electrical systems), you could take a shot at selling on your own. Or if you live across the street from a golf course and people regularly come up to your door, ring the bell and ask politely if your home is for sale, in all these situations you could probably sell on your own. But should you?

They say a doctor shouldn't treat themselves, and a lawyer who handles his own case has a fool for a client. If you want to get maximum exposure for your property it is best to list it with a professional real estate broker who will advertise it, have an open house for both other brokers and for the public, list it in the Multiple Listing Service (MLS) and work with other brokers to show the property to potential buyers. They also help with the negotiations particularly if they are acting as the buyer's agent.

In addition to selling on your own versus broker there's the full service or full price versus discount broker alternative. For my money, go with the full price broker because they have more money to spend on marketing and advertising. They also have more money to put out to other brokers in the multiple listing system. And that will bring more traffic to your house.

Money Sense:

Most homeowners who try to market their property themselves end up listing it with a real estate company—fact not fiction. A real estate broker has people trained to properly market and advertise homes to the public as well as to other brokers in their listing system. They will also qualify the buyer and help you negotiate the best price. As for full price versus discount broker, to me it is all about the revenue sharing. At 6% the listing broker will usually put up to 3% out there for the co-broker who brings a buyer. If you sign an agreement for say 4%, saving you 2%—or so you think—the reality is they put 1% out there for the other brokers to fight over. And if you are taking a client out on a tour of houses are you going to show inventory that brings a 1% commission or a 3% commission. And I think I have answered that question quietly.

SELLING YOUR HOME THROUGH
A REAL ESTATE AGENT

Once you have made the decision to sell through a licensed real estate agent or broker, there are a few things that you'll have questions about:

How Do You Figure Out What Your Home Is Worth? The broker or agent will do a Comparable Market Analysis (CMA) for you. This service is free even if you do not list your house with them. *www.comparative-market-analysis.net/* is one third party free service available if you prefer not to use a broker/ agent. A CMA is based on careful research of other homes similar to yours that have sold in the recent past, homes that are currently under contract and similar to yours and homes that are open listings with the same square footage, bedrooms, amenities and so forth. The CMA will be based on an average of what similar homes either have sold for or are currently on the market for.

How Long Do You Have To Sign Up With the Real Estate Agent? When listing your property, the agent and their company will spend time and money to market it without any upfront money. Newspaper ads, the listing in MLS and on the Internet, open houses, flyers at the house, all of these things cost money. In a hot region/market a 3 month listing is typical but it could take up to six months to sell a house in an average market. In slow markets it takes even longer to sell. So three to six months is a reasonable request from a reputable real estate agent.

What About Commission? Commissions are negotiable and the agent you deal with should tell you what their company charges for services. And if your agent does produce a qualified buyer with an offer at your full list price, you will owe them the agreed upon commission but you won't be forced to sell.

Finding a Potential Buyer Yourself During the Listing Period? Most listings in the St. Louis area are "exclusive right to sell listings". In this instance no matter who sells your property, the listing broker you hired gets paid their full commission. Remember that if you find an interested

255

buyer, there is a lengthy process to go through in purchasing your home. The listing agent helps you establish a price, does the marketing and advertising of your property, qualifies the buyer as to financial and credit worthiness, guides the buyer through the selling process including expediting documents back and forth, guides you in the negotiating and negotiates for you with the buyer. For these reasons, plus the direct and related expenses and time involved, the agent or broker will want to be paid.

Money Sense:

For all the reasons above my preference is to sell through a real estate agent/broker. You may, however, ask to reserve out certain people that have expressed a desire to purchase your house prior to your hiring the agent. In that case, you'll have to name those individuals and also agree to some reduced compensation with the agent.

PRICING YOUR HOME FOR SALE

You have a Comparable Market Analysis from your agent or you acquired one yourself through research and it is time to decide what price to put on the property.

Price It Right

You have the final say. It's important to pick the right number. Compare your house to each of the comparables and consider pricing your property close to the most similar one. If not then a number within the price band of the highest to lowest listings will be a good place to begin.

What Influences the Price?

If the decision is hard and you think the highest priced comparable is worth less or none of the other houses compare to yours, maybe you need to take a drive by to get a better feel for what went into the pricing. In addition to the size of the lot, there are taxes, the schools, the location—main road or side street or dead end, number of bedrooms, number of full and half baths, landscaping, exterior maintenance, condition of the roof if that can be observed and overall curb appeal just to name a few.

Aside from the tangibles in pricing, there is both psychology and human nature at work. The decision of what to offer is up to the buyer. And what to accept should the buyer make a low offer is up to the seller. But what's below the surface can make the difference between a sale or no sale. So pricing is more of an art than an exact science.

For instance, let's say you love your house so much and feel it's so much better than other 3 bedroom 2 bath houses in the neighborhood that you price it higher than all the comparables. Chances are that potential buyers won't look at it. Or if they do come and look, and like what they see, they might be afraid to make what they think is a reasonable offer. They might think you'll be insulted or perhaps angry and to avoid hostility they may simply walk away.

If you are priced at the upper end of the range or even at the same price as the other most similar or most expensive property, buyers will probably come and look. If they like what they see they'll make an offer that relates to the nearest similar house they've seen. And if it is less at least you can make a counter-offer and likely come to terms. But it all starts with the right price.

Money Sense:

Timing is also a factor in pricing. IF you hold out for the price you want, that's assuming you have it priced right in the first place, and the market is just slow or going down, the offers will tell you what the market feels the house is worth. And if your plan is to stick to your guns and hold price, you might just get it. But also think about the opportunity value of the money. If offered $275,000 and you hold out 6 months for $280,000 and finally get it, was the 1.875% difference a real gain or could it have earned more invested elsewhere.

MUTUAL FUNDS ARE NOT ALL CREATED EQUAL

Investing in a mutual fund gives you good diversification with a single convenient investment. A big plus when you have relatively finite amounts of money to invest.

Mutual Fund Selection is Not a "No Mind" Activity

Don't let the convenience or even the diversification make this a one decision or no thought move. With a lot of money at stake there are advisors you can go to who will help you decide how many funds to purchase and what percentage of money to invest in each fund.

DIY Investors' Prospectus Review Plan

If you are the do it yourself (DIY) type, get the prospectus and review these areas:

Management philosophy. Are you looking for aggressive growth (with probably a long way to go until retirement), or a more moderate growth, a value philosophy or a balanced type of fund with growth plus and income kicker. It's all spelled out here.

Portfolio manager (PM). How long has the PM been at the fund? A change here can dramatically affect performance. If a fund has superior performance the past 5 years and a brand new manager, you really have to throw past performance out the window. Find out where the manager has been and check that fund's past performance.

Check performance for 1, 3, 5, and 10 years to gauge consistency over different types of market climates. And on whose watch did the performance occur. This goes back again to the PM.

Money Sense:

You can review the top performing funds in places like Yahoo! Finance,

259

Money or Forbes magazine and of course with your financial adviser or a service like Morningstar. There are also proprietary portfolio analyzers that some financial services firms use—good for you. But check to see if they are set to recommend only load funds v. the entire universe of funds. The difference is that at the end of the day your net real performance will be affected by the front end load you'll pay for too get into load funds. Over the long term it's worthwhile because you can rebalance within the same fund family without paying any further loads once you are invested. However, if you go through the process with a view toward withdrawing funds in a few years, no loads could do the same job without the upfront fees.

MARKET NEUTRAL MUTUAL FUNDS - A TAME WAY TO PLAY TOUGH MARKETS

The appeal of hedge funds has been that they take advantage of or benefit if the market falls. Sophisticated and high net worth investors and institutions gravitate toward them as a risk balancing technique to "hedge" the market.

Taming The Bull And The Bear

The mutual fund industry has created a niche group of funds known as "long/short" funds which use the same technique of holding long positions in some stocks and short positions in others to produce positive if not overly dramatic returns in times when the S&P and other broad market measures decline year to year or move sideways. Unlike the more open-ended and less regulated hedge funds, long/short funds can be a way to make careful bets to preserve capital in a choppy market.

Neutralizing Risk

These funds are popular among individuals looking to smooth out the effect of market volatility on their portfolio or retirement funds. And in theory, long/short funds stand to profit on both sides of the market. However, the reality is some shine more than others in down markets because they can take advantage of certain leveraged strategies and others do better in neutral or sideways markets. The trick is how much of which type and when.

Before you decide on these funds:

- Talk it over with a professional adviser.

- Check the track record of the long/short fund being considered. Their performance tends to be inconsistent.

- Limit your investment exposure in this area.

261

Money Sense:

Here is one of those great sounding investments that tempt most any more sophisticated investor or one with a portfolio of stocks that is relatively larger than most. While these funds "should" and theoretically improve returns overall no matter what the market does, there ought to be a sign out that says approach with caution. Some of the funds track the market closely on the up and down side and others have produced returns that are better, if only marginally, than the overall market. Richard A. Ferri, CFA, author of All About Asset Allocation (McGraw Hill) suggests avoiding them because "their returns are inconsistent and…expenses too high…" A good mix of stocks, bonds and liquid assets can deliver sufficient risk-adjusted returns for my money without having to rely on a portfolio manager to do what's right for everybody in general.

INVESTMENT TECHNIQUES/RETURNS MUTUAL FUNDS; DIVERSIFYING YOUR PORTFOLIO ON A BUDGET

Mutual funds pool the money of many investors under the supervision of a professional investment advisor or analyst in order to invest in a diversified portfolio of stocks, bonds, or other securities. They have been around since the 1920s and more than 80 Million investors are shareholders in over 8,000 mutual funds.

Advantages:

The primary advantages of mutual fund investing are:

- Professional management

- Diversification

- Simple, easy record keeping

- Affordability

- Liquidity

Disadvantages

- No control

- Often high management Fees and expenses reduce returns

- Fund managers are rewarded for both good and bad performance

- Watered down portfolios yield few high impact winners

- Too many choices can lead to overlapping investments rather than diversity

Money Sense:

Starting Up – First: Read Before You Invest. Doing your research on a mutual fund is fairly easy because they are required to publish a document called a prospectus. Among the things you'll find there are—

- Who the fund company is

- Assets in the fund

- History of the fund

- Investment philosophy

- Investment results for the past 1,3,5, 10 years and since inception

- How long the fund has been active

- Charges, fees and costs involved in fund management and operation

- Portfolio manger's name and years with the fund

- Top ten holdings in the latest period

- Securities purchased and sold in the latest six month period

Second: What happens if there is a change of portfolio managers or a restatement of fund investment philosophy? Usually a new prospectus or an addendum to the existing prospectus is sent out explaining major events like changes in portfolio managers, fees, charges, costs, investment or risk approach. A mutual fund is rarely a one decision investment any more. It pays to keep up with the literature or you could be blindsided by a serious decline in performance. If keeping up is too much of a chore, choose one of the newer managed or lifestyle funds. They consist of a portfolio of other funds actively managed by the fund portfolio manager.

MANAGING RETIREMENT SAVINGS

Okay, you have finally done it. Filled out the forms and hung out your "gone fishin'" sign. It's goodbye to the old j-o-b and hello to a life of leisure. No more paperwork. Well, sort of.

You can take a real leave it alone approach to retirement but it could cost you serious hard earned retirement cash, if you do that.

A Minimalist Strategy

Let's just take a look at some essentials in the strategy of making best use of retirement funds.

Decide when you will take Social Security. Since benefits can start anywhere from age 62 to age 70, the longer we wait the larger the checks will be. If you want some independent help with this and your savings are too small to afford professional advice check the internet for some good longevity calculators. There is actually a fun one at *http://www.nmfn.com/tn/learnctr—lifeevents—longevity* from Northwestern Mutual Financial that figures out how long you will live. The bottom line is if you have longevity on your side and family members live till 80 and later, wait for full retirement. If not then early retirement might get you more money in the end. Waiting until 70 doesn't work out best unless you figure on living into your 90s.

Decide when you will start taking withdrawals from IRAs and 401Ks. You have to plan. By 70-1/2 at the latest, if you don't begin taking out money you'll get hit with a penalty of 50 percent of what the withdrawal should have been. That's pretty steep. The amount you must withdraw is based on a calculation the government provides in its publication 590 and one of the formulas is drawn from the Uniform Life Table. A 73 year old person according to that table has a life expectancy of 24.7 years. If they have an IRA with $225,000 in it the required annual withdrawal at that point would be $9109.31 per year or $759.11 per month.

Figure how much of your assets to draw down each year. The generally accepted rule is 4.5% of the balance but some advisers believe more can be taken in early retirement years because expenses tend to go down later on.

Money Sense:

If you are stuck on when to take Social Security, there is a new tool called the Break Even Age Calculator that answers the age-old question of When to Retire.

It's at: *http://www.socialsecurity.gov/OACT/quickcalc/when2retire. html.* And finally, consider converting traditional IRA funds into ROTH IRAs by paying the taxes now and then avoiding them later on. That strategy really needs input from a professional tax adviser

PENSION PLAN CHECKLIST

Pension plans are getting scarcer than hen's teeth these days. They are being replaced by profit sharing plans, and 401 (K) savings plans. If you have on or your prospective employer has a pension plan, here is a good master list of questions to help you figure out its value.

1. What type of pension plan exists where I work?

2. Is it a defined benefit or a defined contribution plan?

3. Who contributes to the plan—employer, employee, both?

4. How many years do I need to work to earn a pension benefit?

5. Will all work years count towards earning my pension? If not, which years won't count?

6. Which years will my plan count in calculating my benefits?

7. How do I meet the plan's eligibility or participation requirements?

8. Will I get a pension and how much will I get?

9. What formula is used to calculate my benefit?

10. Will my benefits be reduced by my Social Security benefits?

11. When am I eligible to receive my benefits?

12. When must I begin receiving benefits?

13. What is the standard retirement age for members in my plan?

14. Can I take early retirement and still receive my benefits? If so, at what age and what will my benefits be?

15. How much will my benefit be monthly if I retire at my "full retirement age"?

16. What are my options for receiving benefits—lump sum distribution, annuity, annuity for life with survivor benefits?

17. Once I retire, will my benefits be adjusted for inflation or cost of living increases?

18. If I die before receiving benefits will my spouse receive any benefits?

19. If I die after I start receiving benefits, will my spouse receive any benefits? What percentage?

20. Has my spouse elected not to receive any pension benefit?

21. What happens to my pension if I divorce?

22. What happens if I change jobs?

23. What happens to my pension rights if my employer terminates me and then I return to resume working for my employer at a later time?

24. What happens if I decide I want to work again after I retire and started receiving benefits?

25. What happens if my pension plan is terminated by the company?

26. What happens if my employer goes out of business? Is my plan insured? By whom? Will I still receive my benefits?

Money Sense:

Armed with this information you'll be able make smart choices about participation, level of contribution, how to get your money in and out and also contrast the benefits of competing employment offers.

RETIREMENT – ANOTHER 60-SECOND TAKE

There was that singer who wrote a hit song about love with lyrics that asked:

"Does the world really need another love song...
here I go again...I love you..."

It's the same with retirement. Does the world need another reminder about planning for retirement? In a word, yes. I can't stress it enough.

Simple But Not Easy

Planning for retirement may be simple. But it's not easy. However, that doesn't mean it has to be difficult.

> ***Start with expenses.*** For a quick top down approach you need to know what your expenses are.

> ***Factor inflation in.*** Then you add in what you expect inflation to be. Could be 2 or 3% per year.

> ***Count in your Social Security***, any pension plan you may have coming, 401Ks, annuities and so forth.

> ***Compare that to your expenses.*** If the result is your expenses are greater than the sum of all the above, you have two choices.

Either live downscale—the least preferred choice— in retirement or if it's not just around the corner, find a way to increase your income sources.

Money Sense:

Retirement is not a clear cut you-have-it-made or it-is-a-hopeless situation. But procrastination is the elixir for an unhappy ending. So get started with this simple but shrewd, quick and easy top down calculation and you'll know what needs to be done next. If retired already and you need more income if working is not an option or desire and you own your own home, you could look into a reverse mortgage which will pay you a certain amount of money each month while you continue to live pretty much as before. What you are doing is living off the built-up equity in the home. Another possibility is to move into smaller less expensive quarters, put the difference in a savings or other fixed income account and make periodic withdrawals. Again, this is a situation that might benefit from the input of a professional adviser. And the advice you get could be worth many times the fee you pay for the adviser's time.

TIRED OF BEING RETIRED? REWRITE THE RULES!

This may seem obvious but many folks over 50 today are able to take early retirement. Others worked in the public sector and can collect a nice pension after putting in the 20, 25 or 30 years of service, still have their health, a lot of energy, and perhaps some time left in the week after enjoying their leisure activities of choice. But they don't know what's out there for them or who is hiring.

Bonnie Lovellette Brooks recently told a Wall Street Journal reporter that at 79 she wants to keep her job at a steel plant because she thinks she'd get bored at home "looking at four walls every day." She's also got young friends and is helping her daughter pay the mortgage and doctor bills. Presidents Jimmie Carter and Bill Clinton are even busy redefining what ex-presidents do.

If this describes you, there is a wonderful site that may open up a world of opportunities. It's called:

www.seniors4hire.org that has everything from articles on employment topics, links to appropriate service organizations and just a ton of helpful information. To quote from the site it is "a nationwide online Career Center and the #1 place on the Internet for U.S. job seekers 50 and over to find job openings from businesses that value a diverse workforce and actively recruit and hire older workers, retirees and/or senior citizens."

For those not into computers, remember to check with your local senior core of retired executives (SCORE) and also your state department of services for older adults. Or have your nearest computer trained relative or friend pull up the seniors for hire site and see what's there.

Money Sense:

You might benefit from one of many good choices out there for folks who have more to offer but perhaps want to change fields or rethink what work direction they take in the future. A couple that were recently recommended to me by fellow seekers are "Too Young To Retire—101 Ways to Start the Rest of You Life," Marika and Howard Stone and "Don't Retire, REWIRE!, 2nd Edition, Rick Miners and Jeri Sedlar.

Both these books are available via Amazon or your local bookstore. Not only are these good reading and helpful if you want to continue in your same field but they are especially valuable if you want to figure out what to do next with your life—or as I'm fond of telling my kids, what I want to do when I grow up.

TALLYING UP YOUR RETIREMENT INCOME

Gathering Assets When You Are Getting Ready To Retire

The day you've been planning on for so long is fast approaching. Now where is your income going to come from?

While working you have a number of investment channels at your disposal to provide retirement income. For instance, employer sponsored qualified plans (401Ks and 403Bs) traditional and Roth IRAs, private savings, annuities and life insurance to name a few.

Let's say you have been building up savings in these plans and now you are thinking it is time to retire and you need a regular monthly income to make life comfortable. You need to set up a systematic payout program that will pay you regularly and yet have the balance of your money continue to grow.

So how do you get your money and keep residual growth going?

Starting at age 59-1/2—or after the penalty period in annuities—you can start taking money out of company plans and IRAs without any penalties, although you will have to pay income taxes on a conventional IRA. On insurance plans (but not term policies where you are just paying for pure death coverage) you can start withdrawing cash value if the policy has been in force for at least 5 to 10 years.

Three Traps to Watch For in Taking Retirement Distributions

- *Taking too soon.* Pulling money before age 59-1/2 will cost you a 10% penalty on top of the tax

- *Taking too little.* Minimum distribution is required on all traditional IRA assets by the year that the individual reaches 70-1/2 or no later than April 1st of the following year

273

- *Taking too late.* Postponing your minimum distribution past April 1st of the year following your turning 70-1/2 will cost you a 50% penalty on the amount not taken that year.

Money Sense:

If you have questions around when or how to take retirement distributions, this would be a wise time to consult with a fee based planner for a couple of hours to help you figure out what's best for your situation. Another issue is which sources of funds to draw down first, retirement funds or regular savings. When you have a choice and aren't banging at the door of mandatory withdrawal of funds, it usually makes sense to draw down taxable funds and available monies first, saving the retirement plan monies and any funds which are tax deferred until taxable funds are exhausted.

WHEN TO START PLANNING FOR RETIREMENT

Smart Money Plans Early

Almost every one of us dreams of a secure retirement, yet most of us fear we will not have enough money to live in comfort. This fear is well founded as the social security administration figures show that without Social Security about 52% of the people who retire would be living below the poverty line. What's more the financial experts tell us that less than 5% of all Americans retire at age 65 with sufficient assets to provide them with a comfortable retirement.

Free Time And Financial Independence.

Nothing sounds better. Free time and financial independence. That's what most of us want. And to avoid becoming a burden to relatives or to society. A 70 year old friend of a client has more than enough money, yet his concern is whether he wants to live a lot longer because he doesn't want to burden his family. It's one or the other or both fears.

The way to get to a secure retirement is to start planning it today, no matter what your age. Here's an example of just how even a periodic system of planning can pay off.

If someone aged 21 starts saving $2,000 per year for the next 8 years and then stops, they will have saved $16,000. Now if they have a friend who is 29 and they start saving $2,000 a year until age 65, they will have saved $72,000. Assume for ease of computation that both these individuals earn 10% per year on their investments. Who do you think will have the most money when they turn 65?

The 21 year old will have $777,732 and the 29 year old will have $658,079.

Money Sense:

Starting retirement savings early beats any other method of saving. So be smart, get ready set and start and get your retirement in high gear this year. It doesn't matter which type of plan you save in. Just do it without fail. Your spouse and family will love you and you'll be the envy of most of your friends. If you are just starting out in the workforce and can't manage to save 10 % or more of your salary in a 401(K) open up an IRA, even if it is just for $1000 per year in the beginning (around $2.78 per day). It's not an all or nothing game. It's an allocation, the regular earmarking of funds for a specific purpose, retirement, and piece of mind plan you'll thank yourself for thousands of times in the future.

START SAVING FOR YOUR 40 YEAR VACATION—
AKA RETIREMENT

Boomers Take Notice

What if you were told that you had a 40 year vacation coming up? What thoughts would that trigger aside from "sign me up." After that there's the normal disbelief or what's the catch reaction? We'll the truth is if you are a baby boomer, there is a very good chance you'll get to have a 40 year vacation. It's called retirement.

Forty to fifty years ago people would retire and in 5 or 6 years they'd be dead. Years a go it was so much fun to hear Willard Scott on the Today Show announce that he'd found a great old man down in the south or heartland somewhere celebrating his hundredth birthday. He'd often make a several minute segment out of the occasion. Today you're likely to hear Willard reel off a laundry list of hundred year old celebrants. Pretty soon there will be a spin off show called 100 something. It's wonderful.

Those of you who have just retired, and those of you who will be retiring from now on need to realize that you may be retired for as many years as you have been working. Also retirement worries are fast climbing to the top of the charts on things most of us worry about. There's no doubt about it, we are living longer; great. But most folks don't have enough money to live longer and better; not so great.

Living Life to The Fullest Takes Planning and Money

Knowing you might have a shot at a 40 year vacation from work, how soon do you think you ought to be preparing for it? If you said yesterday, step up and collect your prize.

Money Sense: by the bushel:

The point is you need to start early to enjoy the fruits of your labor, or in this case your future retirement. Don't leave retirement savings money on the table. Max your 401K savings, your traditional and/or ROTH IRAs and look to a point in time where you will be debt and mortgage free. You need to be secure about your own money if you want to sleep well at night, help your kids or grandkids out and enjoy decades of happy retirement years yourself. You deserve it. And a dollar you save today is worth 4 or 5 times a dollar you think you'll save 20 years from now.

Remember, you don't have to retire completely. You could work part time after retirement doing something you always thought about doing but couldn't because the money wasn't there or the time and expense of re-skilling was not an option. The objective is to be comfortable, not necessarily rich.   You can't enjoy yourself much less enjoy your kids or help them out if you have to live down in retirement. Get a membership in AARP—www.aarp.org—priceless value on insurance, travel and a host of other human interest in retirement issues and SCORE—www.score.org—for a free consultation on re-skilling, second businesses you can start, or starting the one you want. It's darn cheap, darn good advice.

SO WHAT IS THIS THING CALLED RETIREMENT?

Boomers Are Forever Changing Stereotypes

Retirement is not an end. Not by a long shot. Especially with the baby boomer generation—those born between 1946 and 1964. They haven't done anything according to past pattern yet. This isn't going to be their grandparents or even parent's retirement.

Retirement can be a new beginning. In the future retirees will have their post primary career years filled with better health, more in financial resources, and a lot more interest actively exploring their life, family, and community options. You've heard the expression "sixty is the new forty". It's true.

Things to consider in advance of approaching stated retirement age:

1. If this is the first career you are retiring from, consider a second career. What was the second thing you wanted to do or be if the first one hadn't worked out so well or if somebody didn't just push you into it?

2. What are you really "passionate" about doing if the money that you probably don't need now anyway is not the primary consideration?

3. Do you have an avocation you've been pursuing that you would still enjoy if it took up more of your time?

4. Was there a career you wanted but didn't pursue because you couldn't commit the time or the funds to get the education? Perhaps law or architecture or something in healthcare?

5. Is there a creative side of you that got submerged in the rush to corporate life? Like painting, crafts, gardening or writing?

6. What about some pure pleasure activities you never made time for? Sports like fishing, golf, tennis or swimming. Crafts like

woodworking, sculpture. Maybe now with the pressure of earning off your back you'd really enjoy them.

7. If you'd rather contribute in your primary area of experience there are opportunities where you could give back and provide invaluable help to others who will appreciate what you have to offer—like the Service Core of Retired Executives where successful executives help younger business "comers" make their commerce ideas fly.

8. Check with your local senior service and community centers to see what programs or classes you could teach or free services you could provide to other's retired folks who are living on limited or fixed incomes. The psychic income you get from this activity can make you feel like the richest man in Babylon.

Money Sense:

Post retirement is not an all or nothing game. Feel out your thoughts in each of the above areas and see where there might be some connecting threads. If you are a retiring accountant could you provide free tax preparation services to seniors? If you like helping others with healthcare needs but want more work than volunteering offers, perhaps a medical tech job makes sense. If you don't want to seek out professional advice then at least read the following two books: **Rewire, Don't Retire** by Jeri Sedlar and Rick Miners—"traditional retirement isn't for everyone" says it all about this work— and **How to Retire Happy, Wild, and Free: Retirement Wisdom That You Won't Get from Your Financial Advisor**, by Ernie J. Zelinski whose attitude is fully expressed in these words: Retirement does not have to mean the end of life—in fact it can mean a whole new beginning to the life you never had time to explore. Also keep in mind that the author bio states he "works two to four hours a day and doesn't like to work at all in any month that doesn't have an "r" in it."

THREE CLASSIC RETIREMENT MISTAKES
AND HOW TO AVOID THEM

Simple Secret Of The Well Retired: Squirrel It Away In The Last Five Years Before Retirement

Many investors build over 1/3rd of their savings in the last five years before retirement. These are peak earning years. Retirement funds are larger. Assets build more substantially off the bigger base. This is a time to "pour it on" in the savings department.

Avoid Making These Three Mistakes

The naïve belief that you have more than you may need often leads to three costly mistakes that could delay or de-rail your retirement. The three key things to avoid are:

1. Failing to keep saving money at the same or heavier rate than in prior years.

2. Giving money away to family and friends.

3. Over-estimating how much you can withdraw from your retirement nest egg.

What To Do Instead

Keep saving in your 401K, IRA or personal savings plan at the same maximum rate as you have been. However, be sure you are diversified. This is not the time to have all your assets tied up in a single "Cinderella" stock. Sure you might miss a big gain but you could also suffer a big loss and have to delay your retirement altogether. In the dot com meltdown a colleague lost over $300 thousand of his $700 thousand fund because he had over invested in tech/story stocks. Net result: He is still working to make up for it.

Give money away or "loan" it to family and friends—sparingly—under two conditions:

1. You have more than enough money to last you for the next 40 years.

2. You don't really expect the funds to be paid back—or really need them.

The reality is many of these family and friend loans will never repaid. They end up being gifts.

Money Sense:

If you are making $50,000 per year now and spending it all, figure you'll do the same thing in retirement. At least in the early years. And if you think that your $1 Million in retirement assets will fund your annual needs at the same rate as your earnings now—given that you stand a good chance of living another 40 years—think again. A Million won't come close to doing it for you. As Everett Dirksen said, "We are becoming so accustomed to millions and billions of dollars that 'thousands' has almost passed out of the dictionary. So watch your thousands as well as your million.

Finally, if you are taking early retirement—let's say you've been really lucky and blessed with good fortune—at say 55 or even a few years sooner, you'll need more money than you think for yours and your spouse's needs, inflation adjustments, kids, grandkids, relocating and, ultimately, long term care. If you have any doubts about the adequacy of your retirement assets, see a financial planner. Invest in a few hours of their time to provide you with an asset checkup to see objectively where you stand in the asset rankings compared to statistical need.

TO TAKE OR NOT TO TAKE BUYOUT
OR EARLY RETIREMENT OFFERS

For at least a generation now, large companies have been offering very lucrative early retirement packages to get executives, managers, and veteran employees with large salaries and benefits packages off the payroll. A lot people took these packages and were well rewarded. At least in the early years—late 1970s, 1980s and early 1990s.

Gold Pot or Gold Plate?

There are still corporate reorganizations in play in many industries today but the packages have gotten a lot less generous. Now the pot of gold at the end of the rainbow may be gold plate over copper instead. So after you have some mental fun picturing yourself in a chaise lounge on the deck of a luxury cruise ship bound for Tahiti, let's take a closer look at some of the hard facts you need to address to be prepared to take that big leap into the next phase of your life.

What are you going to do with all that time?

Leaving your job is a big deal at any stage of life, but leaving it early may find you very much unprepared. Statistically, people in their 50s are usually in peak earning years. Their life is very involved. They have a very fully organized day around the job and family. If the 50 hours a week or so connected to work and commuting are taken out of the picture, that's a big chunk of space to fill. You may not be ready for the change so soon. This is not a money issue either. It's just not having had a chance to give retirement much thought or planning what to do with such a big blank space on the canvas of life. Ask yourself what you are going to do with all that time now?

Expenses don't change but income does

Your expenses are going to continue but your income will change significantly. In your 50s you could very possibly live another 40

283

to 50 years. And be retired longer than you worked. A number like $500,000—to be generous—might sound like a windfall. However, divide it by 40, if that's your only source of retirement funds, and you're looking at $12,500 per year (not including any growth in this discussion, for added emphasis). You need to project the amount plus the expected annual return, divide it buy your lifestyle and how long you think you will live to see what you will have in hand.

At the end of the day who will early retirement work for?

The best case scenario is the person who already has been thinking about retirement, who has another job in the wings or an avocation they are already pursuing, and enough funds in place that the buyout represents a "bonus" that allows them to get an earlier start on their plan. They, who have the plan, can.

Money Sense:

Even for those with a plan, it's a good idea to spend time with say a fee-paid planner to see if the buyout helps you out with your plan or force you to modify it. And if it has to be modified in the money department, how much of a change can you realistically make. The early out now is great if you won't have to turn out empty pockets later on when earnings power diminishes.

THE TWO MOST SERIOUS AND SIMPLE GUIDELINES EVERYONE MUST FOLLOW PLANNING FOR RETIREMENT

It's hard to distill just two universal guidelines for such an important life event as retirement. However, many years on the battlefront with clients who have done it right and didn't and had to fix it later has taught me a couple of discrete principles I pass to clients and friends that if followed by all will lead to much less post retirement difficulties and post-death stress for our families.

Number One:
Promise To Take Care Of Yourself, First—Always

Now that baby boomers are at the end of the Age Wave, retirement too has changed as never before. We are living longer—some of it thanks to better, more expensive chemistry and equipment—spending more—thanks to greater incomes than ever before— and enjoying life longer—thanks to an I'm not my grandmother attitude. But medical costs are spiraling upward like never before as well. And so are living expenses. Retirees will need more money for more years than ever before. And you can't afford to end up old, infirm—and broke.

Resolve that it is all right to spend your money on you and your spouse. You earned it. You can't take it with you but you'll need it while and for as long as you are here. Now the corollary to number one is number two.

Number Two:
Your Number One Obligation To Family Is To Communicate Your Money Plans.

You must tell your family what you plan to do with your money. If you are going to leave money to them, tell them what they will receive, how it is going to be paid and why. It can be done while you are alive; either face to face or by letter, or it can be done after death through your trust and will. And part two of number two; if you are not going to be leaving any money to your family, they need to know this as well. It's simply not fair to all concerned to hide the truth. There should be no question as to why you did or didn't leave an inheritance, or to whom—and why you are leaving it. There may be unresolved issues among surviving family but there's no reason for them to have to battle over unknowns.

Money Sense:

This could be a good candidate for a video. It blunts the argument of incompetence should there be an intra-family squabble later on.

TAKING INCOME FROM YOUR INVESTMENTS

If you have an investment portfolio and have reached a point where you want to start drawing some regular or serial income or even do a one time withdrawal, most investments make provisions for that.

Some investments pay dividends which are declared and can be distributed every three months. Capital gains can be taken in cash whenever needed. Depending on the investment, income can be streamed from actual income—dividends—selling off shares or a combination of the two. The money can be sent by check or direct deposit into your checking account. Down the road you can increase, decrease or stop your income stream as required. Call either your investment company, or financial advisor, explain the type of income stream or lump sum you want and how you wish to receive it and they'll set it up for you.

Be very careful when taking money out of any IRA investment before age 59-1/2. You are allowed to withdraw a lump sum out of an IRA and not be penalized but it has to be returned within 60 days. Miss the deadline or not know about it and you'll lose 10% of your money plus have to pay taxes at ordinary income tax rates. If you are thinking about making withdrawals of retirement money prematurely or even upon retirement, invest in a little time with a professional to advise you of your options and which alternative might be best for you.

As a general rule, you can withdraw about 5% per year from your investment capital without any likelihood of outliving the money, assuming your investment returns are at least 3% per year. However, please keep in mind that inflation and the length of time in retirement could impact this assumption.

Money Minutes

MEDICARE D-DAY: DELAY AND YOU'LL PAY

January 01, 2006. Call it Medicare D-Day for the new prescription Drug plan known as Medicare Part D. Now for the first time everyone on Medicare can get drug coverage. And no one can be denied coverage due to prior illness or health condition.

Part D was developed to help Medicare participants deal with the rising cost of prescription drug medications. For many it offers an opportunity for substantial savings. That can be important in later life, especially if you are living on a limited/fixed income.

Enrollment is voluntary and there is an additional premium. Also the plan is being offered by more than one insurance company so you'll want to compare them and make note of the differences.

Savings Are Real

Once in a Part D plan you'll use the plans' pharmacies and you'll receive discount prices. The plans negotiate lower prices with the drug companies and pass the savings along. So you'll definitely be saving money on drugs even if you have to pay the full cost of the medication yourself.

If You Make A Bad Plan Choice
You Can Change It In A Year

If after you signed up, you find a better plan elsewhere, don't be too concerned. It's not a lifetime sentence. You can change your plan once a year.

But You Must Enroll As Soon As You Are Eligible,
Or You'll Pay A Price

Procrastinator's alert: Delaying your start date will cost real money. And the price increase is permanent. You must enroll in Part D as soon as you are eligible or Medicare will charge you a premium penalty of 1% per month. Now let's say your premium is $50. Waiting for a year will cost you $50 plus 12% of $50 or $56 per month. Waiting 2 years will cost you $50 plus 24% of $50 or $62 per month. And that surcharge is permanent, year after year.

So you can see the necessity of making a smart and timely choice about your Medicare Part D coverage. Otherwise premium surcharges will rise quickly.

Money Sense:

The three most important things you need to know about Part D

1. Enroll on time or you'll pay a lifetime premium penalty for every month you delay.

2. If you have small drug expenses, you'll be safe with a basic plan. If you have high expenses, comparison shop. Try the *www. medicare.gov* comparison tool.

3. If your health circumstances change, you can switch to another plan each year during the open enrollment period from November 15th to December 31st.

RETIREMENT READINESS QUIZ

So you think you are ready for retirement? Here's a quick 10 question quiz to test to find out how ready you are:

1. What is your retirement age for full Social Security Benefits?

2. How much of your retirement funds—as a percentage of your total living expenses—are you expecting Social Security to provide?

3. How much income do you think you will need in retirement to continue living the lifestyle to which you have become accustomed?

4. How much income will your private pension provide?

5. How much income will your IRAs provide?

6. How much will your Medicare or other Medical Insurance premiums run per month?

7. How long do you think you'll be retired? Or in heavenly terms, how long do you think you will live after you retire?

8. Will you still have a mortgage to pay and are your real estate taxes a reasonable expense?

As the lyrics rightly say money makes the world go round... Your world is no different. You need to know just how much money you'll need to retire stress free and for how long a time. What's more, the sooner you take this test and then get the answers you need, the sooner you can start taking the first steps toward changing what needs to be changed to get you to the retirement destination you've dreamed of.

Money Sense:

First of all be an "A" student. Get all the answers above correct and be honest with yourself. Don't just settle for retirement. Make it your planned retirement by knowing and planning ahead.

TOP TEN RETIREMENT QUESTIONS

Meeting with people everyday from all walks of life and income levels there are certain retirement questions that come up over and over.

- Can I retire?

- What is a good age to retire?

- What does inflation have to do with retirement?

- If I need $60,000 a year how much will I need in 20 years?

- Can my money still grow if I take some out?

- How much income will I need during retirement?

- How much of an emergency fund should I have on hand?

- Is long-term care insurance important?

- Should I keep my life insurance?

- Can I spend down my investment dollars?

If you don't know the answers to 2 or more of these questions, read on and see your retirement problems melt in the face of solid factual advice.

Money Sense:

Based on consensus and experience, if you are thinking about retirement, the above are critical issues to address in advance of the big retirement decision. The retirement race is won by the informed and the prepared. Either prepare and get what you need or what you need will be more than what you get.

Money Minutes

RETIREMENT INCOME: HOW MUCH IS ENOUGH?

I get this question so often. And while I hate to quote rules of thumb here's one where the guidance is pretty good.

Primary Rule: You need 70% of your current pre-retirement income in retirement to maintain your current lifestyle.

If You Think You Don't Need That Much, Think Again!

Now I can hear many readers saying well I won't need as much in retirement as I need now. Are you sure of that? Where are you going to cut back? Is it eating out, vacations, groceries, pet food or what? And what about expenses that you hadn't calculated? Like what you are going to be spending your additional leisure time doing? Will you take more vacations? Entertain more often. Have the grandkids or kids visiting for a week?

Drive greater distances in the car. All of it costs money.

And what about inflation? Cost of gasoline, real estate taxes, cable, phone, water and electric, medical insurance payments. All of it is going up, every year. Do you have a prescription drug plan?

What's the answer? Simple. Increase your savings. Do it today!

Money Sense:

Plan on spending in early retirement years what you spend now and add around 3 to 4% per year for inflation.

Money Minutes

HOW WELL WILL YOU RETIRE?

We've talked about the 70% guideline – needing 70% of your current income to retire and live the same way— and that at least puts a line in the sand. But remember that the guideline is just that and no more. If you are planning to do any of the things on your lifetime wish list—travel to exotic places, take up a hobby, say golf or birding, or take courses toward a new path of knowledge, it's going to take more than just 70%. Think not? Have you priced say greens fees and clubhouse luncheons in recent years?

If you wish to retire and pursue a pro-active lifestyle then what will you need to do to retire without worry?

Know the Facts:

- Social Security and pensions will only cover about one third to one half of retirement expenses for most of us. That's the reality. And it's a pretty big gap to fill.

- The latest Fidelity Retirement index shows the average household is going to replace about 60 per cent of their current income in retirement.

- Social Security Administration data show about 13 Million people would fall below the poverty line without Social Security. Among those: one third depends on Social Security for 90% of their retirement income needs; a third gets half to 90% of their income from the program.

Put it all together and chances are whatever you've got, the data say it's not enough.

How Much is Enough?

More than you've got. At 70% of current income you are probably watching every dollar you get. At 80% or more you are closing the worry gap. At 100% of current income you're smiling and perhaps even enjoying living in the neighborhood of your desire, even if you come from humble roots.

Money Sense:

At 70% of current income, retire adequately. At 80%, retire well. At 100%, retire carefree.

RETIREMENT SAVINGS—WILL YOU SPEND MORE OR LESS?

There are as many opinions about this as there are quills on a porcupine.

The simplest answer is it really depends on you.

You Could Spend Less...

No more lunching out during the week and trips to the cafe in the morning for the designer coffee and scones.

No more new suits to replenish the worn ones each year.

No more shirts to launder, shoes to shine and dry cleaning bills will drop.

Less gas if you drive to work and no monthly commuter fares either.

You Could Spend More...

The nice vacations to far off places that are now on your wish list can be quite costly.

Expensive hobbies like golf that you now have time for will add expenses you didn't figure on and fast.

Getting your grass cut and landscaping or pool care taken care of by service people may be a whole new expense altogether—adding up to hundreds per month in new expenses.

Entertaining more, at home or out, inflates your budget quickly.

Taking new courses even at community colleges can cost a thousand or more dollars more per year.

Money Sense:

If you aren't sure about whether you'll spend more or less, my advice is to start by assuming you'll spend the same. Then look at the factors above and decide yes or no and add any that may have been overlooked. By the time you are done if you are honest and know your innermost desires, you'll know where the give and take is and where to go from there.

RISK

What is risk? How much should you accept?
Risk can be a comfort level. Use your comfort meter as a guide.

If you like bungee cord jumping or climbing mountains, you have a higher risk tolerance. Like to cross at the crosswalk with the green light only when the white pedestrian is displayed? Probable low risk tolerance. Either one is okay. Just know yourself

Money Sense:

What makes you uncomfortable at night? If you wake up in a cold sweat after making an investment decision, then you likely took on too much risk. Just get out of the investment—or at least enough of it to any potential loss tolerable—and you'll feel better instantly.

There are three kinds of risk we'll talk about on following pages:

• Interest Rate Risk

• Inflation risk

• Investment risk

There are times when all 3 factors are in play and it's no wonder most of us desire security. The wisest minds have always known that there's basic security to be found in the trunk of the high reaching tree, but the fruit is always out there on the limb.

INTEREST RATE RISK ESSENTIALS

There are a couple of ways that you can be at risk with rates:

If you have a 5% corporate bond and interest rates go to 10% the only way for your bond to yield the current 10% is for the principal to drop by 50%. Then the yield or return on the principal will be 10%. A $50 dividend on a 1,000 corporate bond yields 5%. A $50 dividend on that bond's current market value of $500 is 10%. That's your risk. If interest rates start climbing your bond will be worth less than when you bought it. So figure out an acceptable loss and either scale back or get out. Of course, if you haven't got much time until maturity and you don't need the principal, you could always ride it out until maturity, surrender the bond and then you will receive the full amount of the principal or $1000 in the example above.

Money Sense:

The best time to be in corporate bonds is when interest rates are at or near their highs. At that point, there is a greater chance that interest rates will decline rather than rise further. Then the principal value of your corporate bond could go up instead of down.

INFLATION RISK ESSENTIALS

If you are in government bonds, you have virtually no risk. Why? The government owns the printing presses and, back-to-the-wall, they can always print money to meet their obligations. So long as you hold the bond till maturity (when it is due to be paid off) you'll collect your entire principal back. Risk? No risk on principal but if substantial inflation comes into play and you hold the bond to maturity your money won't buy what it did when you got into the bond.

Of course you can also buy treasury bonds that are indexed meaning they adjust the principal or face value of the bond to the consumer price index. So your purchasing power will be assured of keeping up with inflation. Not a penny more or less. I think of this part of your investments as running in place. More about these in a separate section.

Money Sense:

What's inflation? Here it is, in a nutshell. In the 1950s a hamburger, french fries and a Coke cost 75 cents. Now a fast food hamburger is a buck, a Coke is 75 cents and French Fries are 89 cents. 75 cents then. $2.59 now. That's inflation.

INVESTMENT RISK

Buy bonds or buy stocks/real estate/private placements. Each investment vehicle carries risks. With bonds you have to watch both interest and inflation indicators. With stocks it's more about growth, earnings and the trend or direction of the market. Pick 'em right and the returns can be substantial. But there is more risk in return for the higher reward. First decide how much of a risk taker you are. Tip: Use the sleep test (see page 34, under risk). Without a doubt the biggest risk takers are our farmers. If they plant corn, when the put the corn seed in the ground in March it is more expensive than when they take it out in June, assuming weather conditions are normal. Now that's risk taking. And you don't have to go that far to make or lose money on your investments. But depending on your age, and lifestyle, a portion of your money should be in the investment risk category.

Money Sense:

Like Alice in Wonderland who was running as fast as she could and exclaimed she was getting nowhere, the Queen told her, if you want to get somewhere you have to run twice as fast. Same with risk. If you want a greater return on your money, you'll have to accept more risk.

LIVING WITH STOCK MARKET DECLINES – A LITTLE STREET SENSE

Sometimes markets go on for so long and rise so steadily, it seems like it could go on forever. Too bad wishing won't make it so.

Market Declines Are Normal

The problem is figuring out whether it is a slight dip or a longer more serious correction. A look back at history gives us a little guidance. For one it shows that since 1900 declines have varied widely in intensity, length and frequency. A routine decline of 5% or more has occurred about three times a year and lasted an average of 48 days. Bear markets—when stocks fall 20% or more—happen about once every 3-1/2 years and last almost a year.

Recoveries From Bear Markets Are Happening More Quickly.

It took investors 16 years to restore their wealth to the pre crash levels of 1929. After the 1987 meltdown it only took 27 months, and in 1990 the recovery was compressed to 8 months. That underscores the increasing volatility of the markets today. While living with market declines isn't easy, once you look at and get to understand the lessons of history it will help you make more thoughtful investment decisions and avoid the crowd mentality that leads to panic decisions.

Money Sense:

Legendary value investor Warren Buffett has ridden out more than a few market declines, successfully. He says he "violated the Noah rule. Predicting rain doesn't count. Building arks does." The moral here is if you have your money invested in the right companies, you can ride out rough seas. And probably come back healthier than ever. But it might also be wise not to have as many occupants in the ark (investments in the portfolio) as Noah did.

305

Money Minutes

REAL "SIMPLE" RISK MANAGEMENT

Five Types of Risk

Risk is a four letter word with a lot of meanings. Most investors don't understand all the risk involved in making a choice about an investment. Altogether there are five types of risk an investor needs to consider:

- Principal risk – the risk to your investment principal and the chance for loss.

- Interest rate risk – the risk that interest rates could change and what effect that could have on a particular investment.

- Market risk—the risk to an investment in a general market decline.

- Business risk—the risk around a particular business. Oil and gas is much more risky than say a utility company investment.

- Inflation risk—the risk of an increase in the rate of inflation that makes the purchasing power of you investment principal worth less.

My Favorite Risk Barometer:

Another thing to consider is risk tolerance and how it can change. The simplest way to get a sense about your risk tolerance is what I call the sleep test. What's your ability to sleep at night and not worry about your investments? Do you have to see closing prices every day and add up the value of your portfolio every week? The more you worry the less of a risk taker you are. The less concerned you are the more risk you can take. To sleep well you need the right investments for you.

Risk Is Dynamic

Risk tolerance isn't static. It can change. Younger investors generally have higher risk tolerances and are more aggressive in selecting investments. Older investors are usually less aggressive. An old Air Force acquaintance of mine used to say "There's a reason why fighter pilots are so young. A single 23 year old jet jockey sees 3 potentially hostile fighter aircraft up there on his screen and he's saying "let me at 'em." A 35 year old pilot with a wife and a few kids at home is yelling for fighter support and starting evasive maneuvers."

Investment Horizon Changes Risk

Market volatility can change risk tolerance. Usually the longer the investing holding period the less risk. The shorter the holding period, the more risk. Day traders, the most aggressive of short term holders, have the highest risk investments and long term investors generally select more conservative investments. Day trading requires nerves of steel and the ability to spend most of the day at the trading screen without flinching. If that's not for you put your money in sound longer term investments and you'll sleep at night.

Money Sense:

Next time you are considering an investment give it the 5 risk once over and you'll have a pretty good idea whether it's a bring 'em on or evasive maneuver situation.

401(K) PLANS – SAVING MAGIC

Ordinary people can accomplish extraordinary things if they just learn to use the right tools in the right way. Really!

A key way to accomplish extraordinary results financially is with a benefit tool called the 401K. If ever there were a way to secure your financial life and accumulate barrels of money at a discount, the 401K is it, along with some other Hardcastle favorites mentioned elsewhere in this guide.

Here's Why 401 K Plans Are The Gold In Your Retirement Rainbow!

First, your money comes directly out of your paycheck before taxes.

Even if you are in the lowest tax bracket—15% every single dollar of savings you put into your 401K account is like saving $1.18 if you had to pay the taxes first and then take it out of what's left in your paycheck. At the end of the year this adds up to a substantial present you gave to yourself. And that's before appreciation. The more money you deposit into a 401K the less you are going to pay in taxes. It is not considered as income and you don't pay any income taxes on it until you start withdrawing it.

Second, 401-K plans often have an employer matching benefit.

Employers will often make a contribution to the employee's account up to a certain percentage of the employee contribution as a sort of incentive for employees to contribute to the plan. Think of this as extra pre-tax compensation. Here's where it gets even more interesting. Let's take the example where a company does a 50% match up to 5% of your pay. In other words, you deduct 5% of your pay pre tax and put it into your 401K plan and your company adds another 2-1/2%(50% of 5%) to that. It's as if you saved 7.5% of your pay. It's more than a gift. It's a Gift Double Play. Gift #1. You put away your money pre-tax (before taxes are paid). Uncle Sam says no tax now. The money can accumulate tax deferred and you can pay me later—when you start withdrawing it. Gift # 2 comes from your company. You save your money pre-tax and we'll add something to it up—the company match— up to a certain percent, free of charge. Your invested money is yours to have any time your wish, the first year or anytime thereafter. The matched money is yours after you have been in the plan for awhile. It depends on the employer. The amount of time it takes to become all yours is called the vesting schedule. It might be 20% per year up to 5 years or some other schedule. Check your company's plan description.

Third, the money you saved plus whatever the company contributes to your savings account all accumulates without any income tax having to be paid until you start to withdraw it, anytime after age 59-1/2.

In other words your money compounds tax free—technically it is tax deferred—until you start to take it out in retirement when presumably you will be in a lower tax bracket. So big tax benefits.

Money Sense:
The 401(K) is about as good a future financial security building tool as you can get. Even a stray cat given a free meal like this would come back for more.

MATCHING CONTRIBUTIONS IN 401(K) PLANS

So What Are Matching Contributions?

A company benefit plan has two types of contributions. One is the money you contribute, known as employee money. Then there is a percentage of money the company decides to contribute to the employee's account in the benefit program. That's known as the matching contribution.

Like Stone Cold Creamery, there are many flavors in the matching store.

Matching is an optional part of the benefit plan. While employees can and should contribute to the plan, the company is not obligated to do so.

For instance, a company may have a 50% match on the first 5% of the money an employee contributes to their benefit plan. Say you are saving 5% of your salary up to the maximum amount permitted to be contributed in the plan. The company will match 50 cents for each dollar you put in, up to a maximum of 5% of your annual salary. If the employee is earning $40,000 per year, and contributes the full 5% or $2,000 to the plan, the company will add 50% or $1,000 to the employee's account.

Do you see why I like contributing the maximum to your benefit plan? The match is like deferred compensation. The longer you stay at the company the better it gets. And if you leave for another company all of the employee money would transfer as well as the entire vested portion of the company's matching contribution.

Does the company have to match contributions?

No, a company doesn't have to match or contribute to the company benefit plan. So when you do get it consider it a gift that rewards you only if you put up money, too.

If the company does match, do they have to continue doing it?

Again, no. And if they do match, they can change the percentage of their match from year to year, or stop matching altogether, and then start up again in the future. Some of this depends on company profits or management assessment of the operations of the business.

Money Sense:

Good money sense says contribute as much as you can to your 401K Plan – at least enough to get the entire employer match. It's an undeclared bonus you deserve as a reward for your saving efforts.

VESTING IN 401(K) PLANS

So What Are Vesting Schedules?

Vesting schedules have to do with how long you must leave matching contributions in the company benefit plan before you can pull them out without any penalty.

All money you contribute, known as employee money, is 100% vested immediately. You either roll it all over into another plan or rollover IRA if you change companies or retire. If you are 59-1/2 or older, there is no reason why you shouldn't be able to get 100% of your money from the benefit plan. Matching contributions refer to the percentage of money the company decides to contribute to your benefit program. Here's where a dollar isn't really a dollar, at least not right away.

Five years is a typical vesting schedule. Here the individual gets 20% of the match vesting each year over a 5 year period. At the end of five years that contribution would be 100% vested. However, it can apply to each year separately and distinctly. Let's say you are in the plan 6 years. Your year one match is now fully vested. Year two's match is at 80%. Year 3, 60%, Year 4, 40% and Year 5, 20%. And so on into the future. There's a trailing vesting schedule and it applies to each year matched.

A Must Read For Those About To Leave Their Jobs...

What if you leave the company and go elsewhere? When an employee leaves the company and the vesting clock is running they can only take that portion of the matching contribution that is 100% vested. The money can be transferred from one company benefit plan to another or transferred from the company benefit plan to a self directed IRA without any charge, fee, or current tax consequences. However, if the employee takes a cash payout, and is under the age of 59-1/2, they are responsible for taxes and will be charged a 20% penalty.

Money Sense:

Resist the urge to cash out your 401K when you leave a company.

Records show many do. Why Not? Don't shoot the golden goose for a temporary cash fix unless there is a real emergency.

SEP: THE SPORT'S CAR PENSION FOR SMALL BUSINESS OWNERS

SEP, or the Simplified Employee Pension, is an ideal retirement vehicle for small business owners.

Three Reasons Seps Get Good Traction On The Retirement Road

#1. It's easy to set up, with IRS Form 5305-SEP;

#2. It's easy to administer— your accountant can take care of it all;

#3. —and best of all—it combines the high contribution limits of a pension plan with the simplicity of an IRA. It can be used by a sole proprietor, partnership or corporation. Even real estate investors qualify.

There are plain vanilla SEPS, readily available, and custom ones. Since the SEP has been around for over 30 years, many of the custom plans—such as those requiring integration with Social Security—are also readily available.

Almost a 'Blank Check' on Contributions

Contributions can be made at up to $46,000 in 2008. For instance, if you earn $50,000 this year you can contribute up to $46,000 to the plan. If you earn $46,000 you can contribute 100% of that compensation to the plan. Maybe a bit impractical but still nice to know, yes?

Other Performance Beaters

The employee is 100% vested right away. They can get in today and out any time and they are still 100% vested.

The employer has no fiduciary responsibility. 100% of the investment decisions rest with the employee.

All funds (including employer contributions) are immediately vested and may be withdrawn by the employee at any time or rolled over to another plan. However, if the employee is under 59½, withdrawals will usually be subject to a 10% federal excise penalty

If you have employees in the company they usually must be included in the plan.

There's Good News On Taxes, Too!

It's good news all around on taxes. All the money going in, either employee or employer contributed goes in tax free and builds up tax-deferred. It is taxable only when it comes out.

SIMPLE IRAS – A STEP UP AND STILL NOT TOO COMPLICATED

Simple But Good For Many Businesses

Simple IRAs are a good option for sole proprietors and small business employers.

Qualifying Requirements:

To use this plan employers need less than 100 employees earning $5000 or more and there can't be any other qualifying plan in existence.
Union and foreign employees may be excluded from the plan.

Setup:

The employer adopts a simple model plan and sets up the IRA accounts for each employee but the plan is owned and operated by the employee.
Contributions are made by both the employee and the employer. They are pre-tax contributions to the employee and tax-deductible to the employer.

Other requirements:

In addition to the employee elective salary deduction contribution, the employer must make a 100% match to the employee account up to 3% of their compensation or instead make non-elective contributions of 2% of each eligible employee's compensation whether or not they contribute to the plan—of up to $225,000 in compensation for tax year 2008. That's an acceptable way of having more money go into the retirement plans of those who make more money. More details on Simple IRA Plans can be found at
http://www.irs.gov/retirement/article/0,,id=111420,00.html#32

Tax Benefits:

For the employer all contributions made to the employees' simple IRAs are deductible on their tax return. Contributions and the accumulated earnings grow tax-deferred until withdrawn at which time they are taxed at ordinary income tax rates.

Money Sense:

There are a few important requirements that need to be followed each year, like notifications and so forth so employers and sole proprietors—all you small business owners—be sure and get the facts straight from your financial advisor or accountant, check the IRS at *www.irs.gov* or call (877) 829-5500 (a toll-free number). The call center is open 8:30 a.m. to 5:30 p.m. Eastern Time. Today's friendlier IRS even takes E-mail questions at: *retirementplanquestions@irs.gov.*

IRAS

Priceless Advice:

So many times I am asked if I think it is beneficial to do an IRA! My answer is an unqualified yes!!!
Anyone who likes to have investment money accumulate before taxes and build up tax-deferred should give IRAs the highest consideration. Over an extended period of time you end up having much more money when it's tax-deferred than when you are paying taxes on the gains made each year. Here we will discuss the two most basic types of IRA accounts, the traditional IRA and the Roth IRA

Who Can Do An IRA?

Simple. Anyone earning an income. For year 2008 you can do the lesser of $5,000 or the amount of your earned income up to $5,000. Over age 50 you can do $6,000 (the "catch-up" provision) In other words, if you only had $5,000 of earned income on which you paid taxes and received either a W-2 or 1099, or $6,000 if over age 50, you could do an IRA for up to $5,000 or $6,000 (over 50). The same rules apply for both types of IRA.

Is there an age limit on contributions?

For the regular IRA you must be under 70-1/2 by December 31st, 2007 but for the Roth there is no age limitation.

Can you deduct contributions to your IRA?

Depending on your income you may be able to deduct contributions to your traditional IRA but you cannot deduct contributions to a Roth IRA.

When do I have to start taking distributions from my IRA?

By April 1 of the year after you reach 70-1/2 you have to begin withdrawing yearly from your IRA but with Roth IRAs you do not have to take distributions.

How will I be taxed when I start taking distributions?

From the regular IRA you are taxed at ordinary income tax rates as it was contributed tax free and grew tax deferred. The Roth IRA distribution or withdrawal is tax free because it was contributed to after tax to begin with.

Is there a special time of year to do an IRA?

Yes. April 15th is the deadline for the previous tax year. So for 2008, the deadline is April 15, 2009. But anytime of year is a good time to do an IRA.

Money Sense:

What's good is worth repeating so anytime of year is good to start an IRA. The only bad thing is procrastination.

TRADITIONAL OR ROTH IRA, WHICH IS BEST?

Choosing which is best depends on a couple of things.

1. Income. All Roth contributions go in after taxes and are tax free upon withdrawal, after a 5 year aging. But someone making less than the minimal amount can put money into an IRA tax-free. Anyone covered by a retirement plan at work can still contribute to an IRA in 2007 at the full rate if they earn up to $83,000, and are phased out over $103,000 (married couples filing jointly, or a qualifying widower) up to $52,000 but then phased out at $62,000 (single head of household). A married individual filing a separate return is reduced or prevented from making a contribution if earning less than $10,000. And up to $156,000 and phased out at $166,000 if you aren't covered by a retirement plan at work but your spouse is and you file jointly. Many people making less than the $83,000 or $103,000 above can put their money in a traditional tax free IRA. Anyone making more of an income would probably choose the Roth IRA.

2. How you feel about the forced distribution you have to take down the line, after reaching 70-1/2. Once an individual turns 59-1/2, they can take money out of either traditional or Roth IRAs but the traditional distribution is taxable and the Roth is tax free. Then at age 70-1/2 with a traditional IRA minimum distribution starts for as long as the person lives and it's taxed. All of any money coming out of a Roth IRA is tax free.

Money Sense:

While no IRA is a bad IRA if you know you'll be in a high tax bracket when you retire and you plan to continue doing IRAs the Roth would be a better choice even though you are putting in after tax dollars because when you do start withdrawals they will be absolutely tax free. And that could make a big difference to you if you are in a high tax bracket at retirement.

Money Minutes

TAKING MONEY OUT OF AN IRA EARLY—
EIGHT WAYS TO DO IT WITHOUT PENALTIES

If money is taken out of an IRA early, prior to age 59-1/2 there is a 10% penalty and taxes are paid on it. But there are exceptions.

You Can Withdraw IRA Money Early If It's Done Right

Here are several ways:

1. First home purchase. But to qualify the person for whom the home is principal residence must be the owner, participant or a family member and they can't use more than $10,000 as "qualified first-time homebuyer distributions".

2. You are disabled.

3. You inherit the IRA from a deceased owner.

4. Your unreimbursed medical expenses exceed 7.5% of your adjusted gross income

5. You've received unemployment insurance for more than 12 weeks and are using the distribution to pay medical insurance premiums

6. It's being used to pay for qualified higher education expenses for either you or a family member.

7. You are receiving distributions in the form of an annuity, such as through a 72T distribution. The IRS section 72T rule requires the individual to take regular, systematic payments for a minimum of five years or to the age of 59-1/2, whichever is the longest period. So be careful of avoiding early withdrawal penalties but being forced to liquidate your IRA early.

8. You are forced to liquidate a part of the IRA to meet an IRS tax levy.

Before taking any distributions for the exceptional circumstances be sure to check with someone knowledgeable about the rules. It all has to be done in the right way to avoid penalties. If done wrong there are no mulligans (do-overs).

Money Sense:

It should go without saying but it's worth saying anyway. If you withdraw IRA money early make sure it's either your last resort or for a really good reason—like a first home purchase, which has many benefits of its own, like tax savings and equity build-up.

IRA OR 401(K) — WHAT'S THE DIFFERENCE

Both IRAs and 401(K)s are retirement plans. Both give you tax-deferred compound earnings growth, a powerful retirement fund builder. You can also save more in an IRA and in a 401(K) if you're over age 50.

The Major Differences are:

Contribution limits. In 2008, the IRA maximum contribution jumps to $5000 and $6000 with the catch up. 401(K) allows larger pre-tax limits—$10,500 up to 25% of your pay inclusive of any employer match.

Ownership. You set up your IRA, select the bank or other custodian and make the investment choices and do the record keeping. The employer sets up your 401(K), automatically deducts your contributions making sure you don't exceed the maximum and issues your periodic reports for the IRS and your records. IRA custodians will also issue the annual reports required but you need to keep track of your contributions, especially for ROTH IRAs which have aging requirements.

Highly compensated employees may be able to do both 401(K) and IRA contributions although IRA contributions will be limited or not tax deductible.

Money Sense:

If you qualify for both a 401(K) and IRA contribution and you can manage it comfortably, both are colossal savings plans. Bottom line: Save in both.

Money Minutes

401(K) ROLLOVERS – THE CHOICES
WHEN CHANGING JOBS

When you change jobs and have a 401(K) account with your former employer you have several choices to make.

1. *Leave the money where it is.* Some companies may require this. You do nothing and nothing changes except you won't be making any new contributions. You'll do that at your new employer. Your ex-employer will continue sending you statements. Just make sure if you work for two employers in the same year and you contribute to a 401(K) that you don't exceed the maximum contribution. If you aren't sure what you want to, you can leave the money where it is and move it later.

2. *Roll it over into another plan.* With this option you will roll over or transfer money from one company's qualified investment plan to another company's qualified investment plan. It could be from one 401(K) to another 401(K). No tax consequences and you maintain your retirement savings status and continue to build a nest egg. If the company you are going to has no qualified savings plan or if you aren't sure whether you are going to work for a company who does have one, you could do an IRA Rollover. Here you transfer the money from your former employer's say 401(K) program to a self-directed IRA. This has to be done properly though or it can cost you big time. See our money minute advice following.

3. *Cash it in.* I list this like I'd list root canal as a dental treatment. It's not something you want to do if you don't absolutely as a last resort have to. Why? Simple. You'll have to pay a 10% penalty on the principal amount for cashing it in. You are also taxed on the accrued gains at ordinary income tax rates. And worst of all you'll have liquidated your retirement plan. Of course, if you are over age 59-1/2 there is no penalty but unless you are retiring you still have to pay taxes on the profit based on your current income.

327

Money Sense:

If you are thinking at all about cashing in, you need to get professional advice first; then act. It's hard to imagine someone picking an option with penalties, taxes and no tax deferral but goals and times change. Here's where objective advice could be worth its weight in gold.

401(K) ROLLOVER TO IRA

Changing Employers Or Becoming Self-Employed

When many people leave their employers and they have money invested in a qualified investment plan such as a 401 (K) plan their new employer may not have a similar plan. Or they may be going into business for themselves and prefer not to leave the money with their ex-employer.

Most Preferred and Most Care-Free Option

On option is to transfer it over into what's known as a self-directed IRA. It's easy enough to set up with a broker or one of the fund managers like Fidelity or Legg Mason, or even though your financial planner.

If you chose this option and many folks do because they like the idea of having control over their own money, the money has to be transferred properly in order to avoid a possible 10% penalty or the triggering taxes to be paid on gains at ordinary income tax rates.

Think Twice About This Alternative

I've had cases where people thought they were doing the right thing taking a distribution of the money from their ex employer's plan and then putting the money into a bank account and several months later they decide to put it into an IRA or want to put it into another employer's plan and find out they have penalties and taxes to pay.

Money Sense:

Before any transfer is made talk to your accountant or personal financial adviser. If transferring into a rollover IRA do it through a reputable broker or mutual fund and have your 401 (K) paperwork with you.

Money Minutes

CAN YOU TRANSFER 401(K) PLAN MONEY INTO A ROTH IRA?

Yes. But It Can't Be Done In One Step.

First you have to transfer money from your 401(K) plan into any self-directed Traditional IRA account. Again, you set up such an account through a financial institution such as a bank, broker or mutual fund. Once the money is in the new Traditional IRA account it can then be transferred to a ROTH IRA. Simple but get some advice before doing it. The reason is you'll have to pay taxes at ordinary income tax rates by including the rollover amount in your income for the year during which the rollover takes place. In other words, at the time you make the transfer from a traditional IRA to a ROTH. Once it becomes ROTH IRA money it is no longer subject to income taxes on any future growth. If it double in 10 years and you take it all out, it is all tax free. But if you have $100,000 in your account when you transfer the IRA to the ROTH account you'll have to add $100,000 to your current year's income and pay taxes at the highest rate even if you weren't making a lot of money when you saved it in the first place.

Once again it's wise to get an objective opinion from an adviser. When rolling over the IRA to a ROTH, the 10% additional income tax for premature distribution does not apply.

Money Sense:

For objective answers to many other questions around the 401 (K) plan conversion to ROTH IRA see: *https://www.financialengines.com.*

Money Minutes

SOLO BUSINESS OWNER OR
HOME OWNED BUSINESS 401(K)

You might be thinking, "Bob, there is already a way to put tax-free money away and shelter earnings from income taxes with an IRA." Sure. You can put away as much as $5,000 in 2008 plus a catch-up figure of $1,000.

But if you are in a solo business and making serious money, or if you have a really good year and the money truck backs up to the home office, you ought to think about an even better alternative—the:

Solo 401(k) Program

Here the maximum deferred contribution is $15,500. There is also a profit-sharing component where the contribution cannot exceed 25% of the individual person's compensation and compensation can be up to $225,000. To highlight the clear advantages of the solo 401(k) plan over no plan, let's take:

> *John Deere, age 54, two dependents, living in Missouri, with an income of $100,000.* After taking out Medicare and FICA and one-half of the self-employment taxes, the net self-employment income comes to $93,192.53. In this example the maximum contribution into a one-person (k) plan comprises two elements, the profit-sharing contribution and the 401(k) deferral. The maximum allowable contribution calculation simply takes the profit-sharing contribution and adds the maximum 401(k) contribution amount to it, and that's the total allowable contribution. In this case, the maximum profit-sharing contribution is $18,638.51 and the maximum 401(k) contribution is $15,500 plus a 401(k) catch-up of another $5,000 for a total maximum contribution of $39,138.51.

Cut Your Taxes and Boost Your
Retirement Savings Big Time

Now that all sounds like a lot of mumbo jumbo so let me put it into terms you'll really like. If you earn $100,000 and can put away the money, in this example you would have $93,192.53 in net earned income. Without any contributions to a solo K plan or any other retirement plan your taxable income would also be $93,192.53 and your taxes due in 2007 would be $24,702.29. With the deductions your net earned income would be the same $93,192.53 less a maximum contribution of $36,638.51 leaving taxable income of $56,554.02. Income Taxes due on that would be $12,343.38 or an annual tax savings of $12,358.91. Would you say that's worth spending an hour of professional service fees to have it calculated for you and then putting an extra 36, 638 dollars and 51 cents into your retirement? You betcha! Or "duh," as my grandchildren would say.

Money Sense:

A great free resource for calculating potential benefits of a solo K plan can be found at *www.pensiononline.com*

THREE BIG WAYS YOU WIN
WITH YOUR COMPANY 401(K) PLAN

There are so many ways to gain by participating in your company benefit plan, it's hard to believe that everyone doesn't invest. Here are the universal ways you win:

1. You are investing pre-tax dollars. Invested money comes right off the top of your paycheck, before taxes are deducted and it goes right into the qualified plan. If you were paying say 20 cents in taxes on every dollar, you'd have only 80 cents left after taxes to invest outside of a K plan in say a passbook savings account. And any interest earned in the passbook account is taxable each year. In the K plan you get the full dollar in and no taxes each year until you either take it out or retire. That's called tax deferral. And the same is true each year on the gains. No taxes until taken out.

2. Savings grow each year in the plan and again no taxes are levied until you take out the money. The compounding here is so much better than regular after tax savings, it's like having a rich uncle send you a greeting card with tax free money every year.

3. If your company has a matching feature—many do—you receive a contribution of money into your account—over and above any money you deduct—according to the terms of the match. That's like getting a tax deferred bonus each year. Let's say you contribute $500 in a year to the plan and the company matches 50% of the first 5% you contribute. The match would be $250. So $750 is credited to your account and grows tax deferred.

Are you beginning to see why I toot the horn so much on this savings plan?

Money Sense:

It's worth repeating the obvious here. Many people don't take advantage of their 401 (K) Plan benefits because they can't deduct the

335

maximum. It's not an all or nothing at all program. If you can't buy the whole pie, at least get a slice. If you can't deduct 5% of your pay, deduct 4% or 3%. Anyone should be able to do 1%. The idea here is to get the power of compound interest working for you on top of the tax savings and free match (equivalent to a bonus).

GETTING INTO YOUR 401(K) PROGRAM

How Do You Set Up A 401 (K) Plan?

New hires usually get the information and election taken care of at hiring. If didn't participate before and now you want to, it is still pretty easy. You simply get the enrollment forms from either payroll or personnel/human resources.

How Do You Get Money Into The Plan?

Once you enroll, the money comes out automatically in each pay period. And you can change the amount or even suspend the contributions any time.

What To Invest In

There are usually a few or more options to choose from ranging from a money market (cash equivalent) account, bonds or other fixed income investments, growth oriented stocks through a mutual fund or index fund and sometimes company stock.

Why I Believe It's A Good Move For Everyone

401 (K) plans are the right choice for virtually anyone wishing to have a successful retirement. The younger you are when you get started the greater the accumulated fund will be. As the ward bosses used to say about voting, vote early and vote often. Illegal for voting purposes but sure great for retirement savings—save early and save often, that is.

Money Sense:

Oh sure, there are a few negatives like the eventuality that you'll have to pay taxes when you withdraw the money (starting at age 59-1/2 with compulsory withdrawals beginning at age 70-1/2), but that's at some future date when taxes may be higher (but your income will probably be less), and you'll also have to make decisions about where to invest the money (seek professional advice if it seems too difficult). Finally if you feel strongly – based on you career track or inheritance and so forth –that your income will be higher at retirement age, think about Roth retirement savings plan alternatives They are after tax investments now but tax free on withdrawal. Either way saving for retirement early and often will make your retirement years more fun. For the more conservative there are even Lifestyle Options Retirement Funds that do the safest less volatile allocations for you. For example if you are planning to retire in 2010, you would buy a 2010 Target Maturity Plan. The closer into retirement year they get the higher the percentage of investments will be allocated toward fixed income like bonds. The farther out you go the more you'll find allocated to stocks. Nice and easy. It passes my sleep test.

401(K) OPTIONS WHEN CHANGING JOBS

Job Changes Mean Decisions
About 401 (K) Funds – Making The Right Choice

Changing jobs is a routine thing in the course of a career these days. But what to do about your 401 (K) plan funds is another matter. *There are basically three options:*

1. Leave it where it is. This may be the best choice if you are unsure about whether your new employer permits rollovers, if you like the performance you've had and don't know enough about the new plan's performance and track record, and if your current employer allows the funds to remain where they are.

Money Sense:

This is not an all-or-nothing choice. If you have a lot else going on you may want to take the easy choice now and "do nothing". Later, once you have settled in to the new job and had a chance to do your due diligence, maybe get some advice from your adviser, you can always initiate a rollover request. Also a smart choice if your new employer has a waiting period before joining their plan.

2. Roll it over to the new employer's retirement plan. The "direct" rollover is an excellent choice if you have done your homework, determined your fund performance won't be compromised by the transfer, and want to take care of an important piece of business without a hitch.

Money Sense:

The cleanest and simplest way to rollover is to do a direct transfer of funds or rollover to the new fund by completing a simple form. If not available, then a check made out to the trustee or custodian of the new fund—mailed to you— will also work. A variation on this is to do an "indirect" rollover where the trustee makes out a distribution check to you, you deposit it and have 60 days to redeposit it into a 401 (K). Not such a good choice for a few reasons. The trustee will have to withhold 20% of the funds for income tax purposes in case you don't make it to the next trustee and if you don't make up the funds you'll be considered as having received a distribution, of the 20% and it's taxable income on your next regular tax return. The key here is to make sure you deposit the distributed funds in the new plan within the 60 days or you trigger a distribution and the 205 withheld will end up being used up in income taxes.

3. Cash out. Figures show this happens all to often. It is simply the worst of all possible choices and the worst of all possible worlds in the future because it can literally derail your retirement plans completely. By taking a cash distribution you lose 3 ways. First the entire amount is considered a taxable distribution and you have to pay income taxes on the amount withdrawn. Second, adding the distribution to your income for the year it may push you into a higher tax bracket. Third, if the first two aren't bad enough for you, there is also a 10 per cent premature distribution tax penalty you'll have to pay unless you are over the age of 55. All I see here is lose, lose, lose. Don't do it.

Money Sense:

Even borrowing against your 401 (K) is generally a bad idea as most loans are made but not repaid and in the end act like a premature distribution. A check of the calculators at places like *www.bankrate.com* and you'll see how, for example, if you had 25 years to go until retirement and borrow $10,000 for 3 years at 7% and pay it back on time, you would still lose $19,100.41 if your K plan investments earn just 9% per year. That's if the loan is repaid. Many aren't.

340

NOW WE FUND OUR IRAS – THE GIFT THAT KEEPS ON GIVING

Every year around the time we start to think about taxes, thoughts turn to IRAs. To keep it simple, let's just look at the why you want to fund your IRA every year. No exceptions.

Let's say you are a nice middler of 35 years. Income and other tax matters aside, you can and will put away the standard $5,000 per year under age 50 and you can use the catch-up provision adding another $1000 per year over age 50. You plan on retiring in 30 years, at age 65. And your return on the accumulated invested money will be a conservative 6.5% per year.

In 30 years you will have contributed a total of $150,000 to your IRA. Not a huge pile if you think you'll be retiring just on Social Security like so many folks. However, with the 6.5% annual return your savings will have grown to $493.000. Now that's more like it.

Even if you were to start drawing 5% per year from that total you would be able to increase your monthly income by over $2,000 plus your Social Security income. So by saving up $5,000 per year now you can withdraw over $24,000 per year in the future, when you retire and want it, and not outlive the money.

If this isn't a perennial gift that keeps on giving, I don't know what is. So don't wait for the end of the year when expenses are typically running high. My advice is put the money in whenever you have extra funds or do it monthly. Treat it like a bill from you to you. And pay that bill first. You'll never regret it.

If you want to refine the IRA calculations to suit your needs, age and savings goal, you can find a free calculator to help at: *http://www. timevalue.com/tools.htm* .

Money Minutes

SECTOR TRADING – RIGHT TIME, RIGHT PLACE FOR EXPERIENCED ACTIVE INVESTORS ONLY

More experienced and active investors know that with over 15,000 stocks, bonds and mutual funds to choose from, not every segment or sector of the market will perform the same way as the general market does. As with the overall real estate market, there will be spikes of upward movement in one area of the country (sector), while other areas will move modestly ahead, some trend sideways and others simply sink.

Sector investing is much more risky than some other types of investing due to the lack of balance usually found in a diversified portfolio but if the investor is trading stocks in the strongest sectors of the market at any given time performance in theory their would be well above the overall market average.

Nothing Stays Hot Forever

Just remember that sectors that are hot now can turn into investments no one wants in their portfolio tomorrow. For instance, technology. Turning the clock back a little we see the ghosts of the past dot.com craze in 1991 that took the whole tech market with it when in tanked. Most people figured all of technology was collapsing. So they sold out. This is what typically happens in sector trading.

There Is No Dozing in the Fast Lane

If you decide trading in investment sectors is for you, only do it with a portion of your portfolio, not your entire stake. Strike a balance that suits your risk and volatility tolerance. If you are right don't let a successful sector you are in take over too much of your total investment portfolio. If a sector grows from 15% to 50% of your assets and then goes down it could be devastating to your portfolio. Take profits along the way.

Stay With The Sectors That are Strong Today And Be Alert For Rotation in Leadership

Sectors can and do rotate so stay with the strong ones. Lately, that's been energy, health and international as well as technology. Drop formerly hot sectors like finance and real estate. Healthcare and energy stocks look like pretty good sectors for the near term future. Real Estate, formerly a hotbed has turned cold. When reading this don't assume the sectors mentioned are still strong. Check the financial pages, and the market reports or your advisor for what's currently strong, how long it's been that way, and what looks like it may be coming back around into favor. In the international arena, BRICK has been a favored investor anagram for Brazil, Russia, China and India but recently Latin America has replaced India.

THE EQUITY SECTOR – HOW TO INVEST IN STOCKS BY TYPE

Investing for Your Type

Some stocks are more appropriate than others for your portfolio or investment type. It depends on your risk profile and financial objectives.

5 Basic Categories Of Stocks:

Cyclical. For instance, airlines, auto, steel, metals and mining are good examples of companies whose performance is closely linked to the economic cycle. In a recession, all of them tend to do poorly. Travel is down, folks hang on to their cars longer, there's less building and industrial output so demand for things like steel and commercial metals declines.

Growth. These are high-quality growth companies the investor can simply accumulate shares of and hold over long periods of time. Blue chip growth companies are either large capitalization—1 Billion or more in sales—medium or mid-cap—500 Million to 1 Billion in sales—or small or emerging companies—sales of less than 500 million.

Income. Stocks for people who want to have some capital appreciation but also want a steady income in the form of a dividend.

Out of Favor or Turnaround. OOF stocks usually have a low price to earnings ratio. Either the company or the industry may be out of favor. If no analysts are covering it on Wall Street it is probably out of favor and the price may be down for a good while.

Value. A little different from out of favor a value stock may just be sitting at a discount to value. Maybe the company and the business assets are worth $25 per share and the company is selling for $18. Or a company that has just had a temporary setback for instance it reported negative quarterly news –perhaps just a penny or two less than analyst were expecting—but the long term outlook is not affected. That could take down the price and make it a good "value".

So Which Categories Should You Purchase?

My "Money Sense" advice is own the ones you like, have a comfort level with their business model, and will enjoy owning. For example, for years Altria has been a favorite of many advisers. However, I have clients who just don't feel comfortable owning a company that gets a large share of their profits from selling tobacco—Philip Morris is the brand.

DIVERSIFY INTO WORLDWIDE SECURITIES
RIGHT FROM YOUR COUCH

Investment vehicles have changed a lot over the past several years. Now you can include stocks of foreign companies in your portfolio, and even invest in international sectors of the market without having to open up overseas accounts.

Here are Two Convenient Ways of Doing this:

1. Exchange Traded Funds (ETFs). A basket of company shares, in this instance, of a group of international companies, is deposited with a trustee in return for units of ownership and these units trade everyday on the exchanges, allowing investors to have a mix or mutual fund like investment in their portfolio. You need to assess the risks here but it's a lot easier these days to invest in a professionally selected basket of global stocks assembled by professional securities advisors like say Merrill Lynch or Barclays, and be able to buy and sell the fund whenever you chose. Also you can go to www.etf.com and get a lot of information about fund selections, whether they trade at a discount or premium to their actual value, and much more. At Smart Money – www.smartmoney.com – you'll even find an ETF screener.

2. ADRs. These are created when a foreign company deposits shares with a US bank overseas and then the certificates representing usually one share are freely traded on one of the U.S. exchanges NYSE, NASDAQ or AMEX. The good news is U.S. investors get to receive dividends and profits already converted into US dollars and net after taxes and currency exchanges, so there are no currency translations or foreign tax forms to worry about. For instance, if you wanted to buy shares of a large foreign integrated oil company, you could own shares of Lukoil, symbol LUKOY, the largest oil company in Russia trading at only 8.8 times earnings. It has more oil reserves than Exxon Mobil is a fully integrated oil company involved in many prospective oil projects in Russia and

347

internationally. A check on www.adr.com will also show you the current top institutional and mutual fund shareholders.

Money Sense:

Two risk advisory comments here: One, you should determine with the help of an advisor what percentage of your portfolio you can afford to allocate to foreign investments and two, there are the added risks of currency fluctuations, political instability and differing account standards, among others, that may influence both price and future earnings.

INVEST IN BOMBAY OR HONG KONG
WITHOUT LEAVING MAIN STREET

We mentioned two ways to add international companies to your portfolio mix using ETFs and ADRs. There is a third way. It's by looking to international funds. They come in a few varieties

International Funds. These mutual funds invest in the major established markets outside of the U.S. like Hong Kong, Germany, France, Japan and Europe.

Global Funds. These funds include companies in the U.S. as well as other established companies worldwide. Because these funds are performance oriented they can and will have a lot of U.S. stocks in their portfolios and depending on what other investments you have may not offer a lot of global diversification.

Regional Funds. Here the focus is narrowed to focus on certain areas of the world, say the Pacific Rim, Europe or Latin America giving the investor more global concentration. Risk goes up here because the investor is targeting one area and hoping to catch a trend. However, the risk is spread by investing in more than one company in more than one particular market.

Country Funds. This is the laser approach. Country funds for example the China Fund, will invest only in companies from a single country and hope to diversify within the country by buying established companies in a variety of favored industries. These funds are often closed end funds meaning their portfolios are fixed and they trade publicly on the stock exchange where their values fluctuate in relationship to supply and demand. So they can actually trade for more or less than the underlying value of the shares in the portfolio. When the China Fund was hot it traded at a large premium to its underlying share value. Some investors look for funds trading at a discount to their value because it is like buying the shares on sale. This is similar to value investing where managers look for companies they feel are trading at a price that

349

is less than their underlying value in the hopes of cashing in when valuations return to normal.

Investing in foreign securities presents certain risks not associated with domestic investments, such as currency fluctuation, political and economic instability, and different accounting standards. This may result in greater asset-price volatility.

INTERNATIONAL INVESTING

Investing overseas has been good practice for many decades. How to do it was the hang-up. No more.

Now with international markets more accessible, freely trading foreign stocks with American Depository Receipts (ADRs) on national exchanges, international mutual funds and exchange traded funds (ETFs), it is pretty easy to bring global exposure into the picture. Of course, with more choices comes more choosing. Now which one is for you?

Diversification Pays

In the past 10 years the U.S. has not been the best performing stock market. Not once. What's more, it has only been among the top six performing markets three times since 1992. In addition, some overseas markets have outperformed U.S. markets since the 1960s. All this data points to the wisdom of having some of your money deployed in international investments.

But Weigh the Risks Carefully

Investing in foreign securities presents certain risks not associated with domestic investments, such as currency fluctuation, political and economic instability, and different accounting standards. This may result in greater asset-price volatility. So while the rewards can be substantial, the investor has to factor in the political uneasiness, the volatility of the situation, and the currency fluctuation into the mix.

This is especially true in emerging country markets, like Asia, Latin America and the Middle East, or in countries with new stock markets, for instance, Indonesia, or in new specialty listings like the China energy companies on the Hong Kong Stock Exchange.

Money Sense:

Clearly, there's opportunity here for the intermediate and long term investor. But international investing is not for the timid or those with limited investment timeframes. That being said, it is well worth exploring by the adventuresome investor with high risk tolerance and an eye toward aggressive growth—at least with a modest portion of a portfolio. And given the broad scope of choices for capital deployment, this is another area where professional advice, if not from a financial planner at least from an account executive with a full service brokerage firm, would be worthwhile.

THE WHY AND WHY NOT OF TECHNOLOGY INVESTING

We've all heard of the famous 6 Ws of investigation: Who, What, When, Where, and Why! And the sixth W is hoW. These are simple yet shrewd diagnostics. When most individuals wishing to be successful in the markets, particularly the technology sector, and particularly over the long term, I ask them to consider my

5 Ts of Successful Technology Investing

Training. You may be a very analytical person or have an MBA. That by itself is not a fully sufficient investment qualification or a guarantee for investment success.

Temperament. Do you have the personality makeup to handle a market that goes up one day and down the next or buy a stock that reports a miss in earnings by a few pennies and goes down 25% the next day? It takes a high emotional threshold to stay the course and not get rattled out of a situation that temporarily goes against you.

Talent. You may have a skill for selecting good companies and have been right on your stock picks in the past. But handling a whole portfolio for say retirement is a pretty big challenge for a working person. It's more than a hobby.

Technology savvy. You may be a company webmaster or in the IT field or have an educational background in computers or feel very comfortable with the technology market. But this sector is more volatile than most others. Knowing when valuations are above or below normal has little to do with knowledge of the field. It's professional investment savvy.

Time. And here is the biggest T of all. Do you have the time to devote to keeping abreast of the market? Even if you have the training, temperament, technology smarts and the talent, most people don't have the time in their busy schedules to devote more than a few minutes a day researching, reading and then

353

making decisions. In the long run, this is probably not a formula for success.

Money Sense:

Retired people may feel they have the time, and the willingness to do it. But once they are handling a portfolio that's fixed, they don't have any more money to add to it, and the game changes. The market may moves against them, valuations go down, and at a given point in time they may not be able to maintain the cool headed comfort level necessary to make the right choices.

This is why I recommend they should work with a financial planner, someone who is full time in the investment and financial planning activity and with the time to do all the research and make the unemotional decisions. And if you are a DIY individual at least avail yourself of one of the technology investment newsletters, one with a good track record according to the Hulbert Financial Digest which has been tracking advisory newsletters for over 25 years.

REAL ESTATE INVESTING — SOMETIMES THE GOLDEN GOOSE , SOMETIMES JUST AN ORDINARY FOWL

Commercial real estate, perhaps for more people than any other investment, has produced a lot of wealth. But always keep in mind it is a cyclical investment with up and down trends. After a historically long run beginning in the 1990s, real estate has come back down to earth, in many cases with a resounding "thud". This time it was fueled by excess speculation and a subprime mortgage meltdown that in the end could be bigger than the S&L crisis of the 1980s. It has produced such huge declines that some prominent Wall Street firms declared their first ever losses.

What does it all mean for this sector? That depends: On the economy; on how long interest rates remain attractive to investors; and on where and how you invest.

We aren't talking about your home. That's not really an investment. It's your family shelter. Although in some cases it could increase your assets more than other investments, the cardinal rule remains. The place you live is not an investment.

Commercial real estate is not a slam dunk. Look at New York City, the jewel in the crown of commercial real estate. The influx of well-heeled foreign investors who like our country's stability, and boomers who want to retire to "city life" with all its conveniences would make it seem almost bullet proof as an investment. However, after a string of record years of unbridled growth, the selling prices are no longer at asking and above because financing is much tougher.

As famed journalist Jane Bryant Quinn recently observed "the best real-estate investments with the highest yields are in working-class neighborhoods, because fancy properties are overpriced." So right now real estate investing boils down to a good bit of knowledge, location as always and guts. If you can sleep nights investing in residential buildings in up and coming neighborhoods that may be on the fringe, your capitalization rate—the annual return on your invested capital—will be higher, the cash flow will be better and the appreciation could work out better in the intermediate term. Getting the right financing in place to cover your anticipated holding period will make a big difference, too. Sooner or later the rates will tend back up from current historical lows though most experts don't expect they'll go a great deal higher at this point.

Real estate investments could be a part of your retirement portfolio but they shouldn't dominate. If a single investment is too much to fund, consider a partner or look at either real estate investment trusts or real estate limited partnerships. Trusts are like closed end mutual funds— portfolios of properties where the income after expenses is paid out to the shareholders. Limited partnerships run by a general partner who is experienced and should have a verifiable track record and you can make investments in chunks of around $25,000 and up. That investment may be partially guaranteed or the properties insured for rental incomes. Of course the general partner who is the property manager and operator will take a good portion of management money right off the top but it's still a conservative way to play the market if you can't afford the ante, or don't have the experience to be a soloist, or don't want the headache of actually managing the properties.

Money Sense:

Your home is not considered a real estate investment but an individuals' home is usually the largest personal asset they make in their lifetime. So treat it like a stealth investment—maintain and care for it and consider it a possible income producer if and when you are ready to move on to a smaller home or retirement situation.

NICHE SECTOR — SOCIALLY CONSCIOUS INVESTING

A growing number of people not only want their investments to do well, they want the companies they invest in to do some good, as well.

Doing Good While Doing Well.

Socially conscious investors seek out companies that meet social performance and product performance standards as well as the standard financial criteria. They are concerned about how companies influence the earth we live on. It's Thoreau (Walden Pond) meets Wall Street.

Who's In and Who's Not

To refine a little here are examples of companies who would be green-lighted for socially responsible investing or not.

Green Light	Red Light
Clean enviromental record	Defense contractor
Widespread advancement of women/ minority workers	Doing business with the military
Safe non-polluting products	Tobaccor or liquor
Active investment in community/ social products	Nuclear power plant
Alternative energy sources—solar, geothermal operators	Product testing on animals
Commitment to worker safety	Casino gambling
Clean constructive industry	Environmental pollution/using child labor

How to Find Socially Conscious Investments

The Counsel of Economic Priorities in New York monitors corporate performance on a broad range of issues. Business Ethics magazine (*www. businessethics.com*) has a list of 100 socially responsible companies each year. Some have repeated for several years.

What About Performance?

On average, socially conscious companies return slightly less to investors than standard investments. This is a small trade-off to those who really care about this issue.

Money Sense:

If it is truly important to the investor that they invest in a company that promotes the right things, the psychic income makes it well worth doing even if the performance isn't quite as good. When choosing among these investments look for the companies that have repeated on performance and returns.

YOUR SOCIAL SECURITY STATEMENT— THE ANNUAL FINANCIAL CHECKUP

If you are age 25 or older, about 90 days before your birthday each year you will receive a personal financial statement from the Social Security Administration entitled "Your Social Security Statement prepared especially for Jane Q. Truly, Taxpayer". Social Security is still the major source of income for most elderly Americans. It plays a major role in keeping many out of poverty in their old age.

The data are brim full of information about your benefits including:

A complete history of your social security earnings. Note this just records your taxed Social Security Earnings, not your entire income if you earned more than the Social Security ceiling, and your taxed Medicare Earnings. If anything doesn't match your actual experience in the statement, or if a year of earnings is missing and you worked, you want to fix it right away by contacting your employer and the Social Security Administration. Your total taxes paid in to Social Security by your and your employers are also shown.

Your estimated benefits are shown for:

Retirement—

If you take early retirement, at age 62, you will receive reduced monthly benefits, as much as 20 to 25% less than if waiting until full retirement.

If you retire at age 65 (if born in 1937 or earlier) or 65+ (varies with each succeeding year of birth until if born in 1960 or later full retirement age is 67).

If you retire at age 70, you will receive additional benefits each month due to special credits you earn for every year you wait to collect.

Disability—What your monthly payment would be if qualified and you become disabled at the statement date.

359

Family—if you receive retirement or disability benefits, your spouse and children may qualify for benefits, too.
Survivors—what your family may receive if you were to die during the statement year.

Medicare—indicating that you have enough credits to qualify for Medicare at age 65.

Money Sense:

If you want more information about your account, visit *www.ssa.gov/mystatement.* or contact your local Social Security office at 1-800-772-1213.

SOCIAL SECURITY AND RETIREMENT NEEDS

The Good News About Social Security:

For over 70 years now Social Security has provided substantial help to millions of people when they reach retirement age or when one of the family members either becomes disabled or dies prematurely leaving underage children and spouses.

The first benefit was the retirement benefit paid to all those reaching age 65. Now retirement age is keyed to your date of birth. If you were born before 1938 it is still 65 years old for full benefits. After 1938 your retirement age for receiving full benefits will gradually rise to age 67 if you were born in 1960 or later.

Social Security has been there for countless millions of people who have suffered the loss of a spouse, the loss of a primary income because of permanent disability and even as a supplement to income under the SSI supplemental income program that is payable to either adults or children who are disabled or blind, have limited income and resources, meet certain living requirement arrangements and are otherwise eligible.

When Can you Collect?

Many people just don't know at what age they can collect full Social Security benefits. It's commonly thought that it's age 65 and we already know from above that it is now variable. The other important fact is you can decide to take Social Security Benefits at anytime between your 62nd birthday and 70th. You don't need to wait for your anniversary date for entry into the system—except for the 40 quarters or 10 years of contributions—or your exact birthday. You can do it at anytime, say 66 years and 4 months or 62 and 6 months. Social Security will calculate your adjusted benefits for you.

The Acid Test: How Much of Your Financial Needs in Retirement Are You Expecting Social Security to Provide?

This may surprise you but many people are thinking that Social

Security will provide a majority of their retirement income. On the other hand, the affluent – let's just call them rich – are expecting just 7% of their income from Social Security and the lion's share to be provided by savings and investments (33%). Followed by IRAs/Keoghs/SEPs, 14%, Private Pensions 14%, 401Ks, 13% and real estate, 9% (Source: US TRUST COMPANY survey of the wealthiest Americans).

Money Sense:

Question: What were you thinking Social Security would provide? If it's a high portion of your income and you are still working get with a confidant, financially smart friend or trusted adviser and see what you can do to change the balance while you are able.

ALL THE SOCIAL SECURITY INFORMATION YOU NEED, RIGHT WHEN YOU WANT OR NEED IT

Being a financial adviser with a lot of clients in the pre-retirement and retirement years, I naturally get many questions about social security benefits.

I certainly consider it part of my job to advise clients on their benefits but did you know that you can now get one of the most complete newsletters on the subject right from the Federal Government. It's true. And it's free.

If you are an e-mail person then go to *http://www.ssa.gov/enews/* to sign up for the newsletter. You'll be very pleasantly surprised at all the information you'll be able to receive. Right now this is the largest online newsletter published with over 300,000 subscribers.

You can receive timely information about: disability, survivor benefits, retirement, supplemental security income, Medicare, new laws and regulation explanations and all the data research and studies done by the government on Social Security. In 1987 the then Director of Social Security, Dorcas Hardy said "The one with the primary responsibility to the individual's future is that individual." At that time the government was much less transparent about information regarding Social Security. Now the individual clearly can receive all the information they need to take charge of their Social Security benefits.

Money Minutes

SAVING ON YOUR TAXES — FIVE OVERLOOKED DEDUCTIONS

"The Hardest Thing To Understand
In The World Is The Income Tax."

Albert Einstein said it, not me. If taxes were such a problem for Einstein where does that leave the rest of us? For sure we aren't going to level the playing field a one minute sound bite on taxes, but you'd be amazed at how much you can save in taxes just by running down this most overlooked list to make sure you aren't missing anything in your records.

Top Five Overlooked Tax Deductions

The top overlooked deductions that can save you a lot in taxes are:

1. Charitable donations. You can deduct cash but you can also deduct wholesale fair market value of non-cash contributions like a car, art, used furniture or computer. Make sure you get a receipt signed by the organization for the items you donate.

2. Credit card debt. Not deductible. But if you get a home equity loan and pay off your credit card debt you may have transferred your non-deductible interest to deductible interest. You get a double bonus here because the interest rate on a home equity loan is less than credit card debt.

3. Expenses in job hunting. Many out of work people spend a good bit of money looking for a job—resume preparation; phone calls, postage and office supplies to copy package or mail data, employment consulting services All are deductible.

4. Investment expenses. Under miscellaneous expenses, did you buy investment newsletters or financial magazines, consult with a fee based adviser, call your broker? All expenses related to

producing investment income are deductible.
5. Tax planning advice. See a tax or investment counselor. Self-employed and pay to have your taxes done. All deductible and can reduce your Social Security and Medicare taxes, too.

Money Sense:

It wouldn't be fair not to say that a sixth overlooked top tax deduction might be the money you spend to get tax advice in the first place. So many clients and other above average income workers and professionals have told me time and again how much money they saved in taxes by engaging a professional not just to prepare their returns but to advise them on ways of saving more income tax. For first timers, you might try a tax preparation service the likes of H&R Block, Jackson Hewitt or Liberty Tax Service. There are online services and AARP has a volunteer staff ready to assist individuals with tax preparation and filing.

NINE MORE OVERLOOKED TAX DEDUCTIONS

Millions of Taxpayers Overpay Needlessly By Not Picking Up These Deductions

You might be saying, Bob, not me. Maybe not, but that's what a former director of the IRS told Kiplinger's, a major financial magazine publisher years ago.

Here are some overlooked deductions he mentioned plus some of my favorite misses:

- *State sales taxes.* This is of most value to taxpayers living in states without income taxes because you get a choice of either the state income tax or the state sales tax deduction and for most taxpayers living in income tax states, the state income tax deduction is a bigger and better bet.

- *Tuition.* You may qualify for a deduction of up to $4,000 of tuition paid for a student—or yourself. Attention late bloomers and boomers.

- *Out-of-pocket charitable contributions.* I'm not talking about the obvious ones where you have written checks but the ones we tend to forget. Like the groceries purchased for making food or baking for the local pancake or spaghetti dinner or bake sale. Or the miles driven while doing good works—14 cents a mile— or stamps and stationery purchased to help a local fundraising effort.

- *Special medical services.* Maybe you have a bad back or you a need a therapeutic massage or other complementary medical treatment (acupuncture or deep tissue massage). The costs are deductible so long as you get a written note from your doctor saying you need such services.

- **Business supplies.** Self employed can deduct all office supplies. If you travel even a business suitcase qualifies as a deduction.

- **Home Office.** IRS Rules have tightened on home offices but one area of choice when you have a home office is whether or not to take the depreciation deduction on your home. If you have a 6 room house and use 1 room exclusively for the business you can depreciate the 16-2/3% of the house that is used for business. It adds up.

- **Catch-up IRA savings.** Maybe you are taking your annual IRA deduction of $5000. But if you are over age 50 + Uncle Sam says you get a bonus catch up deduction of $1000. Never underestimate the value of a tax free or tax deferred saved dollar.

- **Student loan interest paid by mom and dad.** If this ever happened to you in the past the IRS disallowed the interest deduction for everyone concerned. Now it's considered a gift to the child who then gets to deduct the interest on the loan provided the child is no longer a dependent.

- **Refinancing points.** Here's a biggie given the refinancing activity we've been through these past few years. When you get a first mortgage on your home, you get to deduct mortgage points right off your taxes in one limp sum. On re-financings, you get to deduct a portion of the points paid over the life of the loan. On a typical 30-year mortgage you would divide the points paid by 30 and deduct 1/30th of the amount each year.

KEEPING UNCLE SAM'S HANDS OFF YOUR MONEY—LEGALLY!

Render Unto Caesar—But Don't Be Foolish...

Render unto Caesar as the Good Book says, but don't be foolish about taxes. There are certain ways to reduce the amount of income subject to tax to a minimum. We should all be working at tax avoidance. It's earning money by using your noodle, and keeping more of what you earn by paying the least amount of tax possible using the legal means that are made available by law and approved by the U.S. government.

Put Money Into Tax Sheltered Investments

IRAs, Keogh plans, 401Ks and other retirement plans grow and accumulate tax deferred. The same applies to cash value in life insurance plans—tax deferred—and insurance proceeds—payable tax free at death.

Put Money Into Partially and Totally Tax Free Investments

Then there are partially and totally tax free investments worthwhile considering if you are in a higher income bracket. U.S. government bonds are tax free at the state and local level and taxable only at the federal level. It's a good strategy for someone living in a state where there are high state and local income taxes, for example New York or California.

Triple tax free municipal bonds are issued by the city or state you live in and are free of federal state and local taxes. Depending on your tax bracket you would have to be making as much as $200,000 to make tax free bonds really pay for you. However, municipal bonds make a very good investment choice for long term investors looking for low risk, little or no tax obligations and diversification

Money Sense:

Beware The Munie Trap, if you are a prospective investors in municipal bonds: Consider where the interest rate cycle is. Tax free doesn't mean loss free. If interest rates rise a lot while you are holding lower rate bonds, while they tend not to decline as much as regular bonds, the market price of the bond will drop some. So either a long term view, perhaps holding until maturity, if that's possible, or a money market municipal bond fund—lower rates but very short maturities so no danger of a decline in principal in a rising interest environment—would be the way to go here.

HIGH COSTS OF IDENTITY THEFT –
HOW TO FIGHT BACK

The New Epidemic—Hard to Prevent—Costly to Repair

The crime of the millennium's first decade without a doubt will be identity theft with as many as 9.9 Million victims in 2005 and about 25% of credit card losses. That's what the statistics show.

What they don't show is the amount of inconvenience you'll suffer in the aftermath. Every time you go to use your cards once the fraud situation is straightened out—and one estimate says it takes about 400 hours of work to get it done—you'll have to go through phone verifications each time you use your cards and, more to the point, you'll wish you could just change your name to somebody new and start over again.

Simple Advice To Help Keep You From Being An Easy Mark For Identity Robbers.

- *Order checks with just your first initial and last name on them.* If someone steals your checkbook they won't know if you use initials or your full name when signing and they probably won't know your first name. But your bank knows how you sign your checks.

- *Use only the last 4 digits of your credit card in the memo section of your check* when paying bills to your credit card company. Then all the people at the processing company won't see your complete account information.

- *Use your work phone number on your checks* instead of your home phone.

- *Use a PO Box instead of your home address.* Don't print your home address on your checks. For the times you do need it and a phone number, you can either write it out or use a name and address sticker.

371

- *Opt out of pre-approved credit card offers.* They come in the mail all the time. To stop them call the three credit agencies— Experian, Trans Union and Equifax at the following number: 888-567-8688

Money Sense:

I know this one sounds dumb but never print your Social Security number on checks. Also photocopy the contents of your wallet— copying both sides of your driver's license and your credit cards with the contact phone numbers. Copy your passport as well and keep the photocopies in a secure place you can gain access to. Finally, invest in a cross cut shredder and use it for all sensitive mail, especially those blank checks that come with monthly credit card statements. For a more comprehensive approach and understanding of ID Theft see the book SafeGuard Your Identity by Mari Frank, an attorney and certified privacy professional. Because it is such a high probability crime against so many people see the next page for a more comprehensive ID Fraud Prevention Checklist.

PERSONAL IDENTITY FRAUD PREVENTION CHECKLIST

Books have been written about Identity Theft, one of the most prevalent and costly financial crimes of the new millennium. Earlier I presented a kind of mini approach to preventing this crime but due to its increasingly frequency, here is a more comprehensive checklist from the book Safeguard Your Identity by Mari Frank, Esq. which I highly recommend your reading:

Checklist For Reducing The Risk Of Identity Theft.

1. Buy a cross-cut type shredder—cost less than $100. Shred all your important papers and especially pre-approved credit applications received in your name and other financial information that provides access to your private information. Shred credit card receipts.

2. Be careful of "Dumpster Diving." Do not throw anything away that someone could use to become you. Shred anything with your identifiers (cross-cut) before throwing away.

3. Be careful at ATM's and using Phone Cards. "Shoulder Surfers" can get your "Pin Number" and get access to your accounts. Do not leave records of transactions behind.

4. Get all of your checks delivered to your bank - not to your home address.

5. Do not put checks in the mail from your home mailbox. Drop them off at a U.S. Mailbox or the U.S. Post Office. Mail theft is common. It's easy to change the name of the recipient on the check with an acid wash, so use a gel pen whose ink cannot be erased.

6. When you order new credit cards in the mail, or your previous ones have expired, watch the calendar. Make sure that you get

the card within the appropriate time. If it is not received by a certain date, call the credit card grantor immediately. Find out if the card was sent, if you don't receive the card or a billing statement or if a change of address was filed.

7. Cancel all credit cards that you do not use or have not used in 6 months. Thieves use these very easily - open credit is a prime target.

8. Put passwords on all your accounts and do not use your mother's maiden name. Make up a fictitious word, combining letters and numbers of 12 characters.

9. Get a post office box or a locked mailbox, if you possibly can.

10. Ask all financial institutions, doctors' offices, etc., what they do with your private information. Make sure that they shred it and protect your information. Tell them why.

11. Empty your wallet of all extra credit cards and social security numbers, etc. Do not carry any identifiers you do not need. Don't carry your birth certificate, social security card, or passport, unless necessary.

12. Memorize social security numbers and passwords.

13. When a person calls you at home or at work, and you do not know this person, never give out any of your personal information. If they tell you they are a credit grantor of yours call them back at the number that you know is the true number, and ask for that party to discuss personal information. Provide only information that you believe is absolutely necessary.

14. Do not put your social security number on your checks or your credit receipts. If a business requests your social security number, give them an alternate number and tell them why. They do not need that to identify you. If a government agency requests your social security number, there must be a privacy notice accompanying the request.

15. Do not put your telephone number on your checks.
16. Get credit cards and business cards with your picture on them.

17. Do not put your credit card account number on the Internet (unless it is encrypted on a secured site.) Don't put account numbers on the outside of envelopes, or on your checks.

18. When you are asked to identify yourself at schools, employers, or any other kind of institutional identification, ask to have an alternative to your social security number.

19. In conjunction with a credit card sale do not put your address, telephone number, or driver's license number on the statement.

20. Monitor all your bank statements from every credit card every month. Check to see if there is anything that you do not recognize and call the credit grantor to verify that it is truly yours.

21. Order your credit report at least twice a year. You can get a free report at www.annualcreditreport.com. Review it carefully. If you see anything that appears fraudulent, immediately put a fraud alert on your reports by calling the fraud department of the three credit bureaus: Equifax, 800-525-6285; Experian, 888-397-3742; and TransUnion, 800-680-7289.

22. Immediately correct all mistakes on your credit reports in writing. Send those letters Return Receipt Requested, and identify the problems item by item with a copy of the credit report back to the credit reporting agency. You should hear from them within 30 days.

23. Take your name off all promotional lists. Call the three credit reporting agency numbers to opt out of pre-approved offers. Experian, Innovis, Equifax and TransUnion can be notified online at www.optoutprescreened.com

Write to the following to get off promotional lists:

Direct Marketing Association Mail Preference Service P. O. Box 9008 Farmingdale, NY 11735 or www.the-dma.org	Direct Marketing AssociationTelephone Preference Service P. O. Box 9014 Farmingdale, NY 11735 or www.donotcall.gov

24. Write to your State and Federal Legislators to demand stronger privacy protection. Demand that the State Finance and Banking Committees pass legislation to protect consumers from negligent bank and credit reporting practices.

25. Consider making your phone an unlisted number or just use an initial.

26. Make a list of all your credit card account numbers and bank account numbers (or photocopy) with customer service phone numbers, and keep it in a safe place. (Do not keep it on the hard drive of your computer, unless encrypted, if you are connected to the Internet.)

Please visit the Identity Theft Prevention and Survival web site at *www. identitytheft.org.* It has over 70 pages of free information such as sample letters you may use to notify credit card companies about how to handle your account. You may also find more information at www.marifrank. com and www.identitytheft.org.

DAMAGE CONTROL IF YOUR IDENTITY IS STOLEN

Thankfully this doesn't happen very often but in case it happens to you or someone you know, like a friend who had his wallet stolen or another who put those bank credit card checks in the garbage without tearing them into little pieces, here are the steps to take to minimize the damage.

Cancel credit cards immediately. Go to your safe-list of account numbers with phone contacts so you can do this right away. But as a person who has mislaid things occasionally may I suggest you first make sure you have actually lost your wallet or cards before canceling. It can't be undone after you make the call.

Call the police and file a report in the district or town where the wallet or cards were stolen. There probably won't be an investigation but card issuers like to hear that the victim reported the crime promptly.

Last but not least call the three credit reporting agencies and put a fraud alert on your name and Social Security number. The alert puts everyone on notice that your information was stolen. If anyone tries to make an application for credit the red lights will flash and you will be contacted. The lawyer who passed this one to me said he was advised by his bank to do this when he learned an application for credit was made in his name, a new monthly cell phone package had been set up, a credit line approved to buy a desktop computer and even his license information record was changed by the thief who got a new PIN number from DMV.

The vital phone numbers for fraud alerts are:

Trans Union: 1-800-680-7289
Equifax: 1-800-525-6285
Experian: 1-888-397-3742

Social Security Administration Fraud Line: 1-800-269-0271

Money Minutes

AFTER WORD

So many hardworking people think they are financially down a hole or up a tree. It doesn't have to be that way. Just arm yourself with essential information, much of which you'll find throughout the pages of this book. Just taking the time to read up on what's bothering you will, in many cases, give you the information you need to act intelligently or get moving in the right direction. By doing that you avert future problems that cause chronic conscious or subconscious worries

In my profession I get a lot of sophisticated questions around wealth issues of clients. But in over 40 years of being in and loving the financial advisory business, and advising literally thousands of clients and listeners, I have to say that at least 80% of the questions I do get are either addressed or no more complicated than the ones explained in these pages. That's why we chose these topics and answered them. That's also why if you read them you'll find answers to probably many if not the majority of personal finance issues that tend to keep a lot of people from sleeping well at night.

Hopefully, after reading this book, you will have found answers to many, if not the majority of your personal finance issues. If not, my advice is to seek advice from a professional. If you feel like you need to speak to an adviser chances are it would be worth seeking one out. You may contact me at bhardcastle@moneytalk.org to either set up a consultation or get further information on a professional in your area. You may contact Anthony Vlamis at intellagent@att.net

I also want to thank you for reading Money Minutes. By doing so, you have addressed many of your financial problems and concerns before they occur. That is not what the majority of people do. Many wait until the financial problems and emergencies have occurred or are out of control. Then they seek answers that are often too late or much more costly to implement. So by reading this book you are definitely ahead of the game and you'll sleep better at night.

Bob Hardcastle